MARKETING INFORMATION

INTERNATIONAL ENCYCLOPAEDIA OF MARKETING SERIES

MARKETING INFORMATION

Edited by

A. S. BHAMHRA
A.K.CHAUDHARY

ANMOL PUBLICATIONS PVT. LTD.
NEW DELHI-110002 (INDIA)

ANMOL PUBLICATIONS PVT. LTD.
4374/4B, Ansari Road, Daryaganj
New Delhi-110 002

Marketing Information

First Edition 1999

ISBN 81-261-0256-X

PRINTED IN INDIA

Published by J. L. Kumar for Anmol Publications Pvt. Ltd., New Delhi-110 002 and Printed at Mehra Offset Press, Delhi.

CONTENTS

PREFACE

The *Internaional Ecyclopaedia of Marketing* comprises of five volumes, the different core areas of marketing, narrates the business and its marketplace. Here the interaction of buyers and sellers establishes whether the business firm has successfully contributed useful goods or services. In competition with other sellers, each firm endeavours to meet more effectively the needs of buyers and thereby insure its survival. In the early 1950s, largely as the result of a shift from a World War II production-oriented economy to a peacetime market-oriented economy, the business community became increasing sensitive to the problem of interpreting conditions in the marketplace. Out of this era came the 'marketing concept', essentially the notion that a firm's future hinges on an integrated program designed to meet customer needs. Obviously, marketing management problems are broad in scope. Their solution calls for information and insights provided by production and financial management as well as marketing management. It is the particular responsibility of marketing management, however, to interpret conditions in the marketplace. These conditions include such factors as the changing attitudes and habits of buyers, the impact of government regulation, and the prediction of competitive tactics.

In approaching the study of marketing, we shall stress both the formal and informal role of executives. Thus, normative patterns of decision making and planning will be described. As human beings, we would hope that the marketing executive is sensitive to the social problems of our time. As an executive, he should be held responsible or the manner in which he performs his functions.

Editors

1
MARKETING INFORMATION SYSTEMS

Decision makers, to make good decisions, must have relevant information readily available for their use. In earlier years many firms attempted to meet this need by assigning persons, at least part-time, to collect special information and prepare market reports. This was followed in some firms by the establishment of formal marketing research departments. These departments have typically been responsible for securing, and disseminating only a part of the marketing information used within their analyzing organizations. Today, many organizations are investigating the possibilities of integrating their numerous particles of scattered and independent information programs into marketing information systems—and some have successfully completed the task. The fundamental purpose of the new information systems is to be able to discern and provide needed information to decision makers when they need it and in a form they can use to make better decisions.

WHAT IS A MARKETING INFORMATION SYSTEM

One definition states that a marketing information system is

> a structured interacting complex of persons, machines, and procedures designed to generate an orderly flow of pertinent information collected from both intra and extra firm sources for use as the basis for decision making in specified areas of marketing management.

A second definition helps point up other features. Po Kempner has written:

> An MIS is a complex arrangement of well-defined rules, practices and procedures by which men and equipment convert data into information that answers explicit or implied questions of those who manage a business.

Some confusion still arises over the difference and similarities between *marketing information systems* and *marketing research*. Marketing research, the older of the two, is often defined as

> the systematic gathering, recording, and analyzing of data about problems relating to the marketing of goods and services.

The essential difference is that marketing information systems provide *organizational entities for managing marketing information*. They stand between the sources of data and the users and have a goal to discern and to fulfill users needs. In turn, MIS's provide: integrated, analytical, systematic approaches to identify, assemble, analyze, synthesize, process, store, recall, and communicate relevant marketing information to decision makers. In contrast, much of marketing research has focused on the methodology of doing research in marketing and has *not* been organized as a system nor integrated into the larger marketing systems.

The overall objective of marketing information systems is to help decision makers make better decisions. Eskin and Dabbah have explained in dual objectives how this occurs. First, MIS's aid in the decision making and planning process through effective use of available information. Information is broadly defined as knowledge, subjective estimates in the absence of knowledge, and methodology (e.g., experimental designs and decision theory). Second, MIS's can help foster environments in which learning and storage can take place. They provide storage and processing mechanisms that encourage the retention and accessibility of past experiences and allow lessons to be learned and remembered. In addition, they help fight the development of folklore behavior by thrashing out fiction with facts, and they help identify inadequate knowledge areas. In summary, there objectives can be listed as:

1. Aid in the decision making process.
2. Structure and quantify the planning procedures.
3. Effective use of available information.
4. Indicate the need for new information.
5. Serve as communication media.
6. Provide a learning environment.

Another way to help grasp the essence of marketing information system is to review the basic levels or components that frequently comprise a developed system. There are five major components: a general data base, a data reduction unit (sometimes called a statistical bank), an information bank, a model bank, and a display or interface (with decision makers) facility.

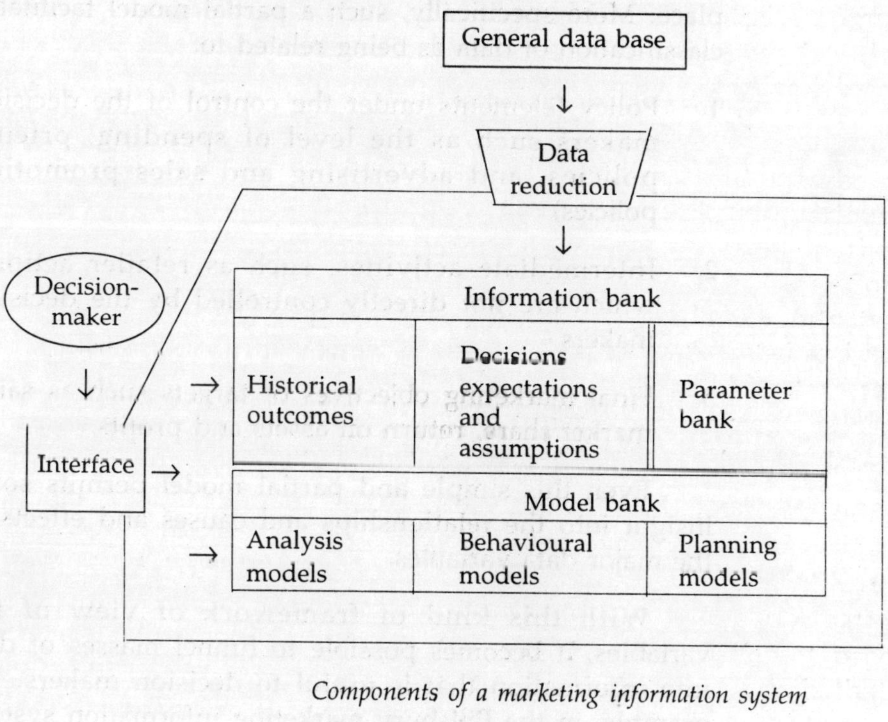

Components of a marketing information system

General data base

The general data base, in this illustration, is considered outside the system since the emphasis is on *marketing* information systems, and the corporate data base includes marketing and nonmarketing data (e.g., accounting data, and inventory). The data base includes activities of data collection, data processing (cleaning and editing), deletion, storage and retrieval. It involves coding and indexing structures to facilities storage and retrieval. And while some data bases are managed by computers, many are flanked by microfilm, associated equipment, and by extensive, traditional library facilities.

Data reduction unit

The data reduction unit is charged with reducing and transforming data into information relevant to the decision makers. Ideally, there would be operational models (pictures) of the organisation's marketing situation to direct this reduction and transformation. Few, if any, organizations presently have the benefit of such models. Consequently, organizations will frequently use a simple and conceptual model that allows then to view each item of data in terms of its role in the market place. More specifically, such a partial model facilitates classification of data as being related to:

1. Policy (elements under the control of the decision makers such as the level of spending, pricing policies, and advertising and sales promotion policies)

2. Intermediate activities, such as retailer actions, which are not directly controlled by the decision makers

3. Final marketing objectives or targets such as sales, market share, return on assets and profits.

Even this simple and partial model permits some insight into the relationships and causes and effects of the major data variables.

With this kind of framework of view of the variables, it becomes possible to funnel masses of data into information that is useful to decision makers. For example, in the Pillsbury marketing information system, detailed price data such as list process, displayed prices, distribution allowances, and deals are transformed (collapsed) into a single index that provides one measure of price-related influences. It is this effective price index that is entered in the information base.

Table 1 data categories: Consumer goods company

I. Internal corporate records
  A. Internal report data
    1. Salesman's call reports.
    2. Marketing mix data by product, time period, and market.
    3. Sales performance information on previously implemented new products.
    4. Life cycle information on products in the line.
    5. Copy and format data on company advertisements.
  B. Judgmental inputs
    1. Forecasts by product, time, and forecaster.
    2. Estimates of market sensitivity of company and competitive marketing activities.
  C. Financial and cost data by product and time period.

II. External data
  A. Secondary data
    1. Government data such as population demographic data by coded areas.
    2. Commercial data such a Market Research Corporation of America, panel data, and Nielsen store audits.
    3. Freight rates.
  B. Primary data
    1. Test market data.
    2. Market experiments.
    3. Market structure analysis.
    4. Competitive marketing activity.
    5. Advertising performance measures such as Schwerin, Gallup-Robinson, Starch.

Informaion bank

An information bank, can be considered to be composed of three principle parts:

1. A historical outcome section or file.
2. A decisions, expectations, ad assumptions section of file.
3. A parameter section or file.

The historical file provides reports on results (not diagnosis). For example, it will include sales results and market share market by market and product by product. These results must be paired with inputs and existing conditions in order to develop insight into the relationships between the marketing policy variables (the controllable inputs) and the marketing objectives (the outputs). This leads to the need for the second file composed of information on past decisions, expectations, and the assumptions that linked the input top the resulting output. Finally, the learning that occurs in the process of relating inputs to outputs is stored in the section or file called the *parameter* file or bank. These entries are basically crude and simple models—they seek to explain and quantify the functional relationships between sets of variables in the marketing system. For example, one parameter may suggest the relationships between cents-off deals, in-store advertising, and sales under a range of circumstances. Another parameter may be concerned with the relationship between the magnitude of spot television commercials and coupons in various situations.

Model bank This component contains models for use in understanding market behavior, discerning factors underlying market results, controlling market operations and planning. While organizations would like to have complete models that integrate all of the input decisions with the environment of offer a complete explanation of the output results, such an advanced state of affairs is not present.

However, models of limited aspects are available and are used. Eskin and Dabbah, for example, have classified the models in the Pillsbury systems as:

1. Behavioral models,
2. Analysis models,
3. Planning models.

Each of these types of models help do a part of the total task.

The behavioral models help fit information together to explain the marketing process. One illustration is shot-range forecasting models based on marketing variables.

Analysis models are mainly concerned with the handling, transforming, and communicating of data to information from sources to users. For example, such models guide the establishment of query procedures that facilitate user access to needed information, and they provide him with analytical packages so he can rearrange and examine information.

Planning models are simply models designed to aid managers in their planning function. They frequently call for the use of information of the major influences in the environment, and select parameters within the organization and historical records. The models are computer-based so the machine plays the role of processor, manipulator and logician while the planner-decision maker calls forth various inputs, generates alternatives, and serves as a synethesizer. More specifically, the planner feeds in various outcomes such as sales and profits. The better planning models also asses store estimates of uncertainty and financial risk that are useful in evaluating alternative programs. Following this pattern, alternative plans are generated and evaluated. The dialogue and output of such a planning model is illustrated in Eskin and Dabbah.

Decision maker interface

One form of decision maker interface with marketing information systems has been alluded to in the discussion of the planning model—the planner interacts with a time-share computer through a remote terminal. He feed in various information and parameter alternatives and calls up various models. He, so to speak, experiments with alternatives and looks at outcomes. This is becoming an increasingly common and practical way for decision makers to interface with MIS's.

Batch processing and output interfaces also continue to play an important role. In this format the decision maker typically receives a printout or display of certain sets of information, but without the on-line opportunity to analyze them further or to call for additional or different information. Finally, not all interface is directly from or through computer-based facilities, as will become clear as more information is presented in some of the following chapters.

CURRENT STATUS

A set of studies dating from 1964 have traced the development of marketing information systems in the United States. In 1964 Brink found that only 80 out of 1000 companies examined had established some kind of formal system, although many more ("a healthy number") had plans to initiate such systems.

In 1967 Cox and Good indicated they had been studying the attempts of major United States firms to develop marketing information systems. The firms included Chemstrand, Coca-Cola, General Electric, General Foods, IBM, Lever Brothers, Pillsbury, Schenley, and Westinghouse. Furthermore, they screened more than 50 companies. From their study they make three summary statements about the current state of the art:

1. Very few companies had developed advanced systems, and not all of these were in operation. Some might even best be classified as sub-systems, since they related to only a portion of the marketing decisions.

2. Some companies, perhaps 15, were actively upgrading their systems to a high level. Of these about half seemed to be progressing well; the others had been much less successful.

3. Many other companies were contemplating plans to develop sophisticated systems.

None of these studies attempted to measure accurately the incidence of marketing information systems. Instead, they reported that marketing information systems were present in a minority of companies; they were receiving considerable attention, particularly by the larger United States firms; and it appeared that many firms would be developing marketing information systems.

The first major contention that the use of marketing information systems was rapidly increasing came in 1971 when a study of Boone and Kurtz reported that "a surprising large number of major American firms have already established marketing information systems and that an equal number are currently in the process of installing systems." More specifically, they indicated that 149 of the 193 (78%) firms hey sampled, from the Fortune 500 list, either had or were building an MIS.

A "State of the Art" paper presented by Brien in 1972 added some additional insight by listing some companies with successfully operating MIS's. The list if of particular interest because it represents many different industries, products, and service. Clearly, operating systems were not limited to packaged consumer product companies.

The most meaningful aspect of the set of studies is that many actual systems have been put under the microscope and have provided insight on their dimensions and why the systems did or did not function.

GENERAL MIS DIMENSIONS

There are many formats for marketing information system. Each firm's management has unique information requirements, since each firm has a unique perspective on both the environment and their firm, a unique order of priorities, and a unique style of management based on the individual makeup and the interaction of the persons in the management group.

Despite these difference, information systems do possess sets of general, identifiable dimensions that permit them to be described, compared, and contrasted. Seven set of dimension are particularly useful—data recency, management access, data aggregation, analytical sophistication, system authority, interface mechanisms, and decision capabilities.

Recency

Data *recency* refers to the lapse of time between when an event occurs and when it is reported in the information system. The recency required of data depends on the use to which the information is put. An airline reservation clerk needs up-to-data or "one-line" information. The sales manager for a washing machine manufacturer, on the other hand, may find biweekly sales reports, for particular districts, sufficient. Boone and Kurtz in their survey found that 17% of the companies updated their data continuously, 36% updated their data daily, with 10% updating weekly and 23% monthly or less frequently. Amstutz found 6%, 32%, 9%, respectively, with 38% updating from 2 weeks to monthly and the remainder quarterly to annually.

Management access This dimension refers to the lapse of time between management's request for certain information and receipt of the requested display or report. Amstutz reported that 9% of the systems he surveyed could provide certain types of information in one minute or less, 28% in one to eight hours, 56% needed from one to five days, while 7% needed two seeks or more. Boone and Kurtz, using different time intervals, indicated some forms of information could be provided in one to 60 minutes by 20% of the companies they surveyed, 17% needed at least from one hour to one day, 46% took from at least one day to a week, and the remainder (17%) required one week or more.

Aggregation Information aggregation indicates the detail in which information is maintained in system storage files. Data can vary from the relatively disaggregated individual item level to highly aggregated data like market share and industry sales statistics. Boone and Kurtz found 52% of the companies complied line item invoice level, 10% at the invoice level, with most of the rest at the salesman sales or product sales level or above. Amstutz reported similar findings. There is normally a relationship between the level of aggregation and the delay in getting information into the system. In general, relatively disaggregated data are reported in the system sooner than highly aggregated, because the highly aggregated information arises out of a longer batch process; that is, it must accumulate before being processed.

Analytical sophistication The fourth dimension refers to the complexity of the structures or models included in a system. At the *lowest* level, a computer only needs to identify a particular file and record, retrieve it, and display its information. At the *second* level of sophistication, the computer must be able to gather data from one or more records and produce a subtotal or total. At the *third* level the computer may be programmed to perform simple arithmetic operations, such as computering averages and differences. The *fourth* level involves logical analysis; in other words, the computer can aggregate data by various classification schemes. The *fifth* level of sophistication introduces analyses such as statistical best estimates, trend estimates, and analyses of variance. At the *sixth* level the computer is programmed to modify values of parameters or structures of models based on the data inputs it has received. The seventh level of analytical sophistication occurs when simulation models are used in sufficient detail and magnitude to represent the real world through the information system. At this level, Amstutz indicates,

> ... the system can provide management with the following capabilities: testing proposed policies and strategies in the simulated environment, choosing between alternatives on the basis of resulting output, implementing the policies in the real world environment, and evaluating the effectiveness of implemented plans through the information system.

At the eighth level are highly sophisticated systems designed to evaluate alternative parameters and models through the use of environmental data. This is called adaptive heuristics because the program can learn from experience. Amstutz reported that about 90% of the systems had capabilities to handle arithmetic computations and logical analyses, with 70 to 75% able to handle various statistical analyses. In contrast only about 36% could handle macro process models and 31% simulation. Boone and Kurtz appear to report similar findings, except for the last two categories, which they have at 6 and 14%, respectively.

System authority

The fifth dimension useful in describing and comparing information systems is the authority granted to the system. Amstutz indicates that it is closely related to the system's analytic sophistication. The levels of authority and their general relationship to analytic sophistication are shown on Figure 1.

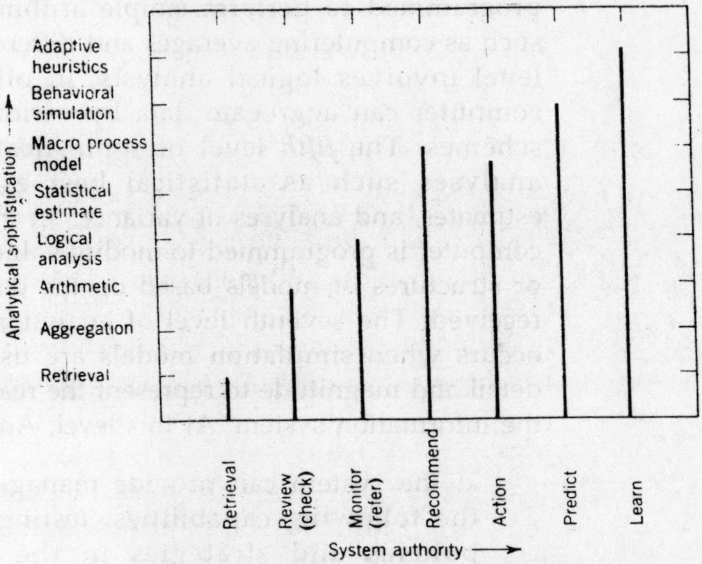

Relationship between dimensions 3 and 4

At the lowest level, decision makers may grant the system authority only to *retrieve* certain information from designated locations. The next level is to have the system *review* (check) the content of each record for reasonableness.

The next level is to have the system perform analyses on records and to *refer* exceptions (as defined by decision makers) for further review. At the fourth step, the further review noted at the prior level is programmed for the system to do and report a *recommendation* for action. When decision makers continually find these recommendations appropriate, they may give the system authority to take *action* on all but exceptional cases (as defined by the decision makers). The next-to-final level of authority occurs when the system is permitted to *predict*. System involvement is greater here than at the prior level because predications are used in planning that affects the future of the company whereas system-directed action related only to current operations. Finally, management may have sufficient confidence in particular heuristics that adapt the system's parameters and models to let them proceed. This clearly magnifies the system's role beyond prediction because the system is evolving the predictive models.

Boone and Kurtz and Amstutz appear to report similar findings on system authority through the first three levels with almost 90% with authority; Amstutz reports 76% with recommendation authority (Boone and Kurtz with only 1%), 22% with some decision making authority, 8% with action authority and apparently 14% permitted to predict (Boone and Kurtz found 25%) but with none granted authority to learn.

Interface mechanisms

Dimension six refers to the interface for developing a close and harmonious linkage between the decision makers and the model bank and the information bank. Two factors that complicate this task are the continuing inflow of new information into the information bank and new and revised parameters and models in the model bank. The objective is to construct a linkage through which relevant information parameters and models can be selected and used by decision makers.

The types of linkage vary fro those where decision makers directly interrogate the computer to those where the decision makers never interrogate the computer, but always look to information specialists, who in turn provide the linkage. With the first type of linkage, the decision makers must have a good knowledge of the content of the information bank, the forms in which data outputs are available, the language needed to communicate with the computer, and the model bank. In the second type of situation, the decision maker needs only a very general understanding of the types and forms of information that are available. The information specialists, through their knowledge of the system and the needs of the decision makers, serve as matchmakers.

The second type of linkage is very dependent on (1) decision makers' ability to provide adequate profiles of their decision making situations and (2) information system specialists' knowledge of the system and its relationship to the decision makers' needs. A few years ago a center director using this linkage wrote:

> Acknowledging the power of the computer, the heart of the system is the technical staff member. He provides the linkage between the... user and the base of information.

Today the direct interface of decision maker to the information system through remote terminals appears to be gaining great popularity.

Decision capabilities

The final dimension for describing and comparing marketing information systems is based on their capabilities to assist in various types of decisions. For example, a system may provide information, parameters, and models for operational *control decisions* and for strategic *planning decisions.*

For control decisions, a system must provide continuous (sometimes employing exception reporting), rapid problem recognition, and trend development. For example, a system with this capability would provide regular reports of company sales by products and territories, together with total annual sales to data, comparison sales figures for previous periods, and forecasted values for the present period. It could report changes in market share, competitive activity, and a host of other information about competition and the environment. A system with planning capabilities would furnish the information, parameters, and models that decision makers needed for planning, with such information generally required less frequently than control information. Simulation models are included in planning systems. They allow trial of alternative plans so that decision makers can make better decisions.

CHARACTERISTICS OF SUCCESSFUL SYSTEMS

Why do some marketing information systems succeed while other do poorly or fail? Can the blame be placed on physical communication facilities, computers or computer programs, storage and retrieval systems, marketing research technology, or other technical problems? Information specialists say that difficulties are *not* due to the technical aspects.

Furthermore, these specialists agree that little explanation can be provided through examination of specific functions and outputs of successful systems, because there are almost as many variations as there are firms with successful systems. Instead, hypotheses for successful systems center in the characteristics of the systems and the environment in which they operate.

Amstutz has commented on four characteristics essential to successful systems.

1. The system is founded on management's conception of the decision environment.

2. The user-managers understand and are involved in the construction of the system structure.

3. The system is based on disaggregated data files.

4. System development proceeds to increasing levels of sophistication through a process of gradual evolution.

5. The system is spawned and managed by a high level director or coordinator.

Finally, we believe there is one other system characteristic that merits discussion.

6. Marketing information audits are a part of the system.

To provide meaningful information to a group of decision makers and planners, a system must reflect those groups priorities. Also, it must provide information of the type and in the amount and form that management wants and can use. Ackoff, in fact, indicates that the overabundance of irrelevant information is a major cause of MIS failures.

An information system, therefore, must be based on models that reflect management's conception of the environment. Management's initial statements must be examined, refined, made less ambiguous, and, in general, be transformed into more explicit statements before they are adequate to help shape the system to provide relevant information.

Management must be involved in establishing and updating the system. Managers must work at the detail level (e.g., they must spell out market boundaries and product groups and define the content of such measures as market share and net sales) as well as at higher levels. They must agree on the dimensions of their environment and must understand and accept the structuring of the system. Only then are they able to define the measures and the analytical activities they need as decision makers and planners. Involvement helps them to reflect their views in the system and to understand the system. As Ackoff has put it: "No MIS should ever be installed unless the managers for whom it is intended are trained to evaluate and hence control it rather than be controlled by it." Also, the more involved they are, the more likely they are to support the system.

Disaggregated data bank

The bank of file of "micro" or disaggregated data is very essential to the evolution of a system. It is the base that is added to over time. Data are recorded and stored in the lowest aggregation or detail level in which they are likely to be used in the future. For example, an individual sale may be recorded by product, location, price, and time of sale.

Amstutz has written:

> At the heart of every successful information system is a disaggregated data file.... The existence of a disaggregative file facilities system evolution.... In the first stages of system development it is simply impossible to anticipate the direction of later advancement.... The disaggregated data file provides the flexibility which is the prerequisite of intelligent system evolution.

The more disaggregated the data bank is, the most costly it is. Therefore, management must consider the cost of the disaggregate data base against the likelihood that future decisions will require the detailed data.

There are three key elements that can preclude a system from evolving. One is a data bank whose leas aggregated data are too aggregated for proposed new uses. For example, a company may want to analyze its sales by counties, but may find that its past information is disaggregated only to the state level. It can start accumulating information to the desired detail, but because of previous state data, he previous sales experience is lost.

Second, a data bank may be so designed that it is not expandable. A fixed-length record bank that initially appeared large enough may not hold sufficient data. An expandable data bank will permit an information system to evolve.

The third factor influencing evolution of a system is the ability of decision makers to understand and use it as rapidly as it can be developed. Cox and Good state that information quality can be upgraded much more rapidly than management quality. They recommend a master plan for system improvement based on the managers' ability to use the improved information.

Organisation and leadership

Successful systems appear to require organization and leadership, both at the development stage and later. Cox and Good report four approaches they have observed with respect to the installation of a system: the fresh-start organization, or, as they call it, the "clean piece of paper"; committee; low-level leader; and information coordinator.

Fresh start

This approach involves setting up an all-new organization for the handling of marketing information. This implies abolishing the traditional information gathering and processing department. Proponents of this approach argue that much information produced by research and accounting departments does not fit the needs of decision makers and planners. Furthermore, the information parts have *not* been sufficiently integrated to be ready for use. Therefore, the argument goes, the "ideal" procedure is to abolish the old. This approach is not feasible in most companies. Cox and Good, reporting on the firms they have studies, say:

> Traditions and positions are too well entrenched. Furthermore, it would note solve all the problems... it would not ensure the development of an MIS geared to management needs. For another, no management information department could supply all of the data the system needed.

Committee approach Some firms have tried committees composed of members from key information supplying and using areas to study and establish marketing information systems. Such an approach can gain involvement of many appropriate persons and serve to bring forth the unique information problems of various areas.

The typical committee, however, does not get the job done. Development and operation of an information system requires much time—far more than busy managers will spare for such committee work. Also, a committee usually lacks sufficient leadership and authority.

Low-level approach Some firms have shown a lack of understanding of the difficulties of organizing marketing information systems—they have assigned a junior member of the marketing research department to the task. The key man needs perspective, knowledge, and power. A junior man, at best, may possess tow of these.

Coordinator approach Some firms have used a top-level executive as a "coordinator" or director of marketing systems and retained traditional department boundaries. He works somewhat like a "prime contractor," in that he develops the information system plans and specifications and coordinates and inspects the work of various suppliers who contribute or subcontract to the program.

Cox and Good point out that such a coordinator must have cost control. That is, he must be responsible for the overall budget and must negotiate with decision makers and planners to establish their marketing information needs and the funds they must provide for their needs. On the supply side, he arranges with various departments to provide needed information and services and to compensate them. Firms using this approach have usually located the coordinator within the marketing department, not in central or corporate systems departments. This placement results in the coordinator's representing the area that uses and pays for the information system. The major reasons for this placement are:

> Effective development of... systems requires a management, rather than a technical support systems, orientation. Furthermore, effective MIS can be developed only by people who understand users' problems and who can be responsive to users' needs.

This approach to leadership and organization has been the most successful of those studies. Its success is largely dependent on the "right" man filling the job. He should have the full support of top management and be a person who is capable of understanding decision makers' information needs and systems problems.

Marketing information audits

A sixth characteristic of successful systems is marketing information audits. Ralph Cordiner while not specifically talking about MIS, sounded the need:

> What is required... is a... penetrating and orderly study of the business in its entirety to discover what specific information is needed at each particular position in view of the decisions to be made there.

A marketing information audit is a systematic, critical, and impartial review and appraisal of the total marketing program. It is concerned with the basic goals, objectives, policies, and assumptions underlying the information activity, as well as with the methods, procedures, personnel, and organizational structures used in the activity. It is both diagnostic and prognostic in that it search both for malfunctions and for new opportunities. Specific objectives of audits are to pinpoint (1) users' information needs and supplies, (2) unnecessary duplications (including users' "needs"), (3) various information producing activities within an organization, and (4) inefficient and efficient performance of information activities in an organization (from users through to data sources). A marketing information audit is made up of three major phases-a demand audit, a supply audit, and a management audit.

Demand audit

The information needs of each decision maker and planner depend on his tasks and role within the organization. An auditor cannot proceed by simply asking each person to specify his information needs. Some demand for more information than they need while, at the other extreme, others simply do not realize they need information. An auditor can *help* various managers see their needs in terms of type, form, and amounts of information. The individual manager contributes a detailed view of his situation, and the auditor contributes a view of divisional specializations, accompanying organization structures, and functional relationships in terms of the total performance of the organization.

Early reviews with information users are in terms of the information wanted and the estimated value of various information items. Later in the audit, when more meaningful information cost estimates become available, the earlier "ideal" wants are tempered by what decision makers and planners can afford.

Supply audit

The second audit phase is concerned with supplying marketing information. The auditor's starting point is a listing of his firm's information wants. Then he seeks possible sources of data and appraises the alternative processes and costs of transforming them into available, needed forms of information.

The auditor needs to be familiar with the activities and roles of each organizational unit within his firm in order to evaluate internal supply capabilities and capacities. Once again, he works with the managers of the various departments. Supply audits are not limited to assessment of capabilities within the organization. Internal information is supplemented with knowledge of outside data and information supplies and of services and their costs.

Management audit The third and final phase is the managing audit. This is an assessment, review, and evaluation of the information-managing activities. Put more specifically, such an audit is concerned with (1) the balance between needs and supplies, (2) duplications, (3) misallocation of information activities, (4) inefficiencies, and (5) the relationship between information benefits and their costs.

The demand and the supply audits provide the base for assessing the balance between information needs and supplies. Needs that are matched with appropriate information supplies provide one indication of adequate management. However, unmet information needs (that can and should be met) are indicative of difficulties.

Unneeded duplication of activities is also indicative of weak information management. For example, an advertising manager may want market share data by media markets for a specific product and seek it through an advertising agency. The sales manager may need similar market share measures by sales territories and have his sales force seek it. In addition, marketing research may want similar data and, accordingly, proceed to seek it from still other sources. Such a situation needs attention to see if one measure from one source is adequate.

Misallocation of various data processing and information supply activities is also an indication of difficulties. The concern is to see that the right specialists are performing each activity. For example, large tabulation jobs should not be hand-tabulated within a department (because it lacks computer knowledge), but should be handled by the computer center.

Inefficient performance of information activities is a fourth identifiable sign of poor management. Such defects are difficult to identify because, normally, they do not stand out as do cases of poor balance, duplication, and misallocation. Instead, each supplying activity must be analyzed to ascertain the degree of efficiency being attained.

Information benefits and costs

A part of the management audit is continuing review of the relationship between information benefits and their costs. Specifically, management would like to know (1) how much an item of marketing information will cost and (2) the change in dollar profits (the benefits) that will result from the use of the information. What will it cost—what will it accomplish?

Information costs. There are four somewhat distinct costing situations. In the first one, ready-to-use information is purchased in total from outside sources. Then, the paid price, for all practical purposes, becomes the cost. For example, a company may need an estimate of its current flow of products at the retail level and contract with a commercial audit and survey firm. When additional costs are directly associated with this information (e.g., transmitting, analyzing, or storing), they must also be charged against the information.

The second situation is concerned with data secured and handled solely within the organization. For example, prices of competitive products may be needed from all outlets, and the information office handles the entire job. Then all of the direct and separable cost associated with the various tasks would be recorded and charged against the job. The costing procedures involved are very similar to cost analyses of other marketing activities.

In a third type of situation, part of the information task may be handled outside the company and part inside. For example, a company may want to query a representative group about purchasing behavior. The specific questions are to be developed in the company, but the fieldwork and tabulations are to be handled by outside organizations. Then further analysis and communication are to be handled within the company. In this common type of situation, the prices paid to the outside groups are added to the incurred internal costs to arrive at a total cost.

Finally, the costs of not having the information facilities available for other activities (opportunity costs) must be considered.

Information benefits. When information benefits exceed accompanying costs (and there are no better alternative uses for the funds), the information should be secured. In some situations there is little need to undertake detailed evaluation of benefits, in that they clearly do or do not exceed costs. Often, however, information mangers must attempt to assess information benefits. Estimating the usefulness of marketing information presents problems similar to those found in attempts to evaluate the effectiveness of advertising and other marketing activities. Only in a few simple situations is the dollar contribution either easily discerned or obviously sufficient. In most situations, the dollar contribution must be inferred from some intermediate measure. In advertising, for example, Starch and other postreadership recall tests are used to help evaluate the "effectiveness" of advertising. They measure recall, which is not equivalent to measuring effectiveness in terms of contributing, but it provides a useful inferential base.

It was indicated that information benefits vary with the degree of uncertainty with regard to outcomes, the economic consequences of an incorrect decision, and the amount by which the information can reduce the uncertainty. Multiple-use information extends the benefits to a number of uses and, in turn, tends to raise the total benefits received. For example, detailed information on company and competitive sales would probably be used by at least the sales manager, the advertising manager, and the marketing manager in planning and controlling their activities. In contrast, a special-purpose piece of information may be used only by one manager, who alone must pay out sufficient benefit to cover the cost. Multiple-use information normally includes estimates and measures of potential, product sales by markets (and other breakdowns), competitive product sales, distribution expenses by major categories, and channel and other promotional mix knowledge.

2

ORGANISING FOR MARKETING INFORMATION

Whenever a group of people work together to achieve a common set of goals, problems of organization are present. Organizations arise to provide working arrangements. There are obviously alternative ways to do this. Organizations can be broken down into four basic parts: (1) tasks—the things they do with purposes in mind; (2) structure—the most or less permanent framework of people, materials, and processes in their sequences and hierarchies, (3) tools—from physical tools to technology for helping get things done; and (4) people. An organization's task is not the sole determinant of its shape. Instead, the relationships of all four of the parts run in both directions resulting in a great variety of organizations.

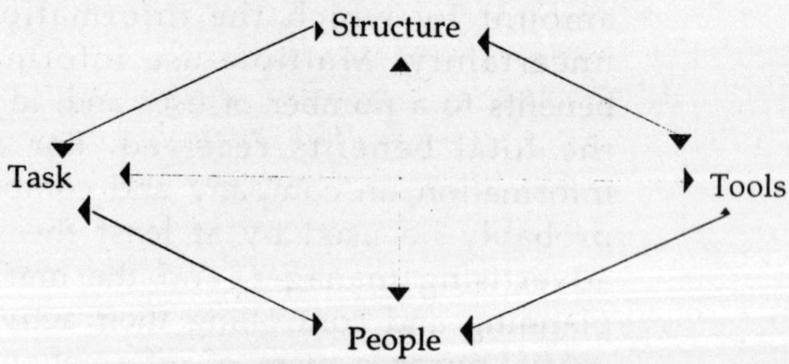

This chapter is concerned with marketing research and information organization to help firms meet their marketing needs. In the first section we consider several concepts that are universally important to organization design. In the second section we examine four ways to orient marketing and marketing information organizations: function, product, customer, and region. We discuss existing organizations and, when applicable, also explore the dimensions that future marketing information systems may take. The emphasis is an analysis, not on prediction.

Before discussing some of the alternative organizations, we should briefly review tow concepts of organization design—specialization and coordination. Specialization brings substantial gains in productivity. As Adam Smith pointed out long ago, this is due to increases of dexterity, saving of time by not passing from one type of work to another, and development of machines to abridge labor. Later writers have added that differences in peoples' natural abilities and reduction of wasteful duplication of tools and facilities are also important. Overspecialization, however, brings rigidity and leads to worker boredom, loss of interest, and poor job performance. Finally, the gains to be achieved through specialization are conditioned by the task of *coordinating* the outputs of specialized activities into usable forms.

The principal purpose of organizations, such as those described in this chapter, is to facilitate the achievement of tasks by providing structures and tools that do not create artificial barriers to the interaction between people. Our concern is to apply the major concepts or principles of organization to the problem of designing effective marketing research and information organizations. We need to examine the ways in which the advantages of specialization may be achieved.

There are numerous concepts of organizational design where the best principle is far from clear (centralization versus decentralization). Also, students of organization must remember that every formal organization is intertwined with many informal relationships and groups that influence organizational performance. The "official" organization does not always (if ever) reflect the "real" system. However, to paraphrase Leavitt, Dill, and Eyring, it is dangerous to conclude that the informal system constitutes the "real" organization and that the formal rules, responsibilities, and duties are merely ritualistic nonsense with no purpose and meaning. The formal organization is extremely functional and it is quite effective in keeping the organization going.

Informal relationships

Marketing information flows both vertically (formally) and horizontally (informally) within marketing organizations. Andersen and Cundiff report that in four Texas-based companies informal information flows were the most important. This informal communication took place in four ways. First, there was the voluntary exchange of information through information copies of correspondence. Second, special-purpose committees such as new product committees facilitated horizontal flows. A third type of information flow took place during staff meetings. Finally, the most frequent was the informal, nonperiodic exchange of information when executives met to discuss matters in general.

Andersen and Cundiff also indicated that there was little *requirement* to exchange marketing information. Most of it flowed at the discretion of the individual managers. Furthermore, specialized information was sought from the managers, who served as the centers of communication for the specialized areas. This left the attainment of coordinated decision making up to the individual managers.

Marketing pressures

Marketing organizations must accommodate four basic sources of marketing pressures: various functions, products, regions, and customers. These four pressures get accommodated in various ways in different industries and even by different firms within industries.

The resulting marketing organizations often are unique. Rarely are all four pressures accommodated equally. Instead, the believed to be the most important receive major attention in the organization and the others receive limited attention or are completely ignored. When companies sell numerous and varied products to relatively homogeneous markets, the organizations are likely to orient around the products. When regional difference in marketing are considered the most important, regionally oriented organizations are likely to develop. Customer-oriented organizations may arise when different customers must be treated in vastly different ways. Finally, a functional framework may develop when the other three pressure may be built in on a subsidiary basis.

These four pressures influence the organization of marketing research and information activities as well as the overall marketing organization.

FUNCTION-ORIENTED MARKETING ORGANISATION

Function-oriented organization has been popular with many firms that have recognized marketing as an important problem and decision-making area. Under this arrangement marketing specialists have taken on responsibilities for marketing research, advertising, sales promotion, sales, and other functional specialties. Normally, no one of these specialists has been specifically responsible for a given product or market. Instead, the top marketing manager has been ultimately responsible for the integration and coordination of the individual efforts into sound marketing programs. Consequently, he has held ultimate responsibility and, for practical purposes, sole responsibility for the success or failure of his firm's products in each geographical area.

In this type of organization, managers of the functionally specialized units are often responsible for the determination and assembly of much of the marketing information they need. Starch Reports, for example, are usually bought by advertising managers or their advertising agencies. Sales managers usually require direct reports from their salesmen, and so forth.

In many firms the marketing research specialty is not even formally recognized. The most recent American Marketing Association report of marketing research activities in the United States indicated that 45 per cent of the responding companies did not have a formal marketing research department. An additional 24 per cent of the responding companies had only one person assigned to the activity.

The quality of marketing research departments within different companies varies immensely. Usually they are shown on organization charts on a common plane with the advertising and sales departments. In practice, however, some are shrouded in their organizations with few people, little budget, and little influence. To quote William R. Davidson, a past president of the American Marketing Association, "... the typical corporation's investment in marketing research is minimal... and it indicates a reluctance within industry to invest in research dealing with people, markets and marketing...."

In such situations the departments are concerned with a small part of the total marketing information needs of their firms. Lee Adler has provided a particularly lucid portrayal of the plight of such marketing research departments:

> The research director inherits a legacy of practical difficulties. Gaps exist between marketing research needs and fulfillment—and there is one major explanation. Marketing management problems are broad-scale and complex. However, researchers define such delimited problems for investigation that the findings either deal with too small a part of the total problem or cannot be related to the total problem. As a result, researchers have little link with reality as far as marketing executives are concerned.

On the other hand, many marketing research departments regularly provide continuing data bases, as well as large quantities of special-problem information for their decision makers. The American Marketing Association study cited earlier listed 34 types of marketing research activities. The four most common in order of importance) were: determination of market characteristics, development of market potential, market share analysis and sales analysis.

How do function-oriented marketing research departments organize to provide such activities. The organization of the Market Research Department of The

Maytag Company provides one case in point. This department provides three major types of activities. It analyzes, compares, and reports on company sales by product and by market; it engages in nonroutine, special-problem research; and it prepares sales forecasts.

Function-oriented information system

The Maytag company illustration pertained only to what that company has termed "market research." What about a more complete marketing information system that could handle many of the activities. What might it look like and how could it function? Once again, there are organization alternatives. When certain pressures are particularly demanding or critical, they may include a new product information group in an otherwise function-oriented structure. Instead, it suggests one form for a function-oriented marketing information system.

A look at one of the groups within the office suggests the degree of specialization that is possible. The Field Projects group would be responsible for all field studies, that is, for studies taking place in the marketplace. When outside field forces are needed, the Field Project group would be responsible for their retention and supervision. The Field Project group would also provide special training and other help in the design and implementation of field studies to inside group (e.g., the sales force) and they may conduct field work themselves. In each instance the Field Project group is the field work specialist.

Lest this organization be misperceived, a few observations are needed regarding the relationships among the various functional groups. Some of the groups would tend to be more information-using and condensing than generating or consulting. For example, the Numerical Analysis and Data Control group, for the most part, would provide services for the other groups. In contrast, information generation as well as considerable condensation would take place in Sales and Distribution Cost analysis, Market Measurement, and Customer Evaluation groups. Further information condensation and use would occur in the Long-Range Planning and the Product Planning groups as well as in the director's office. Finally, the director's office would coordinate activities, assign priorities, arbitrate disputes, and, in general, plan and control the marketing information office.

Selection consideration

When would a function-oriented organization by used? It appears most advantageous for short-to-limited-line firms selling their various offerings through essentially similar channels. That is, this structure is appropriate for firms like The Maytag Company, Schlitz Brewing Company and the numerous other firms that have (1) relatively few products or product lines and (2) relatively similar and related marketing problems even among their somewhat varied product lines. In these cases this orientation is particularly effective, because it permits a maximum of information specialization and, therefore, the advantages of specialization. In addition it affords extensive perspective throughout the marketing information function.

This structure does not provide the most effective orientation for the multi-product firms or firms facing heterogeneous marketing problems. It simply cannot provide sufficient attention to individual product lines, individual customers, or regional differences without overwhelming problems of coordination.

Product-oriented marketing organizations can be built in a number of different ways. Large companies that are highly diversified, such as General Electric, General Motors, DuPont, and Ford Motor Company, and example, has nine car, truck, and body divisions, automotive component divisions, one household appliance division, four engine divisions, and four other non-automotive or defense divisions. General Electric is divided into six product groups or divisions: Consumer Products, Aerospace and Defense, Components and Construction Materials, Electric Utility, Industrial, and Information and International.

The following figure shown a general product division model. While this model shown marketing research and advertising activities at both corporate and product division levels, not all firms are organized in this manner. Some place one or both functions at only one of the levels.

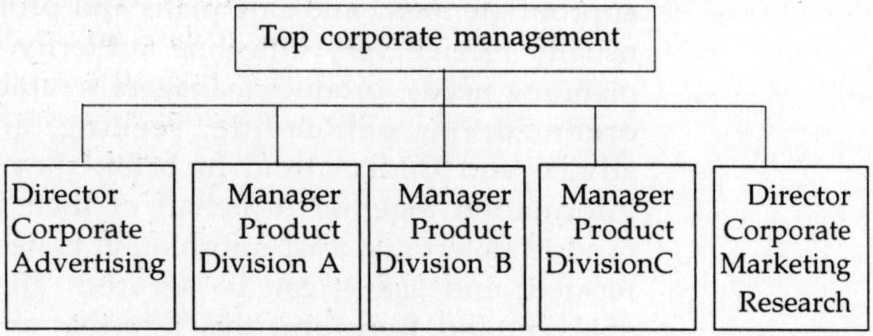

When marketing research appears at both levels, the relationships between the two levels as well as the division of duties varies among companies. Some divisional research offices report to the corporate research offices. In other cases the relationships between the two offices are on a voluntary basis.

Kotler has indicated the major factors that influence location of the marketing research activities. Some economies may be gained by placing marketing research at the corporate level if it (1) minimizes the duplication of personnel, space, and equipment, (2) permits the hiring of a few extremely competent persons, or (3) facilitates better coordination of separate product programs. On the other hand, if marketing research problems of individual product divisions are radically different, or if the corporate staff lacks adequate acquaintance with individual products, divisional operations are advantageous. Of course, to get adequate product attention, the corporate marketing research office could be oriented by products.

The Mennen Company organization, indicated another way to gain product attention. This type of organization makes major use of product managers. All of the products are distributed through one sales force, advertising is handled by one advertising manager, and there is one manager of marketing research.

Under this type of organization, each of the many products in a firm's line has a manager-guardian, and supposedly there are no orphans to be lost or trampled in the mass of products and functions. Individual product managers are usually charged with preparing appropriate merchandising plans and proposals, but they usually receive very little line authority. To accomplish planning needs, product managers scramble among their organizations persuading, seeking, and assembling advice and information. In brief, they pull scattered information together in behalf of their products. They need to determine *what* information is needed, *where* it is located, and *how* it can be secured. They then secure, analyze, and transform this information into proposed marketing plans. Thus product managers are very much involved in the management of marketing information.

The marketing research office is usually retained in the product-oriented organization. However, the advent of product managers has resulted in some changes. Marketing research activities have become more operationally oriented (product managers, e.g., have typically prepared their own sales forecasts). The marketing research units have become more technique, method, and "doing" oriented. They serve more as operational arms by helping in research design, information collection, purchase, and analysis.

Some marketing research departments have been product-oriented. In this, new product research is assigned to a new product research manager. The three product research managers use the specialized research activities of the behavioural research manager, econometrician, field administrator, and librarian. For example, the grocery products market research manager may turn to the librarian for sources of published relevant information or other information stored on magnetic tape or disk files. If such information process inadequate, the product research manager may decide to design a research study that will provide the needed information. The various information specialists would likely be involved in various phases of the study design, implementation, and analysis, both individually and in term efforts.

As a research office is broadened, each additional information activity might be placed either under individual product information managers or separately as a specialized composite whole (like the econometrician) available jointly to the product managers.

For example, where might a marketing sales and cost analysis section be added to a product-oriented information system? Conceivably, such a section could be added to each product line area. However, sales and cost analysis is quite specialized, and both machine and men utilization advantages accrue to a consolidation. In addition, no special advantages are likely to result from physically locating this information activity in each of the several product areas. Regardless of where it is located, one segment of analysis must be by products. Consequently, it appears that this activity can be best managed as a specialized whole rather than as a part of each of several product areas.

As a second example, where might a brand or product manager activity be added? Conceivable, this activity could be consolidated in one specialized merchandising office or it could be added as a part of each product information section. Because of the prior concentration of information activities by products, it appears that this planning activity could best be managed as a part of each product section.

The specialized nature of the sales and cost analysis activity and the product manager function makes their placement within an information system relatively clear. Not all information activities fit so positively.

In this structure there has been centralization of (1) numerical analysis and data storage, (2) sales and cost analysis, (3) management of incidental and secondary data, (4) specialized consultation on behavioral research and operations research, and (5) administration of field projects. Most of the other information activities have been assigned by product lines.

The typical product group contains (1) a section manager, (2) an information coordinator, assisted by product planning managers, (3) project directors (to initiate and carry through special-problem-focused research), assisted by research analysts, and (4) market estimators (to provide market measurements). The various product information managers would be charged with fulfilling the corporation-wide marketing information needs for their assigned products. However, the actual information may be stored, analyzed, and so forth in several locations. Finally, various product group managers would use the specialized services of the nonproduct-oriented information managers (e.g., the behavioural and the operation research consultants) in their activities.

Selection consideration The product-oriented marketing information organization may be an appropriate alternative for firms with many products whether they use product divisions or one centralized organization. Companies organized by product·divisions that want a centralized information system (or part of it) at their corporate level are likely to use a product orientation. Also, other multiple-product companies (without product divisions) that face unique markets and marketing techniques, because of their different products, are likely candidates. The product orientation is appropriate in both of these situations, because it focuses attention on individual products (or product lines). When product marketing problems give the most pressure, product orientation is appropriate.

Small, short-line firms, or company divisions with few products, do not need a product orientation. They are likely to have sufficient attention already focused on individual products because of their few numbers.

Regionally oriented marketing organisation Companies selling over a wide geographical area will usually have regional specialization of at least their field sales. In some situations entire marketing organizations may be structured predominantly along regional lines. This is most likely to occur when regional problems dominate and customers and products are relatively homogeneous. A regional orientation, for example, has been used by at least one large brewer who though that regional brewers provided the major competition.

In regionally oriented organization, four regional vice-presidents report to the executive vice president. Reporting to each regional vice-president is a regional marketing director, who in turn has reporting to him an advertising manager, market research and planning manager, service manager, and field sales manager.

At the corporate level there is a vice-president of marketing. He has a staff that includes directors of advertising, marketing research, sales promotion, marketing education, trade relations, and market administration.

When marketing research appears at both levels, the relationship between the levels as well as the division of activities varies among companies.

The marketing research offices are regionally oriented in the sense that they are principally concerned with the information activities within their regions. However, it would be a most unusual situation where a centralized, regionally oriented, company-wide information system would be appropriate. Instead, the offices would normally be organized by functions, products, or customers.

A customer-oriented framework may be particularly appropriate for firms that market to various customer groups who are distinctly different in their buying behavior or product need. The Scott Paper Company, for example, has divided its marketing into two distinct customer groups at the top level—retail and industrial. It has further divided the industrial customers group by three customer types—government sales, national accounts, and other industrial customers.

Some of its customers are in separate categories, because their product needs are distinct and selling to them required specialized product information. Other customers (government) are in separate categories, not necessarily because they buy different products, but because their buying behavior is such that different marketing activities are required.

The Scott Paper Company organization shows a corporation-wide location of marketing research and several other marketing activities under a corporate director of marketing services.

Customer oriented information system

With a customer orientation, the marketing information organization focuses principally on the various customer groups rather than on functions or products.

In this hypothetical organization, three of the four managers are charged with the information activities for individual customer groups (government, industrial, and consumer). The fourth manager (numerical analysis and data control) provides his specialty to the three other groups.

The three different customer groups contain somewhat different activities. The government group, for example, is the only one with a Washington, D.C., office and the consumer group is the only one with a behavioral study unit. Sales and distribution cost analyses units have been appended individually to the industrial and to the consumer groups. Such an arrangement is likely to arise only when sales and cost analyses problems are vastly different from one customer group to another. Normally, as observed earlier, this activity would be consolidated in one specialized department.

Selection consideration

The customer-oriented information system is a very appropriate alternative for firms that have oriented their other major marketing activities along customer lines. It continues the alignment.

In addition, firms that feel pressure for more customer orientation, but cannot achieve it in terms of field sales or other activities, may use it for obtaining information. Such situations may arise may arise when distinct customer groups are present but are too small and widely dispersed to support specialization in selling activities. Also, customers may fit in several customer categories and not want several different salesmen from one company calling on them. In these situations, customer-oriented information organizations may provide just the necessary attention. Finally, some customer-oriented firms divide the information activity between the corporate level and customer groups. Basically, the same issues that were discussed.

There is a considerable diversity of informed opinion and business practice with respect to answers to the question: "Where does marketing research best fit into the company's organizational structure?" Some consideration was given to this subject when the delegation of marketing activities between the corporate and divisional levels was discussed. The remaining major question is: Should the marketing information system be under the jurisdiction of marketing people or under that of other (whether centralized or decentralized)?

A number of studies have indicated the most frequent arrangements for marketing research offices. They agree that approximately 50 to 56 per cent of all marketing research managers report to sales or marketing managers. One of the studies indicates that about 37 per cent of the managers report to top corporate, nonmarketing management, while Twedt reported 23 per cent in 1963, but 30 per cent by 1968.

Prescriptive advice, which is still relevant, about where marketing research offices should report has been given by Lazo and Corbin and The Conference Board. They appear to agree that if the research activities are confined to those associated with sales or marketing, the department should report to a. sales or marketing executive. The major reason has been that such a marketing information department works primarily with and for persons in the marketing division. The work of the department, as a member of the marketing division, may be enhanced if it is viewed and treated as one of the family. Furthermore, being a member of the family, an information department may better understand the marketing decision's information problems and needs.

When the activities of the research department are more inclusive and the department serves other parts of the company, it is likely to report to a top-level, nonmarketing executive. To paraphrase a comment from the The Conference Board Study, a marketing research department that has expanded its activities so that it serves the financial, production, and administrative parts of the company as well as marketing is often placed directly under a top (non-marketing) corporate executive. The Conference Board Study proposed several criteria to determine the placement of a marketing research department within a company. The location should provide: (1) freedom from the influence of those whom its work affects, (2) maximum efficiency of operations and (3) the cooperation and support of the manager to whom it reports.

Based on the criteria, findings and comments of Lazo and Corbin, kegerreis and a new study of The Conference Board we expect, in general, that the more broadly based, multiple-activity research and information systems will report to top corporate management and, as more departments undertake more information activities, more of them will report to top corporate management. The organization and location of integrated marketing information systems certainly need more real-world trial and error before much can be said. Cox and Good, who have screened more than 50 companies and have reviewed over 100 articles on information systems, have commented:

> Many companies we have observed have not really come to grips with the difficult problem of providing the organizational arrangements and leadership necessary for successful MIS development.

However, they have recommended that the head of the MIS represent the area that uses and pays for the information services. And, finally, an observation by a leading authority in accounting provides some thought for the future:

> Advanced business systems tend to break down traditional department walls and tend to redefine managers' duties—freeing them for more attention directing and problem solving.

3

THE MARKETING INFORMATION MANAGEMENT SYSTEM

A marketing information management system can be defined as a structure designed to implement the research process. As such, it includes all personnel, equipment, and procedures developed to produce information for managerial decision making. The purpose of the system or structure is to perform certain functions necessary in carrying out the research process. Research, as previously defined, is used broadly to include all information-generating activities. The ultimate purpose of the information is to improve the decisions made by the managers receiving the information. The functions involved in carrying out the research process are collecting data, processing the data to transform it into useful information, and transmitting the information to the manager.

An illustration of how one of the pioneers in this area developed his information system may be helpful in understanding the concept. The development of information systems at Pillsbury from 1956 to 1966 was described by Mr. Terrance Hanold, executive vice president, Finance and Planning, as follows:

> From 1956 to 1961, the bulk of our efforts were directed at the immediate savings which systems staff could realize from reflowing paperwork and at the further savings more slowly obtainable from substituting primary data processing equipment for clerical procedures. These efforts centered on the primary accounting levels in the central and branch office areas where paper flourished,

> where the targets were clusters of people employing the lowest routine skills, and where the savings were directly demonstrable.

While they seemed hectic and adventurous at the time because of the novelty of the systematic approach and the drastic dislocations of personnel which their rigorous application always seems to threaten (without quite accomplishing), in retrospect they were halcyon days when we lived with clearly quantified ideas and produced crisply measurable results.

This was the period of simple substitution, when we replaced one method of doing things with another and better method, but the frame of things remained essentially unscathed.

Overlapping the latter end of this five-year period and continuing in the five-year span that followed was the trend toward consolidation of identical operations into fewer locations.

So long as the orders, invoices, and accounts receivable are processed by clerical routines, it seems to make little difference whether they are concentrated or dispersed, and tradition held that they were best done in intimate relation to the field sales force and in proper subordination to the necessity of its optimum use made plain the economics of more limited geographic locations, so we gradually shrank our grocery products branch accounting offices from 33 to 4. An when the advent of our first computer made it possible in 1960, to a single location in Minneapolis.

After our transfer to [our fist computer] a centrally operated GE-225 computer in 1962, we made parallel consolidations at Minneapolis of our field sales accounting operations in our refrigerated and flour milling products divisions as well.

The order-invoice cycle is the operation critical to any total systems treatment of our main business areas. The programming of this cycle has been repeated, laborious, and continuous. It was achieved in primitive style as we moved from manual to automatic data processing in more advanced form when we changed to our first computer; in far more comprehensive shape as we moved to the GE-225; and is being expanded again as we have transferred this summer to a large-scale GE-635 [a time-sharing system with 92 remote terminals]. Experience, experiment, and discovery are forever disclosing new potentials for information, analysis, decision, and control as logical by-products of the process. And more of these values came properly within our reach until central processing was fully attained.

But the progress of this primary consolidation of a few operations brought more than enhanced informational and analytical capabilities in its train. It also started a current of fundamental shifts in the management structure of which the meanings are only beginning to be perceived. One immediate results was the removal of a very large administrative function from the branch sales manager, and of a very large administrative supervisory job from his superiors. Another result was to relieve the information flow of the frequent and varying modifications which branch managers habitually had given to the data before transmitting it to the divisional office.

With the addition of a Datanet-30 communications computer to our Minneapolis center, an effort of like character began in our plants and mills, and is just now coming to completion. Only original entry data of materials received, of ingredients processed, and of shipments initiated is recorded at these points, and then as a rule only in a form sufficient for transmission to the computer center. All inventory, payroll, costing, scheduling, and other accounting and control procedures are maintained by the central electronic apparatus with such informational returns to the plant office as operations may require.

Again, the administrative load of the plant manager is lightened, and his concentration on production and engineering matters is encouraged.

Nothing the disappearance of several echelons in the chain of command, we discovered the compacting effect on organization of more advanced computer programming, and because of the length and vertical reach which this advance gave managers, the executive level found itself much nearer the field of action than it has formerly been.

Next, computer disciplines began to infiltrate areas in which the judgments of specialists and technicians has technicians had enjoyed unfettered play—those of nutrition, formation, traffic, quality control, procurement, and many others. In these enclaves, where the tangled threads of decision embraced many factors and infinite interrelations between them, which prevented either adequate direction of evaluation by conventional methods, linear programming techniques are providing both guides to decision and measurements for review.

Dimensions of the information management system

Before going into a detailed discussion of the nature of an information management system, some of the general identifiable dimensions of a typical system should be understood. There dimensions permit different systems to be described, compared, and contrasted on a common basis even when each marketing manager has unique information requirements and unique perspective of both the environment and of the firm. In this context the following dimensions are significant:

1. Management access.
2. Information recency.
3. Information aggregation.
4. Analytical sophistication.
5. System authority.

Management access. The first dimension of evaluation measures the time lapse between management's request for certain information and receipt of the desired report or display. Measurements along this dimension range from several months for manual compilation of extensive statistics, to fractions of a second for on-line computer access, to information in primary storage.

Information recency. Information recency refers to the time lapse between the occurrence of an event in the environment and inclusion of data describing that event in the system. This may range from several weeks for certain market developments to a few hours or minutes for automated inventory control.

Information aggregation. Information aggregation describes the detail with which information is maintained in the systems data bank. Inventory control systems in which information on product components or subassemblies is maintained at the item level represent relatively disaggregate (micro) data maintenance, while industry market share statistics (developed through trade associations) represent highly aggregate (macro) measures.

Analytical sophistication. Analytical sophistication represents the complexity of models or statistical procedures encompassed by the system. Several levels of sophistication are possible within an information management system. At the lowest level of analytical sophistication, the computer retrieves a specified record and displays the information it contains. The second level involves aggregation, gathering numbers from one or more records to produce a total or subtotal. At a higher level the system may perform arithmetic averaging or compute differences. The fourth level, introduces classification schemes through which data are aggregated within subsets or conditionally segmented. At the next level, statistical techniques are used to develop extrapolations from historic data, statistical best estimates, analyses of variances, or trend estimates. Macro process models may be used at the sixth level to relate multiple factors in the management environment to current or expected future conditions. At the higher levels of analytic sophistication, micro analytical behavioral models are encountered. These behavioral simulations may be used to produce an artificial environment paralleling the real world environment monitored by the information network.

System authority. The final dimension of evaluation, authority delegated to the system, is closely associated with analytic sophistication. Management is more willing to delegate authority to sophisticated systems and conversely, as management places greater demands on as information management system, a greater level of analytic sophistication is required.

The need for information management systems

The system approach to marketing management is a way of viewing and analyzing a marketing organization so that the manager can improve the performance of the major marketing activities. A systems analyst or manager in attempting to group major marketing management activities should consider (1) the general area that the decision concerns, (2) the time dimension of the decision process, and (3) similar requirements for information in the decision process. Using these criteria marketing management can be grouped into the decision areas of market analysis and formulating the marketing mix.

The system must be able to trace all information flows associated with these management activities and with the decision-making processes involved, regardless of the organizational boundaries that must be penetrated. The network of information flows that is outlined for each group of management activities forms the basis of the information management system. The focus of the information system activities is on the generation and management of the necessary information flows. If the system is to be an effective information network, it must deal with all major information flows. An information flow is essentially the movement of data from its source to the manager and includes the processing of data to convert it into usable information. In considering methods of getting timely and accurate information to the marketing manager, the two major information flows must be considered. These are marketing intelligence and the internal information flow.

Marketing intelligence is the flow of information from the environment to points within the firm. This information comes from such sources as wholesalers, competitors, customers, and the government whose actions affect pricing, advertising, and other marketing management decisions. Marketing intelligence is a term used to encompass raw data, statistics, inferences, opinions, impressions, and rumors from outside the firm. The idea of marketing intelligence is borrowed from the military. "The high level military decision maker is usually far removed from the battlefield and therefore is totally dependent upon secondhand information in directing the battle," thus, he uses hunches and rumors as well as hard facts. The marketing manager is in a similar position; he is fighting for sales in the market place with allies such as suppliers, channel members, and complementary producers against the competitive enemies. Action is also constrained by the external environment within which operations must be conducted. Information from outside the firm is essential in effectively conducting the essential managerial activities.

The second flow is the internal marketing information flow which consists of the flow between relay points within the firm. This includes the marketing intelligence after is has entered the firm. The internal flow is comprised of downward, upward, and horizontal flows. The downward flow consists of communications from top management to subordinates. The upward flow is made up of "grapevine" as well as requisitioned information moving from the lower levels of the organization toward the top. The horizontal flow consists of information passed between employees on the same level.

These marketing information flows are shown in Figure 1. The flows are initiated with the collection of data from internal and external sources. Internal sources are within the firm and provide such data as performance reports and decision rules. External sources, outside of the firm, provide data relating to the customers, markets, the competitive situation, and environmental constraints. Data from these sources typically flow into some type of storage network. The data may then be analyzed by the application of model or statistical techniques before transmission to the

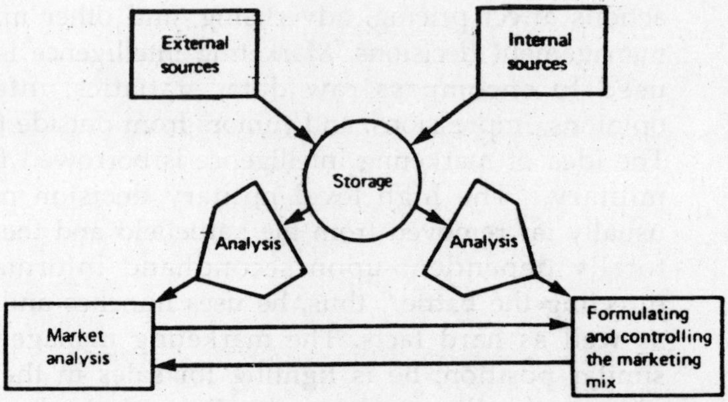

Marketing information flows

manager engaged in some specific type of decision making. These transmissions form a flow of information to the managers responsible for conducting each of the marketing management activities involved in market analysis and formulating and controlling the marketing mix. The types of data collected and the nature of the flows and analysis depend on the needs of marketing managers in conducting these activities.

Problems in management of information flows

Several factors have worked to inhibit the development of well-managed, integrated information systems. First, marketing information needs have usually been satisfied on a piecemeal basis by using data sources and reports designed for other management purposes, such as financial reports, production control, and accounting. This "hand-me-down" method sometimes looks like an economical way to solve continuing marketing information problems. Basic information needs to unfulfilled, however, since important aspects of customer identification, cost allocations, and external market conditions cannot be captured unless special provisions are made for doing so.

Secondly, EDP techniques have been successfully applied first where dollar savings or operating advantages have been easily recognized; accounting, inventory control, order entry, and production scheduling usually get top priority. The benefits of better information for the marketing function are difficult to quantify in dollars and cents.

Finally, the concepts behind a marketing information management system may be misinterpreted by senior executives. At one extreme, they may expect such systems to deliver the answers to the most difficult kinds of questions—the effectiveness of advertising and promotion, for example. At the other extreme, the systems approach may be dismissed as just another sales reporting scheme. Neither concept is correct.

The lack of an effective information management system can lead to many problems. There such problems which may arise with an unmanaged or poorly managed information management system are:

1. *Information disappearance*. A salesman obtaining information about a competitor's activities may forget to relay the data, may not know who should receive the data inside the organization, or may purposely suppress the information for personal reasons.

2. *Information delay*. Marketing intelligence and internal information may take longer than necessary to travel from the original relay points through the handling system to the decision makers. Thus decisions may be delayed and lose their effect or may be made without sufficient information which can lead to poor decisions.

3. *Information distortion*. Data may be changed or misinterpreted in the process of being encoded, transmitted, processed, and decoded. This can result in a poor managerial decision even when accurate data is being gathered at the collection level.

These problems may arise when a marketing department has an inefficient or unplanned information system. Additional problems may be generated, of an equally serious nature, if a narrow view of information flows is adopted. The narrow model for a traditional information flows within the business organization. The network supporting such a closed system contains both vertical and horizontal flows. The characteristics of a closed system suggests that the organization is situated in a constant type of environment and that the management process can be conducted in a specified manner. This viewpoint suggests that within the time frame of one planning cycle, management does not intend to respond or react to changes in the raw materials markets, the external environment, the finished goods market, or actions by competitors.

The implication of a closed network is that the overall business system does not need to react or respond to external changes; and that the nature of business activity is such that all phases of the planning process can be completed before any of the activities in the time period covered by the plan begin. This means that the control process begins only after the planning process (strategic and management) has been completed and that management control seeks conformance of activity to the plan. All aspects of the planning process must be performed within the time frame of the cycle. Once the complete planning process has been performed, the process cannot be repeated during the time frame of the cycle. This means that based on changes in the environment under conditions of a traditional information management system, it is not possible to quickly change the assignment of resources or personnel for purposes accomplishing a new order of identified tasks.

A more realistic approach is to view planning and control as continuous and overlapping operations. Time requirements for information vary considerably: at one extreme, information may be required continuously (for management control) and at the other extreme some information is needed only once (for strategic planning). To meet the needs of effective management, the general model for a marketing information management system must be open. It must cover all major information flows within a marketing organization and between the marketing organization and its environment. It must also be flexible regarding the time requirement for obtaining and processing information.

The need for an information management system

There is a need for a set of procedures to diagnose and solve the basic informational problems arising in the management of an organization. The information management system provides a systematic method for accomplishing this task. The systems analyst (should attempt) to identify, observe, analyze, and specify and requirements for information (for the management) activities throughout the business organization, to determine the sources of data, and to match the information requirements with the appropriate data sources by employing some of the current management science tools and techniques.

The aim is to establish the ideal system that is compatible with the major management requirements in the existing unique environment of a particular business firm. In one firm the ideal system may make use of computer equipment, communication facilities, and operations research techniques; however, in another firm, limited use may be made of these items. The need is to develop a unique system in each organization that is appropriate for the unique conditions in that organization. This ideal system for a given organization should attempt to balance the most timely, the most efficient, and the most economical arrangement of information flows for that organization. Thus, management will have better information for particular management activities and can establish control devices for dealing with recurring types of problems on an exceptions basis.

Functions performed by the information management system

In order for the total information system to operate effectively, certain basic functions must be performed. These functions maybe grouped into three sets:

1. Data collection
2. Data processing
3. Information transmitting

Data collection. The first step in data collection is a careful specification of pertinent data needed by management in each phase of the management process. This should be provided by the information audit. A data search should then be conducted to locate the sources of the necessary data. Data may be available in journals, government publications, internal reports or other secondary sources. These should be used whenever possible in order to reduce cost and increase the efficiency of the system. When secondary sources are not available, primary data must be collected or purchased. Procedures should be developed in securing relevant data, and screening to filter out unimportant material. The system must also be able to retrieve stored information from the data bank in order to produce periodic reports and form a basis for various types of analysis.

Data processing. A second important function is that of data processing. The data processing function includes the elements of storage, manipulation, and movement of data. Systems may be organized in various ways to accomplish this function. A centralized system is one in which all of the processing is performed by an organization clearing house of information. All data collecting and processing within the organization is done by a centralized system, where data is stored and used to prepare the required reports. A decentralized system involves several rather autonomous parts serving functional departments or suborganizations within the enterprise. Each of these gathers its own data, produces reports as needed by the department it is serving, and stores data accordingly. Another form of system is a distribution-oriented one whose operations emphasize the transmission of information to managerial stations throughout the organization. The opposite is the storage-oriented system which is more concerned with the efficient storage of data than with its transmission to information users in the managerial system. Retrieving information from such a unit may require an excessive amount of effort on the part of the manager who needs the information. "An information (... storage unit) is considered small by authorities... if it has access to 50,000 or less records. A record is an amount of information pertinent to something or somebody about which the organization needs information." Units that store and have available up to 1 million records are usually considered to be medium sized, and large systems contain over 1 million records at any one time.

Most information systems include data-retrieval and document-retrieval procedures which aid in the processing function. Data-retrieval procedures take many different types of data, kept in storage devices, and manipulate them in such a way that a desired report can be produced, usually involving mathematical calculations. Document-retrieving procedures are able to produce a given document upon request but with little or no manipulation of data. This type of procedure sometimes makes use of microfilm and other recording techniques that use miniatured reproduction in order to store documents and records.

Almost every system uses both manual and automated techniques in getting its work done. It is possible to develop a system that is entirely manual in which all of the storage, manipulation, and movement of data is accomplished without the use of any automated devices. This is usually seen only in very small businesses. The degree to which a system should be automated depends upon the speed with which the data must be processed, the amount of data to be processed and stored, and the value of the information to the managers compared to the costs of automating the system.

The key aspect of processing is the manipulation of data in such a way as to transform it into useful information. This manipulation is carried out by the application of various statistical techniques and models to the raw data. The appropriate techniques and models vary with the managerial activity under consideration.

In terms of computer procedures the most common data processing techniques are those that make great use of batch, or sequential processing techniques. A batch technique is one which gathers and saves all transactions affecting a file of data, and after a certain period of time or after a specified number of transactions have been accumulated, the file is updated making use of the transactions that have been collected to that point. Real-time systems do not gather transactions for processing at some later time, but process each transaction as it occurs."

Information transmitting. The third function of the marketing information management system is to deliver needed information to the manager and aid him in using the information. The manager needs the information either in the form of periodic reports or special project data, depending upon whether the decision under consideration is strategic or managerial. In addition, he may need a research specialist to help him interpret the information delivered to him. Help may also be required in formulating problems and specifying the types of information needed. Finally, the manager may find computer program assistance of value. Specialists in the computer field can help the decision maker in understanding the computer and the kind of things it can do. These various types of technical assistance should enhance the manager's ability to secure and use information to make accurate and timely decisions.

A framework for the information management system

Five basic elements or components are key functional parts of the typical information management system. These components perform the necessary functions of the system and include: the data collection procedures, data bank, statistical bank, model bank, and display unit. This flow is initiated by questions arising in the management process. These questions which may relate to either market analysis or formulation of the marketing mix were collected by a unit designed to handle the interface between the system and the managers. Such a mechanism is usually referred to as a display unit.

These managerial questions are the basis for determining data requirements for the system. The output of the system should be information designed to aid the manager in answering questions related to the decisions he must make. Data may be needed to answer questions of a major nature which arise only occasionally as in the case of strategic decisions or to answer questions which arise on a regular basis as n the case management decisions. After the data requirements have been established, the question should be asked, "Are the data in the data bank?" In many cases, date which has already been collected for some other purpose can be used in answering new questions. If this is the case, the precollected data should be used to avoid the cost of duplication. With management decision data requirements standard collection procedures can be established to collect and feed data into the data bank. In the case of strategic decision data needs, the question must be asked—Are standard data (collected for operational questions) sufficient? If the answer is yes, the data will be generated through standard collection procedures. If the answer is no, a second question must be answered—Should we buy information or design our own research.

If the decision is to design research, data collection procedures must be selected to collect and feed data to the data bank. The method for using the system's analytical capabilities must also be determined and programmed into the analytical bank. If the decision is to buy, the purchased data flows either into the data bank or the analytical section. Data may then flow from the data bank directly to the display units or to the analytical unit for processing. Processing may take place in either the statistical bank or the model bank. Data may pass to both of these banks in order to complete the processing. After the information is processed, it may flow back to the data bank for storage or to the display unit. From the display unit, information goes to the manager to answer specific questions which aid him in the decision-making process.

Data collection procedures. Data collection procedures consist of all methods of gathering relevant data. Such data might originate at numerous sources, and the collection procedure should be varied depending on the source and type of data needed. Typical data classified by source include the following:

1. Secondary data: Internally generated (sales records, cost-price data, advertising expenditures, etc.)

2. Secondary data: Externally generated (economic data, legal regulations, Nielsen Retail Index, competitors' product data, etc.)

3. Primary data: From qualitative approaches (this is subjective data basically in the form of hypotheses generated by focus group interviews, depth interviews or protective techniques).

4. Primary data: From quantitative approaches.

   a. Survey Data (sales surveys, consumer characteristics and buying behavior, competitive price and distribution analysis, etc.).

   b. Experimental data (awareness tests, price sensitivity tests, dales promotion effectiveness, etc.).

   c. Simulation data (data generated by simulation models).

Data bank. The data bank serves as a memory unit for the system. It holds the sum total of past information available to the organization. Such information is a vital input into the management process. In order to facilitate the storage and handling of this information, an attempt should be made to classify and index information along relevant management dimensions (in the case of marketing management these dimensions are market analysis and formulation the marketing mix). Some data cannot be placed in any one area and must thus be stored in a common unit.

Since the volume of data in any one area of the data bank may be quite large, an attempt should be made to compress information. This data compression may be achieved by filtering out insignificant information, aggregation of data and/or conversion of data into probabilistic terms.

Statistical band. The statistical bank should contain those techniques needed for the statistical manipulation of data. These may include several basic procedures such as cross-classification, chi-square analysis, and regression. Statistical techniques may be used for several different purposes including description, building tailor-made models, and setting the parameters of generalized models. These techniques, because of their broad applications, are not normally segmented by decision dimensions but form a general statistical bank.

Model bank. A model may be defined as "a simplified representation of the relevant aspects of an actual system of process." Many types of models, the product life cycle model, break-even models, media selection models, and numerous others can be very useful if the models parameters can be established. These models can be segmented by management activity and selected models used to analyze data for specific types of marketing decisions.

Display unit. The display unit is the point of interface between the information mechanism and the manager. It receives and routes questions from the manager and provides him with the informational outputs of the system. The display unit should provide aid in the utilization of the information. The format for the presentation of information is dependent upon the nature of the problem and the sophistication of the system. Whenever possible, data should be presented in simplified tables and/or graphs for ease of interpretation and use by the manager.

The information management system as it relates to the research process

The information management system is a structure within the organization designed to carry out the research process. Its basic components work to accomplish the functions required of the system. The data collection procedures perform the data collection function; the data bank, statistical bank, and models bank work together to perform the data processing function; and finally, the display unit performs the information transmission function. When these functions are carried out effectively the research process of generating information can be accomplished. Thus a flow of information is provided to the decision makers within the organization.

BUILDING A MARKETING INFORMATION MANAGEMENT SYSTEM

The modern marketing information management system is capable of providing valuable information for the marketing manager. Yet certain questions pertaining to the information management system seem to perplex those who are willing to build such a system in their companies. Some of the important questions raised by marketing managers are:

1. What development strategy should be followed?
2. Should the attempt be to build a total system in one mover or in stages?
3. What should be the major characteristics of the system?
4. How much should be spent on developing and operating the system?
5. What kind of behavioral problems are likely to arise in the development process?

READING THE ORGANISATION

The starting point in development of an effective and efficient system should be a review and appraisal of the entire marketing organization and the policies that direct it. As one marketing executive pointed out, "We realized we couldn't develop a marketing control system until we had clearly and sharply defined the responsibilities of our marketing manager... (the purpose of the) system was to measure their performance against plans, we had to specify precisely what each man was accountable for." This statement holds for the development of any type of information network and its subparts. In fact, the specification of who is responsible for what automatically determines many of the characteristics of the decision-making process and thereby; many of the dimensions of the information management system.

ORGANISING FOR DEVELOPMENT

Management must next decide how to organize the development activities. Cox and Good observed that this is a much more complex problem than might be assumed. Sophisticated systems require the coordinated efforts of many departments and individuals including top management, marketing management, system designers, programmers, computer equipment experts and suppliers. The contribution of each group depends on its specialized talents and interests in the system. As an example, programmers cannot define the marketing manager's information needs and managers usually cannot program. It is virtually impossible to find one person within an organization with sufficient knowledge of the organization and expertise in technical areas to accomplish all facets of the development of a desirable system. Therefore, the question to be answered is who should be responsible for design, planning, and development? The approaches which have been tried to solve the problems of organization and leadership can be characterized under the following categories:

1. *Clear piece of paper approach*. This involves drawing a new organizational chart. The idea procedure is to abolish the traditional information gathering and processing departments and establish a new management information department.

2. *Committee approach*. Under this approach some companies have established marketing information committees. They are designed as vehicles for communicating points of view and for joint learning and sharing in the experience of developing of compatibility and coordination problems and of the need and means to resolve them.

3. *Low level approach*. Some companies, on the other hand, have assigned the task of development to a junior member of the marketing research department, often as a part time assignment. This reflects a total lack of understanding of the difficulty of the task. The low level approach is the least satisfactory of the typical approaches.

4. *Information coordination approach*. Finally, some companies while retaining traditional departmental boundaries, have appointed a top level executive to

the post of information coordinator. His job is to bring together the necessary resources (human and physical) to develop an effective and efficient information network. Such a coordinator is sometimes called a director of marketing systems. This approach has the advantage of leadership with sufficient authority to get things done within the organizational framework. The information coordinator approach had met with considerable success in the business community.

The level of sophistication of the system must now be decided. This decision should be based on a review of the information needs of the management process and the cost of meeting those needs. To develop and use effectively some of the more sophisticated models and statistical techniques the managers must be able to: define specific information needs; develop analytical approaches (statistical and model); make explicit their decision-making procedures; and be able to interpret and use sophisticated information. One of the characteristics of more advanced systems is automation of certain aspects of the marketing management process through the use of decision rules. It is essential to make the process explicit before such advanced procedures can be used.

The key to the decision on the degree of sophistication is system-manager balance. It is necessary to maintain a balance between management sophistication and the complexity of analytical techniques employed in the information management system. The fact is that information quality can be upgraded much more rapidly than management quality. It is relatively easy to throw the management system out of balance by installing procedures which are too sophisticated for the managers. A more positive approach is to develop a master plan for upgrading the system gradually over several years so that management has sufficient time to adjust to the changes.

While an attempt to develop a highly sophisticated, total marketing information management system at the outset has a high probability of failure, it is desirable to develop a complete framework in one move. This will generate a more integrated structure than a fragmentary approach. Additional sophisticated procedures can then be developed and instituted within the overall framework at a rate which will allow management to fully absorb and utilize them.

Apart from decisions on the general characteristics of the system to be used, the micro specifications must be determined. In addition to the type of system to be developed, other important considerations are the nature of the data bank, the form and the method of data displays, and computer selection.

1. *The micro data bank*. In designing the data bank, it is important to provide for common denominators in different sets of data so that the full analytical potential of the system can be realized. This means that such elements as the geographic, time, and responsibility boundaries of different types of data must be compatible to permit meaningful comparisons.

2. *Data display*. Developing an effective system includes resolving the questions of what information should be presented, how it should be presented, and to whom it should be made available? One important aspect of these questions is the degree of manager-system interaction desired. At the extreme of "distance" managers receive information in the form of regular reports. With somewhat closer but not complete interaction, the manager can make special requests for information from the data bank. At the extreme of "closeness," the manager can obtain almost instantaneous computer response with a time-sharing or on-line system. Given the current state of the art, regular reports supplemented with special request procedures appears to be the most practical arrangement.

3. *Computer selection*. The computer requirements for the information management system will depend on

the system's performance specifications and the decision management has made on each of the preceding design problems. While technical help is usually necessary in the decisions on hardware, management has the responsibility for making certain that the equipment chosen will meet the system needs both at the time of installation and in the future when the system becomes larger as well as more sophisticated. In this respect the system designer should recognize that the managers will learn many new ways to use the computer as they become more experienced in the use of the new procedures and thus room for expansion is essential.

It is extremely difficult to generalize about how much an advanced information management system will cost or how much it will be worth. Usually, there is little increase in data collection costs since most companies already collect much of the raw data required. Cost increases result mainly from increased requirements for data storage and transforming the raw data into useful information. The difficulty in determining past development cost arises from the fact that many companies lack accounting arrangements (such as interdepartmental billing) which would allow them to keep track of the total cost of the manpower contributing to the program.

Usually computer-based information systems, such as those used for accounting, have been justified on the grounds that they reduce personnel and other administrative costs. Advanced marketing information management systems could be justified on the basis of cost reductions, but a more meaningful justification is improved marketing management. Determining how much the new information will increase marketing effectiveness is again a difficult task. The involvement of management in developing overall specifications, in terms of the management needs for information, should help in making an estimate of the total system benefits.

Individuals have a natural tendency to resist change; thus unfavorable behavioral consequences often accompany the introduction of a sophisticated information system. In order to minimize such unfavorable consequences the manager must not only recognize that such problems are likely to arise, but must also understand the basic factors underlying such behavior:

1. *Changes in the formal organizational structure.* Most organizations have definite departmental boundaries and divisions of formal responsibility. Changes in these boundaries and divisions often occur in connection with the introduction of a new information system, and as these formal lines of responsibility are violated resistance becomes inevitable.

2. *Changes in the informal structure.* The informal relationships which develop within any organization may be highly complex and of importance to the individuals involved. Informational and social ties develop; breaking such relationships can generate adverse reactions.

3. *Personal characteristics.* Personal characteristics and background of the particular individuals affect their behavior toward new developments. Younger people with fewer years of service tend to be less opposed to change than older people with more years of service. Besides this, many people see the computer as the most recent intrusion of the machine into man's domain and to them it represents a danger to their status and perhaps their job.

4. *Managerial climate.* The members of an organization are more likely to respond favorably to a proposed change if the managerial climate maintains open communications and permits all grievances to be heard. The method used by management to introduce change is another significant variable affecting its likelihood of success.

These and other underlying factors may generate various forms of dysfunctional behaviour. Usually such dysfunctional behavior takes one or more of three forms depending upon the individual's position within the organization.

1. *Aggression.* Aggressive behavior represents an attack intended to injure the object causing the problem. The most dramatic aggression toward the system occurs as sabotage (when people attempt to destroy the system's components). A less dramatic but more common form of aggression occurs when people attempt to "beat the system."

2. *Projection.* Projection exists when people blame the system for causing difficulties that are in fact caused by something else. In many instances the system may be blamed for failings actually caused by too rapid an implementation or the incompetence of the individuals involved.

3. *Avoidance.* people may defend themselves by withdrawing from the frustrating situation. In the area of management utilization this behavior often takes the form of ignoring the system output. This is particularly the case when the system does not totally fulfill information needs.

The manager must attempt to minimize dysfunctional behavior. To do this, special attention should be given to the following:

1. *Proper atmosphere.* Critical aspects are the attitudes of both management and any affected employee, organizational cohesiveness, and organizational culture. The attitude of top management should be one of full support for the system. There shouid also be open lines of communication between different levels of management, between management and employees, and between line and staff employees.

2. *Participation.* Which items will be included, what information will be given to whom, and possible job modifications are the important considerations. The specialists must not dominate the installation; more responsibility should be given to the operating

managers than has often been the case. An attempt should be made to achieve harmony between individual and organizational goals.

3. *Clarity of the system*. The purpose and characteristics of the system should be as clear as possible to those who have direct contact with it. This means that the nature and detail of a system must be fully explored and discussed with those affected before, during, and after installation. Another factor of importance is minimizing initial system errors. Frequent mistakes can delay or even completely undermine a potentially good system.

4. *Plan scope*. The fact that a computer has the ability to do something does not necessarily mean that the computer should do it. Attention should be paid to the possible need to deliberately expand the scope of activities for the individual within a computer-controlled system resulting in a calculated inefficiency that can save the humanity within the system.

5. *New challenges*. New challenges may be opened up by the installation of a sophisticated system. A look should be taken at what management and employees ought to be doing that is more important and satisfying than what they did before. The manager should discover and emphasize these new challenges in discussions with individuals at all levels.

6. *Re-examine performance evaluation* There will likely have to be a shift from rewards based on individual accomplishments to rewards based on group achievements if integrated programs are to be useful.

7. *User orientation*. The design of the system must fulfill the needs of the user if he is to be satisfied with the output. Otherwise he is compelled to maintain his own system which defeats the basic purpose of the installation. The system should be

carefully developed so as not to overwhelm the user with a large volume of output which the user either cannot understand or cannot use effectively. This is why user orientation is the *key factor* in attempting to minimize dysfunctional behaviour.

Marketing managers are faced with increasingly complex problem situations. The development of sophisticated marketing information management systems is a logical response to the increased information needs generated by these problems. Thus, it seems reasonable to suppose that business will continue to implement advanced information systems and that the successful manager of the future needs to be able to understand and operate efficiently within such an environment.

The information management system within an organization is the machinery (procedures, personnel, and equipment) set up to do research. Research in this context means any type of information production activity. Information is, of course, a vital ingredient in the decision making of marketing management. To carry out the research process and insure an orderly flow of information within the firm, the system must perform three basic functions: data collection procedures to collect data; a data bank, statistical bank, and models bank to process data; and a display unit to transmit information to the managers. These components form the functional parts of the system. Its inputs are raw data and its outputs are information for decision making.

A careful reading of the organization is the key to building an effective information management system. To work well, the system must be user-oriented; it must serve the needs of the decision makers. The building process should thus start with a careful information audit which locates the relevant decisions, who makes each decision, and what information is needed.

4

INFORMATION FOR MARKETING DECISIONS

One of the principal functions of management is to make decisions Drucker has acutely observed:

> Whatever, a manager does he does through making decisions....management is always a decision making process... the important and difficult job is never to find the right answer it is to find the right question. For there are few things as useless—if not dangerous—as the right answer to the wrong question...nor is it enough to find the right answer more important and more difficult is it to make effective the course of action decided upon. Management is not concerned with knowledge for its own sake; it is concerned performance.

Marketing management has to accept responsibility for making complex decisions these cover factors such as the nature products, product mix, pricing policy, distribution strategy, promotional activities, etc. In order to make decisions that are likely to lead to successful business, marketers need to assess:

1. the extent of their existing information specific marketers
2. relate this store of knowledge to the types of decision they have to make
3. specify the nature of additional information they will need before particular decisions could be made within an acceptable degree of risk.

Robert Schlaifer has described marketing as the place where the most money is risked on the least information. Admittedly, a substantial amount in advertising appears to be undertaken with more optimism than actual knowledge or reasoned argument about the likely pay-offs. In the majority of marketing problems. It is usually possible to collect data that will enable decisions to be based rather more firmly on fact. Information is the raw material of management productivity; marketing management should be alert to the need to acquire and use intelligently, information about the markets in which they are operating or plan to enter.

Need for discipline

But management information should not be gathered indiscriminately or viewed merely as a 'play-safe' strategy. Russell Ackoff has pointed out that many people demand more and more information, when, in fact, they already have more paper coming into their offices than they can possibly read effectively. As the result of carefully analyzing the type of decisions which executives had to make, Ackoff found that a very great number of these could have been taken quite reasonably with more limited and selective information. Yet, paradoxically, there are occasions when executives are badly served with information: the symptoms shown are of malnutrition rather than of over-indulgence. The right kind of information is not always to hand at the time is wanted; it needs to be available not only in adequate quantity, but it should also be relevant to the decisions under consideration.

Before seeking information, marketing management should first of all define the nature of the problem facing them. This disciplined approach will help to clarity information needs, and avoid wasteful use of management and other resources in acquiring data which may not be really relevant to the problem in hand. Too frequently, managers seem to be seeking solutions to problems, the nature of which they have never taken the trouble to identify and analyze. Instant solutions are demanded for problems which themselves are never actually clarified.

Only by defining be known can the constraints in certain marketing situations, for example be known, and research directed to these specific areas. Roll's-Royce used of years to congratulate itself because it had half the world market for civil airliner engines. But this true fact concealed the vital information: What was the company's share of new business? The answer wasn't a half or even a quarter: Pratt and Witney had been clobbering Rolls-royce all over the airways and failure to recognize that fact was as fatal to the company as deadly nightshade.'

Categories of information needs

Information for marketing decision could be usefully classified in three broad categories:

1. Information for strategic decisions (e.g., whether or not to enter a particular overseas market; or to diversity into new markets).

2. Information for tactical decisions (e.g., planning of sales territories).

3. Information to provide a data-bank; this will require periodic updating to endure that it retains its usefulness (e.g., details of competitive products, market share analyses, VAT requirements, etc.).

Collection of information in any of these categories should be under taken systematically and according to the nature of individual companies and the types of commercial or industrial activity in which they are engaged. As companies develop, new needs for information will tend to arise; hence data should be reviewed from time to time and evaluated for its contribution the specific decisions now being undertaken by management. Some data may require to be improved in quality, e.g., markets may have become highly segmented and relatively superficial market assessments may be of tittle value as more sophisticated competition emerges.

Impact of dynamic environment

The dynamic nature of many markets underlines the need for managers to keep their information up-to-date. Marketing information interprets the changing environment and its needs so that the right kind of decisions can be taken affecting production and marketing the *microenvironment*, specifically the economy, technology, law and culture and the *task environment*, specifically buyers channels competitors, and suppliers.... A major task of an effective marketing information system is to provide speedy, accurate, and interpretative information to its decision makers.'

Two-way flow of information systems

Marketing management information flows are two-way: from the organization to the environment and from the environment or market to the organization which seeks to service specific needs in that market.

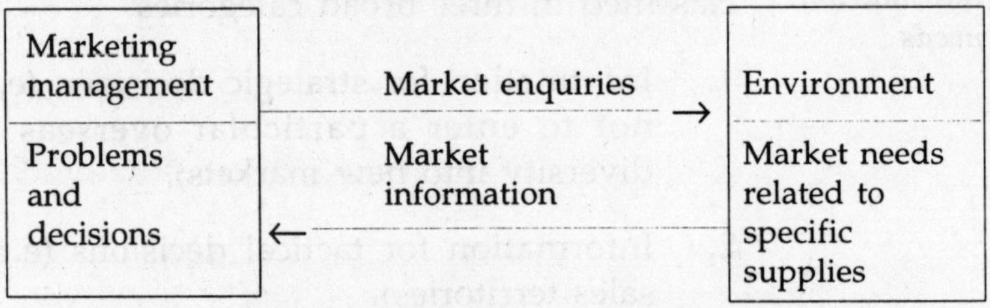

Two-way flow of marketing information systems

Marketing information should be gathered methodically both from within the marketing organization using the accounting and financial control system, as well as from market sources. Many firms do not coordinate the information which is the accounting department with the data needs of marketing management. At a relatively small extra cost, invoices and other financial could be designed so that provide useful analyses of sales product type, region or territory.

In defining information needs, marketing management should not fall into the trap of demanding limited data. Levitt has stressed the difference between data and information. The enormous prodigality of the computer has so accelerated the process of data accumulation that we often actually know less than we did before. Great masses of data are disgorged...What is needed is discrimination in the case of data, not its sheer abundance information is usefully only if it is relevant.

There is no shortage of information in many organizations; the trouble is that is often the wrong kind of information excessive, irrelevant and incompatible apart from being out-dated. Robertt Heller vigorously comments: 'Managers are to information as alcoholics are to booze. They consume enormous amounts constantly crave more, but have great difficulty in digesting their existing intake.'

Mr Harold MacMillan's famous observation about the value of official statistics to management of the British economy—that using them was like planning a train journey with last year's Bradshaw guide—could equally apply to the value of out-dated management statistics. Inevitably, statistical and other data are historic but with effective planning the time intervals between collection and presentation can be shortened.

To be really useful, marketing information does not necessarily have to be sophisticated or expensive to produce. Relatively simple but up-to-date information is preferable to sophisticated information which has lost most of its value because of the long time taken to collect and present it to management.

The incompatibility of data originating from various departments of an organization may be frustrating. For example, if weekly or monthly statistics are kept by production marketing and financial sections of a business, do they relate to the same bases? Some companies have special accounting periods which may not coincide with the records kept by the production management or by the marketing people. Personal investigations with the Board of Trade were, in a particular instance, considerably frustrated 'because half the figures relating to staff were collected on a calendar month basis and the other half on a four week basis.' A similar problem has been experienced with sales statistics and the financial records kept by a manufacturing firm.

The collection and dissemination of information for managerial guidance should be designed so that full value can be derived from departmental statistics. Marketing management should become acquainted with the various statistical returns made, for example, by the production controller to the financial department. Stock records should be compared against market targets and actual sales performance. The profitability of an organization may be increased if managers in all functional areas are more willing to exchange information and to perceive that a parochial use of statistics is a short-sighted earlier than an audit of information available within an organization would be a worthwhile management exercise. It might reveal (and often has) that records of very similar nature are being kept by different sections; that duplication of this nature has grown up from either ignorance or managerial competitiveness; and that some of the information assiduously collected serves no real function. It may have been demanded some years ago when markets were different, but no one in authority had issued instructions to stop this routine production of data. From time to time, therefore, organizations might usefully check the application of the data which at today's staffing costs, entail considerable expenses. Inadequacies may be discovered in the existing data because of changes in the environment and which may require additional analyses; for example, expansion in overseas markets, formerly analyzed by broad regional breakdown, may now require the collection of more elaborate data. Essentially, a marketing information system should be flexible to retain its value. Special data may be necessary to supplement information so that specific marketing problems can be approached objectively.

Role of marketing research

Collection of data from the environment should be undertaken on a planned and objective basis. Marketing research involves a disciplined approach to the various problems of marketing goods and services of *all* kinds.

'Marketing management have the responsibility of identifying customers for their products and services, of evaluating their present needs, and predicting their likely future requirements.' Marketers largely control the destinies of their companies, and it is no longer defensible that their decisions should be based on inspired guesswork or hunches. Objective, systematic research into market opportunities should become the first step in forming the marketing plan. Research should include economic and business analyses, technological evaluations assessment of competitors' activities, analyses of political, social and other environment factors —particularly where overseas trading is concerned—and an overall appreciation obtained of the factors affecting or likely to affect a company's market.

Robert Buzzell, in an article some years ago in the *Harvard Business Review*, expressed concern that 'the term "research" ever came to be used to describe the activities of most marketing research staff units'. He suggested that a much more appropriate designation would be 'marketing intelligence', since its function was analogous to military intelligence in warfare. "Military intelligence personal are not expected to develop a science of warfare. Their mission, instead is to obtain complete, accurate, and current information.'

It could be argued, of course, that the label is of little consequence, that it is the function that matters. On the other hand, misleading descriptions can put people off products. Research may suggest, to some management, esoteric enquiries undertaken in the cloistered calm of an academic institution far removed from the hurly-burly of commercial life. This view is enhanced by the academic aura which surrounds the function of learned research.

Marketing research has a practical purpose: to provide reliable knowledge about specific aspects of marketing. It is nearer to the function of field intelligence than of the research laboratory. But its function is not just to provide intelligence or information, but to *interpret* these data. To be of value, research into marketing should be based on years of experience in a particular industry, but they tend to be subjective views. Marketing research is scientific enquiry: science may be at-least partly defined in terms of the outcomes of scientific investigation....science deals with the unembroidered fact rather than with opinion and belief.

Marketing research is not a substitute for decision-making, it is an aid to making *better* decisions by providing additional information in defined areas of investigation. Far from being theoretical, marketing research applies in real-life conditions some of the techniques of scientific analysis to provide management with up-to-date marketing knowledge. It forms, therefore, the cornerstone of a successful marketing strategy; applying marketing research does not guarantee success, but it *will* narrow the field of uncertainty which surround many marketing decisions. Marketing research is not an end in itself: it is not some kind of expensive peripheral activity which only organizations with substantial resources can indulge in. Decisions have to be made in organizations of all sizes; if they are based on accurate knowledge it is reasonable to surmise that they are more likely to be sound than if they rely solely on managerial experience and inspiration, or what a salesman said when he last visited the works. Marketing research should not be regarded as a luxury service but as an essential method of acquiring facts which were not available beforehand. Marketing research is not magic: it is the expression of management logic.

Several attempts have been made to define marketing research in formal terms. At one time, 'market research' and 'marketing research' tended to be used to describe particular activities; the former referring merely to enquiries into market size and related statistics whereas 'marketing research' covered a far fuller area of enquiries involving for example, behavioural factors, advertising strategy, etc., as well as measurement of market demand. This pedantic distinction is now largely discarded, and nowadays the terms are used indiscriminately.

The American Marketing Association (AMA), in 1961, defined marketing research as:

> The systematic gathering and analyzing of data about problems relating to the marketing of good and services.

In 1962, The British institute of Management (BIM)

followed closely the AMA's definition: The objective gathering, recording and analysing of all facts about problems relating to the transfer and sales of goods and services from producer to consumer or user.

Kotler has drawn attention to marketing research's role as 'systematic problem analysis, model building and fact finding for the purposes of improved decision-making and control in the marketing of goods and services'. This definition emphasizes the end-purposes of marketing research activities.

Marketing research related to industrial products has been defined by the Industrial Marketing Research Association (IMRA) as:

> The systematic objective and exhaustive search for and study of facts relevant to any problem in the field of industrial marketing.

These various definitions emphasize that marketing research involves objective analysis and fact finding for marketing effectiveness related to supplies, either consumption by individuals or to be used in production of other goods.

Marketing research has tended to be closely associated with consumer products in the past. Studies of the effectiveness of research techniques have normally been confined to markets other than industrial and the impression may have been formed that the field of marketing research is limited to products which can be bought in supermarkets and other retail outlets. But this underestimate the value of marketing research to industrial markets. The problems of marketing industrial and technical products are certainly no less complex than those faced when devising the launch of a new soap powder or soft drink. Many industrial managers would say quite strongly that they face far more difficult problems which demand considered technical knowledge, apart from commercial acumen and experience.

Marketing research can make a real contribution to

the marketing of organizational supplies. By their training scientists, engineers and technicians demand objective facts which are subjected to close scrutiny and analysis. This objective approach should not end at the laboratory or factory door: it should be extended to include objective analysis and interpretation of all those factors which are likely to affect the profitable marketing of industrial products. This is the key role of marketing research - and it can be applied to companies of all sizes.

Political and Economic Planning (PEP) surveyed the attitudes of British management over several industries. Their report stressed the need for industrial firms to develop through marketing research, a positive customer-orientation. Many firms investigated displayed an apathetic attitude towards the techniques of marketing.

The commercial manager of one large firm in the machine tool industry, which had a comfortably sized order book, replied to the question whether he ever estimated the annual growth of the market by the comment: 'Now, we have perhaps been spoilt over a period of years. We've on average been more than able to sell our output, and we tend to leave it at that.' For most firms however, competition has been increasing causing shorter order-books... and a change in business methods'. A medium-sized earthmoving equipment manufacturer was reported to have told a PEP interviewer: We were a small company and our products had virtually no competition, so that when a man went to build a dam, he just looked in the that was that. The last ten years it's been such a competitive business that you simply can't do business that way.'

Since the date of the PEP report, competition in all markets has increased enormously and so has the risk attached to marketing decisions in particular. British industrial managers generally seemed to be a pretty complacement lot from the PEP research findings. Since then, many of them have had to endure a lot of corporate suffering before they have been willing to change their ingrained managerial habits. The impression that marketing techniques are unnecessary with industrial products has been reluctantly abandoned, although even now the old prejudices against systematic investigation of markets still linger in many organizations.

Marketing research techniques can also be applied productively in the planning of non-profit making activities such as the social services public transport, education health services etc. Unless reliable information is used at the design stage of these services, it is clear that public resources may be unwisely committed. To serve people's needs it is advisable to identify these as closely as possible; mere conjectures are not good enough. Objective research will also be of value in assessing the effectiveness of existing services and may identify new areas which could legitimately be the concern of public authorities. Far greater use of marketing research could therefore result in better utilization of scarce resources and improved benefits to the community. In some directions services may be adequate to meet the needs of particular sections of the community. There may be need for new types of public services where a district is changing its character because of industrialization or the arrival of immigrant populations.

Planning is accepted as an important element of public administration Marketing research is not confined to commercial investigations; it evolved in fact, a substantial part of its methodology from the pioneer social investigations made, for example, by Bowley and others in the early part of this century. Since that time, techniques have been refined and extended, and the strong link between marketing research practitioners and social investigation continues with several research agencies specializing in medical and social welfare investigations.

The process of marketing research can be conveniently divided into five steps which lead logically to the survey report. These phases apply irrespective of the nature of the market—consumer, industrial or public service. Professional skill is needed at every stage of the research programme to ensure that the findings of the survey are based on objective data which have been obtained representative samples of a specific population.

Research brief

This initial crucial stage will decide the nature and direction of the whole research programme. It entails defending clearly and in specific terms the marketing problem to be investigated. With industrial products, market research objectives may be focused on the needs of particular customers for machines of special capacity or for specific formulations of chemicals. The extent stock levels needed), the nature sales-service support expected by some industries or the type and level of competition are a few of the problems which industrial researchers continually tackle.

Before clear definition of the marketing problem is feasible, it may be necessary to make exploratory enquiries in certain areas of the organization, e.g., selling arrangement publicity methods, pricing structure, etc., This preliminary work should gain researchers valuable back-ground knowledge, and may, in fact point to the real problem which has to be investigated. The marketing problem may relate closely, for example, to production methods and some degree of integrated research may be necessary.

At this critical briefing stage, both management and researchers should endeavour should be prepared to take researchers into their confidence and present them with an unvarnished picture of their organization and the kind of marketing problems which face them. Marketing researchers have the duty to probe and ensure that they have been given adequate between client and researcher is similar to that of a barrister and his professional client. Unless the briefing is through, misunderstanding and even catastrophe could result.

If the proposition put forward by a seems unrealistic, a reputable marketing researcher will point out the constrains which, inevitably govern the nature of research activities. Like all products and services research costs money: it involves time and professional skills. Before a research brief is accepted both parties should agree on the level of accuracy required, the date by which the research report will be available and the approximate price to be paid.

A great deal of thought, time and care should be given, therefore to the marketing research brief. Clients and researchers should be prepared to spend some time on defining the precise terms of reference which will guide the research programme. Slip-shod thinking at this initial phase will set the whole research off course, and probably cause deep annoyance to both parties later on.

Work plan

At this stage a research should be developed which, by means of a simple model of the problem will specify the data to be collected and the methodology to be adopted. It is important to check that the proposed research strategy will satisfy the objectives set out in phase one. These objectives should be developed and refined into one or a series of working hypotheses which can be tested during the research programme. These hypotheses arise as a result of *a priori* thinking about the subject, preliminary investigation of available data and material (including related studies), or advice and counsel of experts or interested parties. Like the formulation of the problem, such hypotheses are most useful when expressed in precise clearly defined terms'.

A research schedule should be drawn up giving timing for the various operations. This will take account of the methodology to be used and the time constraints imposed by the client.

Collection of data

The research programme having been agreed, the next stage is likely to occupy a considerable amount of time. The relative efficiencies of collecting data by alternative methods will have to be checked. Complementary data may be describe in some types of market investigation. Sampling procedures need to be thoroughly planned to avoid some of the biases which make research such a precarious profession.

Analysis and evaluation of data

Every stage of the research programme is inter-related. It is no use applying sophisticated techniques of analysis and statistical tests of data at this stage if the original research design did not ensure that, for example, the sample methodology was soundly based.

Data are the raw material of the research programme; they have to be refined by means of tabulation, analysis and interpretation. During these processes, significant relationships between variables may be discovered; these require objective discussions and evaluation related to the problems which the survey had undertaken to study.

System of data storage and retrieval may also be incorporated in this stage of the research. Provision should be made to up-date information so that market knowledge on critical factors in buying behaviour retain their value for management decision-making. New competitors may, for example, enter the home or an overseas market. Different distribution strategies may radically alter the nature of competition. A comparatively low-ranked competitor may be taken over by a large industrial group which is prepared to invest substantial funds in an aggressive bid for a larger market share.

Computers have revolutionized data processing which in a comparatively short period has progressed from hand analysis to systems of mechanical tabulation, eventually to arrive at the speed, flexibility and diversity of modern computerized systems. The attractions of such a flexible and speedy system may conceal dangers: a careful check is needed to avoid the GIGO effect (garbage in-garbage out).

Questionnaires can now be read mechanically and at great speed. Sophisticated analytical techniques such as factor analysis are no longer fairly tedious, if not prohibitive, methods of analyzing certain kinds of data.

These improvements in the technical efficiency of research data processing are of direct benefit to clients. Speedier and more elaborate surveys are possible and at very economic cost.

Preparation and presentation of research report

This stage completes the research programme; it deserves professional attention because faulty communication can undo a lot of the good work done earlier.

Researchers should develop their managerial expertise in presenting the findings of research surveys so that they are fully understood by clients. 'Interpretation of survey findings is a matter on which experts express strongly conflicting views. Some would have researchers give their own interpretation of the findings of surveys, while others, equally dogmatic, believe that researchers should limit themselves to reporting the facts discovered through the survey.'

The question of interpretation should be discussed at the time the research brief is agreed. Clients as well as researchers may have different views, so some clearly agreed policy is desirable. To discourage researchers from exercising their professional knowledge in the interpretation of a surveys findings would seem to be a rather short-sighted policy. They may be able to suggest alternative marketing strategies as the result of approaching problems with professional objectivity. For several months the clients problems will have become the focus of intense commitment: It would be unproductive not to exploit this valuable of creative managerial inputs.

In preparing a survey report, researchers should keep in mind those who will read it'. Both the content and the style should be designed to satisfy the needs of particular readers. Clear, grammatical language should be used with data shown attractively in tables and diagrams. The format, printing and binding are factors that can help considerably in making the contents of a report intelligible and acceptable.

Some industrial marketing research reports substantial technical data which in detail, may not be required by commercial management. In such cases, it is often advisable to prepare two editions. One to be read exclusively by technical specialists and which contains a detailed technological assessment; the other to be intended principally for commercial management would cover technology in less depth and would concentrate more an commercial implications of the marketing developments studied. Where separate reports are not desirable care must be exercised to ensure that any technical terms used are defined so that the report would be understood without undue trouble.

Because delays may occur in production of the main report, clients may find it helpful to have a preliminary report which distils the research findings. In addition to the final report, some clients invite researchers to discuss the survey findings preferably after all involved have carefully studied it.

Scope and responsibilities of marketing research

The diversity and complexity of marketing decisions have been discussed earlier; these factors demand better knowledge. Information needs it has been noted, fall into three broad classes; strategic tactical and 'data-bank'.

In organizational affecting buying preferences. The time scales of consumer and industrial markets are, in general vastly different. In non-profit making activities such as the social services the role of marketing research was discussed earlier in general outline

There are, therefore, many areas in which the techniques of marketing research can be applied with the objective of improving marketing productions. Costs are escalating in all directions and in all types of organizations. Improved methods of serving customers' needs must be found; new ventures require evaluation before committing heavy investment; better systems of selling and distribution should be devised and tested objectively.

That marketing research techniques used by profit-oriented firms are of use in the public sector, where primary motivations tend to be different should not be regarded as a bizarre proposal.

Research techniques by which profit-making firms measure the market ability of their products and improve the effectiveness of their services distribution and communications, are applicable to projects concerned with education culture, health, environments and energy supply. New standards may thus evolve to help measure the effectiveness of such non-profit organisations in achieving goals that do not pertain directly to such economic goals as sales and profits.

The needs of people deserve objective analysis; managerial account ability for the effective use of corporate resources applies equally in both sectors of the economy. In the opening chapter, human needs were seen to be capable of almost infinite extension. Marketing research attempts to track these changing needs—sociological, political technological, environmental, psychological, legal and a esthetic-and to evaluate and relate them to the resources of organizations which could serve them.

Marketing research is the route towards a deeper understanding of customers and clients and of the environment in which they live, work and play. It is more than just a set of techniques: it is the foundation of marketing strategy.

The development of effective marketing strategies is based upon tan understanding of the consumer and his or her behavior. But consumer behavior cannot be absolutely measured not, can one predict with certainty how any group of people will interact. This is one of the major problems facing marketing managers. With all of these unpredictable people, how are they supposed to make decisions based on their probable future behavior ? Part of the answer lies in marketing research

The American Marketing Association defines marketing research as *The systematic gathering recording and analysing of data about relating to the marketing of goods and services."*

The task of the marketing manager is decision making. Managers earn their salaries by making effective decisions that enable their firms to solve problems as they arise and by anticipating and preventing the occurrence of future problems. Many times, though they are forced to make decision with limited information with inadequate facts. Marketing research serves to present pertinent facts, analyze them and suggest possible action.

All decision areas for the marketing manager are candidates for marketing research investigations. A marketing research efforts are commonly centered around developing sales forecasts for the firm's products determining market and sales potential designing are products and packages analysing sales and marketing costs, evaluating the effectiveness of the firms's advertising and determining consumer motives for buying products.

Marketing research is a relatively new field that traces its origins in the United States to 1911 when Charles C. Parlan was appointed as manager of the Commercial Research Division of the Curtis Publishing Company. Much of the early research represented little more than testimonials received by writing purchasers of the firm's products.

Research became more sophisticated during the decade of the 1930s, but mistakes were still made. The *Literary Digest* conducted a major national study of 10,000 households selected at a random from lists to telephone numbers and reported that Alf Landon—not Franklin D. Roosevelt—would be elected president. The fiasco resulted from a failure to realize that many voters (Apparently, most of whom were Democrats) did not have a telephone in 1936.

The development of statistical techniques during the 1930s led to further refinements in sampling procedures and improved accuracy in research finding. By 1973 the American Marketing Association reported that 81 percent of the nation's leading manufacturing firms had established formal marketing research departments. Total research expenditures in 1977 were estimated at more than $1 billion.

It has been said that the recipe for effective decisions is 90 percent information and 10 percent inspiration. Figure 3-2 separates the management decision process into a series of stages and indicated the type of information that is crucial at each stage.

MARKETING RESEARCH PROCEDURE

Most marketing research investigation begin with an awareness of a problem or opportunities. The first task of the researcher is to define precisely the problem or opportunity.

By now reader is perhaps envisioning a long of steps involved in a research study with the idea in mind that the longer the list the more difficult it will be to remember them and the greater the possibility that the instructor can subtract five or more points from the examination paper. The reader is perhaps thinking "After all, everyone knows what the problem is. The task of the researchers is to determine methods of solving it. So why don't we eliminate step one?" The following example should shed light on this question.

Anne Stewart has been the management department program with Columbia Corporation for sixteen months when she received a two-month assignment in Columbus marketing research department. Prior to this she had worked with he sales representatives who called on wholesalers and supermarkets that handled the firm on household cleaning products.

The marketing researchers is confronted with a number of problem symptoms such as low sales. In order to solve the problem or enable the firm to take advantage of a potential opportunity, a search must be conducted for causes. The purpose of the exploratory research is to give the researcher an intelligent understanding of the problem area and some insight into its causes and effects. It consists of discussing the problem area with informed executives, sales representatives and other sources of information within the firm. *Wholesalers retailers customers* and others outside the firm and the examination of secondary sources of information..

Utilising internal data

Valuable sources of information are contained in the existing records of the business firm. Analyses of these records should provide a basis for obtaining an overall view of company efficiency and often provides clue to the problem under investigation.

The basis for analysis of internal data is traditional accounting data provided by the accounting department, which is usually summarized on the firms's financial statements.

Basic financial statements are often too broad to be very useful in marketing analysis. Where nondetailed accounts are used their main contribution that they assist the analysed in raising more specific questions.

Table 1: Topics for the Exploratory Analysis

A. The Company and Industry

1. Company objectives

2. The companies comprising the industry (size financial power) and industry trends

3. Geographic locations of the industry

4. The company's market share as compared with competitors

5. Marketing policies of competitors

B. *The* market

1. Geographic location

2. Demographic characteristics of the market

3. Purchase motivations

4. Product use patterns

5. Nature of demand

c. *Product*

1. Physical characteristics

2. Consumer acceptance and as a promotional weapon

4. Manufacturing processes production capacity

5. Closeness and availability of substitute products

D. Marketing Channels

1. Channels employed and recent trends
2. Channel policy
3. Margins for resellers

E. *Sales* Organization

1. Market coverage
2. Sales analysis by number of accounts per salesperson size of accounts type of account etc.
3. Expense ratios for various territories product types account size etc.
4. Control procedures
5. Compensation methods

F Pricing

1. Elasticity
2. Seasonal or special promotional price cuts
3. Profit margins of resellers
4. Legal restrictions
5. Price lines

G. Advertising and Sales Promotion

1. Media employed
2. Dollar expenditure as compared with competitors
3. Timing of advertising
4. Sales promotional materials provided for resellers
5. Results from previous advertising and sales promotional campaigns.

Comparison of the 13 percent selling expense to sales ratio with previous years may hint at possible problems but it will not specifically reveal the true cause of the variation. To discover the real problems, a more detailed break-down is necessary.

Sales Analysis. Table 2 illustrates a typical breakdown of sales by territories. This kind of breakdown becomes a part of an overall sales analysis. The purpose of the sales analysis, the in-depth evaluation of a firms sales is to obtain meaningful information from the accounting data.

The sales analysis, easily prepared from company invoices that are stored in computer tapes for billing purposes, can be quite revealing for the marketing executive. As Table 2 shows, the sales force in Territory 4 has a much higher cost-sales ratio than the sales representative in other territories.

Table 2 Sales and Expense Analysis by Territory

Territory	Average Salary	Average Expenses	Total Sales costs	Total Sales	Cost/Sales Ratio
1	$ 13,600	$6,400	$20,000	$385,000	5.2 %
1	11,9000	8,800	20,700	320,000	6.5
3	17,200	9,100	26,300	512,000	5.1
4	15,700	8,300	24,000	114,000	21.1
5	14,200	7,700	21,900	355,000	6.2

In order to evaluate performance of the salespersons in the five territories the marketing executive must have a standard of comparison. Territory 4 may consist primarily of the Mountain States containing large amounts of territory but relatively fewer industrial centres. Consequently the costs involved in obtaining sales, of necessity will be higher than for other territories.

This standard by which sales forecast by territory products customers salespersons and other breakdowns. Once the sales quota has been established, it is a simple process to compare the actual results with expected performance. Table 3 shows a comparison of actual sales for each sales representative in Territory 4 with the quota established for each person.

Even though Shapiro had the smallest amount of sales for the period, her performance was better than expected. The regional sales manager should investigate the performance of Chandler since his performance resulted in the territory failure to meet its quota for the period.

Table 3 Sales Breakdown by Representative in Territory 4

Salesperson	Quota	Actual	Performance to Quota
Holtzman	$ 36,000	$34,000	94%
Thompon	28,000	31,000	111
Shapiro	18,000	19,000	106
Chandler	46,000	30,000	65
Total	$128,000	$114,000	89%

Marketing Cost Anulysis A second source of internal information is marketing cost analysis which is the evaluating of such items as selling a costs billing warehousing advertising expensive in order to determine the profitability of particular customer territories and or product lines. Conducting a marketing cost analysis require a new way of classifying accounting data. *Fundamental accounts* must be established to replace the traditional natural accounts used in financial statements. A natural account, such as salary, must be reallocated to the original salary account will be allocated to selling inventory control, storage billing, advertising and other marketing costs. In the same manner an account such as supplies expense would be allocated to the functions that utilize supplies.

The costs allocated to the functional accounts will equal in total those in the natural accounts. But instead of merely showing total profitability they can be used to show the profitability of particular territories, products, customers, salesperson, order sizes, or any other breakdown required.

The most common reallocations are to *products customers* and *territories*. Table 5 shows how such a reallocation may be made.

Table 4 *Allocation of Marketing Costs*

Marketing Costs	*By Customers* Large	Small	*By Territories* A	B	C
Advertising	$ 14,000	$ 30,000	$20,000	$10,000	$14,000
Selling	52,000	62,000	38,000	38,000	38,000
Transportation	33,000	26,000	28,000	14,000	17,000
Credit	400	2,600	1,600	600	800
Total	$99,400	$120,600	$87,6000	$62,6000	$69,800

The marketing decision-maker is now in a position to evaluate the profitability of particular customers and territories based on the sales each produced and the costs incurred in producing the sales.

Marketing cost analysis is similar to sales analysis in that both provide burning signals of deviations from plans and allow the marketing executive opportunity to explain and possibly correct the deviations.

Secondary data

An extremely important source of information for the marketing researcher is to use of secondary *or previously published* data. In fact, so much data of this future is available at little or no that the researcher faces the problem overwhelmed by the volumes of collected data. In the era of the formation explosion one of the marks of a good marketing researcher is the ability to select *pertinent* secondary data.

Government Sources The federal government is the nation's signal most important source marketing data. The most frequently used government source is census data. Although Population, the information is available for use at no charge at local libraries or it can be purchased at a nominal charge on computer tapes for instantaneous access. In fact, the Bureau of the Census products seven different censuses.

The 1970 Census of Population data is so detailed for large cities that breakdowns for population characteristics are available by city block. Thus the local retailer or shopping center developer can easily gather details information about the immediate neighborhood that will constitute his customers without spending time or money in conducting a comprehensive survey.

Census of Population. Conducted once each decade. It provides a count of all residents of the United States by state, city, and country and in large cities by census tract and city block. Data is also gathered on age, sex, race, citizenship, educational levels. Occupation, employment status income and family status of inhabitants.

Census of Housing. Since 1940 combined with the Census of Population to gather information regarding the housing conditions of Americans such as value of the house, number of rooms type of structure race of occupants and year built.

Census of business Information regarding retail trade, wholesales trade, and selected services. The data is broken down by countries and by large cities and includes such facts as number of stores of a particular type operated total sales employment and legal from of organization.

Census of Manufactures. Covers approximately 450 industries revealing the value of products produced by industry cost of materials and equipment number of establishments and ages paid.

Census of Agriculture Data regarding the number of farms number of person residing on farms (by age and sex) value of farms products sold acreage of each major crop, number of tractors number of livestock present of electricity and running water for each country in the United States.

Census of Minerals. Data on employees wages quantities produced cost of materials and supplies types of equipment used and manhours worked in over sixty industries.

Census of governments. Data every five years no number of public employees payrolls value of taxable property and financial asserts of state and local governments.

So much data is produced by the federal government that the marketing researcher often purchases summaries such as the *Monthly Catalog of United States Government Publications* the *Statistical Abstract of the United States* the *Survey of current Business* and the *Country and City Data Book*. The *Statistical Abstract of the Unites States* is published annually and contains a wealth of current data.

State and city governments are other important sources of information on employment production and sales activities within a particular state. In addition, university bureaus of business and economic research often collect and distribute such information.

Private Sources Numerous private organizations provide information for the marketing executive. for activities in a particular industry trade associations are excellent resources. Advertising agencies continually collect information on the audience reached by various media. In the annual *Survey of Buying Power* Published by *Sales and Marketing Management* Magazine the marketer will find a wide range of illuminating and valuable data. Figure 3-4 illustrates the information for each of the states of the United States and the Canadian provinces.

Several national firms offer information to business firms on a subscription basis. The largest of these, A.C. Nielsen Company collects data every two months on products sales retail prices display space inventories and promotional activities of competing brands of food and drug products from a sample of approximately 1,6000 food stores and 750 drugstores.

Market Research Corporation of America (MRCA) gathers information on consumer purchases of food and other household items from a panel of cover 7,000 households throughout the United States. The *panel* (or continuous sample) periodically reports to MRCA a detailed list of all food and other household products purchased during a particular time interval. Viewed over a period of time this information can be extremely useful in determining brand preferences effect of various promotional activities on retail sales in a particular region or age group, and the degree of brand switching that occurred for different products.

Planning original research—the research design

The use of secondary data offers two important over that of primary data (*data collected for the first time a marketing research study*):

1. The assembly of previously collected data is almost always *less expenses* than the collection of primary data.

2. Less time is involved in locating using secondary data.

The researcher must be aware of two potential limitations to the use of secondary data: (1) the data may be obsolete, or (2) the classifications of the secondary data may not be usable in the study. Published information has an unfortunate habit of rapidly becoming obsolete. A marketing researcher analyzing the population of the Orlando, Florida, metropolitan market in 1977 discovers that most of the 1970 census data is obsolete due to the influx of residents attracted by the development of the Disney World complex. Also, data may have been collected previously on such bases as country or city blocks or census tracts. In such cases the marketing researcher may not be able to rearrange in a usable from the secondary data and must begin the collection of primary data. Data collection should be preceded by a detailed research design which can be defined as *a series of advanced decision that taken together comprise a master plan or model for the conduct of the investigation*. By developing a comprehensive plan for performing the research study the researcher can control each step of the investigation and can avoid potential problem at the outset of the study.

Collecting primary data

The marketing researcher has three alternatives in the collection of primary data: observation survey, or controlled experiment. No one method is best in all circumstances, in fact any one may prove the most efficient in a particular situation.

The Observation Method Observational studies are conducted by actually viewing (either by visual observation or through mechanical means such as hidden cameras) the overt actions of the respondent. This may take the form of traffic counts at a potential for a fast-food franchise, a check of license plates at a shopping center to determine the area from which shoppers are attracted the Nielsen Audimeter that when attached to the television set, records the times when the set is turned on and the channel being viewed, or (as in the case of the famous study reported in the Hidden Persuaders) a special camera equipped with a telephoto lens that records the number of consumer eye blinks per minute and indicates the mild hypnotic trance of a housewife who is "overcome" by the complexity of colors and packages on the supermarket shelf.

The Survey Method Much information cannot be obtained through mere observation of overt consumer acts, the researcher must ask questions to obtain information on attitudes motives and opinions. The survey method is the most widely used approach to collecting primary data. There are three kinds of survey telephone, mail, and personal interviews.

Telephone interviews are inexpensive and fast in obtaining small quantities of relatively impersonal information. Since many firms have leased Wats services, a Seattle call adds no further cost than would an across-town interview. Telephone interviews are limited to simple, clearly worded questions. Such interviews have two drawbacks: it is extremely difficult to obtain personal characteristics of the respondent, and the survey may be prejudiced since two groups will be omitted-those households without telephones and those with unlisted numbers.

Mail interviews the marketing researcher to conduct national studies at reasonable costs. Whereas personal interviews with a national sample may be prohibitive in cost, the researcher can reach each potential respondent with the price of a postage stamp. Costs may be misleading however, since *returned* questionnaires for such a study may average only 40 to 50 percent, depending upon length of the questionnaire and respondent interest. Unless additional information is obtained from nonrespondents through telephone interviews or other methods, the results of the study are likely to be biased since there may be important differences between the characteristics of nonrespondents and those people who took the time to complete and return the questionnaires. For this reason a follow up questionnaire is sometimes mailed to nonrespondents to telephone interviews may be used to gather additional information.

The *personal interview* is typically the best means of obtaining more detailed information since the interviewer has the opportunity to establish rapport with the respondent. The interviewer can also explain questions that might be confusing or vague to the respondent. Mail questionnaires must be carefully worded and pretested to eliminate any potential misunderstanding by respondents. but misunderstandings can occur with even the most clearly worded questions.

But the personal interview is slow and is the most expensive method of collecting survey data. Its flexibility coupled with detailed information that can be collected, however, often more than offsets the time and cost limitations. Information is rarely gathered from all sources during the survey. If *all sources were contacted in a survey* the results would be called a census. but unless the number of sources is quite small the costs are so great that only the federal government can afford it- and then only every ten years. Instead the researcher selects a *representative grown* called a ample. *If chosen in such a way that every member has an equal chance of being selected* the sample then is a simple random sample of students at Florida international University in Miami may be drawn by obtaining a list of names from the college registrar and assigning each a number, then selecting numbers on the list from a table of random numbers and using those selected to be questioned.

A second method of obtaining a random sample

where population lists are unavailable is by area sampling. Here *blocks instead of individual are selected at random for the survey*. Then everyone on the selected blocks is interviewed or, in some cases, respondents are randomly selected from each designated block.

The experimental method The final and least-used method of collecting marketing information is through the use of *controlled experiments*. To data, its most common use has been in test marketing.

Marketers face great risks in introducing to the American market. They often attempt to reduce this risk by *introducing the new untried product into a particular metropolitan area and then observe its degree of success*. Frequently used cities include Peoria, Wichita, and Columbus, Ohio. Consumers in the test market city view the products as any other new product since it is available in retail outlets and is advertised in the local media. The test-market city becomes a small replica of the total market. The marketing manager can then compare actual sales with expected sales and can project them on a nationwide basis, if the test results are favorable the risks, of a large-scale failure are reduced. Many products fail at the test-market stage, and thus consumers who live in these cities may purchase products that no one else will ever buy!

The major problem with controlled experiments is the difficult task of controlling all variables in a real-life situation. The laboratory scientist can rigidly control temperature and humidity, but can the marketing manager determine the effect of varying the retail price through refundable coupons when the competition decides to retaliate or deliberately confuse the experimental by also issuing competitive coupons?

In the future experimentation will become more frequent as firms' develop more sophisticated simulated competitive models requiring computer analysis. Simulation of market activities promises to be one of the great new developments in marketing.

The problems of questionnaire design, selection, training and control of field interviewers, editing, coding, and tabulation of the data, interpretation presentation of results and follow-up are discussed in derail in numerous marketing research books, which should be consulted by the interested reader.

It is crucial that the marketing researchers and the research users cooperate at every stage in the research design. Too many studies of unused because marketing management views the results as too restricted due to the lengthy discussion of research limitations or use unfamiliar terminology, such as levels of confidence and "Type 1 errors." Recommendations should be given so that the written report may be explained expanded, or clarified. This increases the possibility of positive use of the report by management.

While most larger companies have their own marketing research departments, many smaller firms depend on independent marketing research firms to conduct their research studies. Even the largest firms typically rely on outside agencies to provide interviewers and they often out some research studies to independent agencies. The basic criterion for the decision to conduct a study through an outside organisation or internally through the firm's marketing research staff is usually cost. Other considerations should include an estimate of the reliability and accuracy of information collected by the outside agency.

Research is likely to be contracted to outside groups when the following requirements are met:

1. Problem areas can be defined in terms of specific research projects.

2. There is need for specialized know-how and/or equipment.

3. Intellectual detachment is necessary.

For example in depth studies of consumer motivations in the purchase of the firm's products may require the use of trained psychologists and expertise not available in the firm's department. Also, the use of outside groups aids in ensuring that the researcher is not conducting the study in an attempt to "prove" the wisdom of a favorite theory or a package of his or her own choosing.

Many marketing managers discover that their information problems result from an overabundance-not a paucity-of marketing data. Their sophisticated computer facilities provide them daily with literally a deluge of printouts about sales in thirty different market areas, a hundred different products, and 6,4000 customers. The marketing manager solves the crisis of too much information of the wrong kind in the wrong from each morning by gently sliding the ominous stack of computer printouts to the edge of the desk, where it is speedily deposited in a certain circular file.

The solution to the problem of obtaining *relevant* information appears simple-establish a systematic approach management through the installation of a planned marketing information system. Establishment of an effective marketing information system is, however, much easier said than done, as documented by the large number of firms who have attempted to develop an MIS and have only succeeded in increasing the amounts of irrelevant data.

The ideal marketing information system should be a designed set of procedures and methods for generating an orderly flow of pertinent information for use in making decisions providing management with the current and future states of the market and also providing indications of market responses to company actions as well as the actions of competitors.

Properly constructed the MIS could serve as the nerve center for the company, providing instantaneous information suitable for each level of management. It would act as a thermostat, monitoring the marketplace continuously so that management can adjust its actions as conditions change.

The analogy of an automatic heating system shows the role of marketing information in a firm's marketing system. Once the objective of a temperature setting (perhaps 68 Fahrenheit) has been established information about the actual temperature in the house is collected and compared with the objective and a decision is made based upon his comparison. If the temperature drops below an established figure the decision is made to activate the furnace until the temperature reaches some established amount. On the other hand, a high temperature may require a decision to turn off the turnace.

Deviation from the firm's goals of profitability return on investment, or market share may necessitate changes in price structures, promotional expenditures package design or numerous marketing alternatives. The firm's MIS should be capable of revealing such deviations and possibly suggest tactical changes that will result in attaining the established goals.

Many marketing executives feel that their company does not need a marketing information system for various reasons. Two arguments are most often given- (1) the size of the company operations does not warrant such a complete system, and (2) the information provided by an MIS is already being supplied by the marketing research department.

These contentions arise from a misconception of services and functions performed by the marketing research department. Marketing research has already been described as typically focusing on a specific problem or project the investigations have a definite beginning middle, and end.

Robert J. Williams, creator of the first marketing information system in 1961 at the Mead Johnson division of Edward Dalton Company Evansville, Indiana, explains the difference in the manner:

> The difference between marketing research and marketing intelligence is like the difference between a flash bulb and a candle. Let's say

> you are facing in the dark. Every 90 second you are allowed to set off a flash bulb. You can use those brief intervals of intense light to chart a course, but remember everybody is moving too. Hopefully, they'll accommodate themselves roughly to your predictions. You may get bumped and you may stumble every often, but you can dance along.
>
> On the other hand, you can light a candle. It doesn't yield as much light, but it's a steady light. You are continually aware of the movements of other bodies. You can adjust your own course to the courses of the others. The intelligence system is a kind of candle, it's no great flash on the immediate state of things but it provides continuous light as situations shift and change.

By focusing daily on the marketplace, the MIS provides a continuous systematic and comprehensive study of areas that indicate deviations from established goals. The up-to-the minute data allows problems to be corrected be fore they adversely affect company operations.

Marketing information systems have progressed a long way from the days when they were primarily responsible for clerical activities-and usually at an increased cost over the old method. Today, managers have available special computer programs, remote access consoles, better data banks, direct communication with the computer, and assignment of authority to the computer for review and referral. In some instances the computer simulates various market conditions and makes decisions based on the results of the model. But just how common are these computer-based marketing information systems in company offices?

A 1972 of the 500 largest firms in the United States revealed that 75 of the 193 responding companies possessed an operational computer-based MIS. Nearly two-thirds of the firms had established their MIS within the past five years at a typical development cost of between $50,000 and $500,00. Data were most often recorded at the line, item invoice level (sales of each product, salesmen, customer type of sale, price), and printed reports (not computer terminals) were the most frequently used method for transmitting data to the marketing decision-maker.

CONSTRUCTING AN MIS

The first step in the construction of the MIS is obtaining the total support of top management. Management not only must be truly enthusiastic about the potential of the system, but also must maintain the belief that it is top management's place to oversee its development. Too often the technical staff are left to build such a system.

The next step involves a review and appraisal of the entire marketing organization and of the policies that direct it. The marketing manager's responsibilities must be clearly defined. If the system is to measure their performance against plans, then it is necessary to specify precisely each person's areas of accountability.

Once the organization is readied for the development of the system, the level of sophistication of the MIS must be determined. Before this can be done the company needs and the costs of meeting these needs must be carefully considered. The abilities of manager to develop and effectively use a sophisticated system must also be considered. Managers must be able to define their specific information needs.

Management must also be able to state explicitly its planning decision making and control processes and procedures. If managers are able to verbalize a specific set of decision rules, an automated exception reporting system may be developed for the manager who states "I always like to know about all situations in which sales, profits or market shares are running 4% or more behind plan. Furthermore, in any exceptional cases I also require the following diagnostic information prices distribution levels, advertising and consumer attitudes".

Sales forecasting

An extremely vital form of marketing information is the sales forecast—the estimate of company sales for a specified future period. In addition to its use in marketing planning the sales forecast also plays a critical role in production scheduling financial planning inventory planning *and* procurement *and in the* determination of personal needs. An inaccurate forecast will result in incorrect decisions in each of these areas.

Sales forecasts may be either short-run or long-run. Short-run forecasts usually include a period of one year, while long-run forecasts often cover a longer period.

During periods of steady growth the trend extension method of forecasting produces satisfactory results. But it implicitly assumes that those factors that contributed to the attainment of a certain level of output in the past will continue to operate in the same manner in the future. When conditions change, the trend extension method will often produce incorrect results. For this reason forecasters are increasingly utilizing more sophisticated techniques and complex mathematical models. Inputs-ouput models which depict the interactions of various industries in producing goods, are being developed by the U.S. Department of Commerce and by private agencies. Since outputs (sales) of one industry are the inputs (purchases) of another industry a change of outputs in one industry will affect inputs of other industries. These models show the impact on supplier industries of increased production in a given industry and can be used to measure the impact throughout the economy of increased demand in any industry.

The task of management within the modern corporation is extremely complex. Firms have many goals which are usually pursued simultaneously. Some of the more apparent one are profits, market share, geographic expansion, growth, dominance, satisfied customers. Social responsibility, and in this era, a desire to conserve scarce resources. The goals which are emphasized at any given time depend on a number of internal and external factors and how management reacts significant elements in goal attainment. Marketing manners reacts to them. The marketing strategies of a firm have become increasingly major responsibility toward that end since they are concerned with the problems and decisions which shape marketing strategies.

Marketing management as a unit must assume responsibility for such diverse areas as: product development, pricing, sales, market research, advertising, promotion development, physical distribution, and channel structure. In doing this, the managers must develop answers to questions such as the following related to advertising.

1. Out of your total budget for daytime TV spots, should you divert S1 million to nighttime network television...and if you do, what changes well you make in your pattern of daytime TV?

2. Results of new advertising copy run in three test markets are satisfactory, but not outstanding. What will increase its effectiveness and how will you test the changes in time for national expansion a year fro now?

3. You except to have an improved produced ready for distribution in six months. What ideas should the agency creative people be developing now to generate a strong positive consumer reaction to the product changes?

The answers to such questions will help determine the degree to which the firm is able to meet its goals. Marketing managers are responsible for making appropriate decisions. The kinds of decisions they make are influenced by a number of factors such as:

1. The volatile nature of buyers.

2. The geographic dispersion of markets.

3. The variability of people in the marketing organization.

4. The dependency on people outside the organization.

5. The diversity of alternatives in terms of marketing mix and promotion mix.

These factors and many others contribute to the risk and uncertainty associated with marketing decision making. Decisions concerning new-product development, advertising campaigns, pricing strategies, and market research efforts, expensive advertising campaign, and expenditures for new-product research represent significant with risk and uncertainty, it becomes obvious that the quality of decisions made by the marketing manager is critical in determining the firm's success. How can marketing manages function effectively in this highly complex decision environment?

The answer lies, at least in part, in the effective application of scientific methods to marketing decision making is predictive in nature. In making a decision, the manager is predicting both the outcome of a number of alternative solutions, and that the course of action chosen represents the optimum among the available alternatives. When selecting among alternative advertising campaigns, there is an implicit prediction as to use a particular marketing mix implies a prediction about future profitability resulting from the particular alternative selected.

The aim of science is to facilitate more accurate decision making by providing more nearly perfect knowledge. The ability to predict the outcomes of particular alternative courses of action more accurately reduces the risk associated with uncertainty. Of course, perfect knowledge is not a practical reality. However, the more nearly perfect the knowledge, the less uncertainty in the decision-making process and hence the less risk in predicting outcome. Harper W. Body and William F. Massey point out that,"...many years will pass before enough is understood about marketing factors and their interrelationships to permit the making of nearly perfect predications whenever they are needed for problem solving in marketing and the use of scientific methods can facilitate marketing, decision making.

The purpose of this chapter is to establish a conceptual frame work for treating decision making information generating in a scientific fashion. A more detailed discussion of selected areas of this framework will be presented in later chapters.

Today's business organizations need highly structured methods to cope with the significant increase in size, complexity and diversity of operations. These factors are moving management away from the art that has existed in to a new arena. What management needs today is an underlying science, or at least a very structured approach to decision making. This approach has been given the name "systems". The systems approach provides a mean for accommodating increasing organizational complexity. It provides a framework for visualizing both internal and external environmental factors in an integrated fashion. In short, the systems approach is a structured way of thinking about managing.

The systems concept

The word system can be defined in many ways depending upon the purpose for the definition. For our purpose the following definition seems best: a system is a structure which implements a ongoing process. The structure may be formed by many diverse parts, but the parts work together toward a common objective. The world system connotes order, a plan, method, or arrangement.

A dictionary definition of a biological system can serve in explaining the concept: "An assemblage of parts or organs of the same of similar tissues, or concerned with the same function; e.g. the nervous system, the digestive system. Similarly, a marketing system consists of diverse parts (a structure) which are concerned with the same function-the process of generating the desired quantity and type of transactions.

A system can be thought of as having certain basic aspects. Any system whether mechanical, biological, or behavioral can be viewed in these terms.

1. The central focus of a system is that the internal parts or components which carry out the process. Seymour Tills defends a system as "a set of interrelated parts". These parts must work together

to efficiently carry out desired process. The parts of the system and relationship between them are controllable elements for a manager. The managerial role within a system is as a coordinator of controllable factors. A manager must monitor and control the operation of the functional parts and system's inputs in such a way as to achieve the desired results.

2. Inputs are the other controllable elements of a system. The inputs flow into the central processing unit and either act as support in building or developing the functional parts or act as raw material for the purposes. Inputs can include people, money, equipment, information, and many other elements depending upon the nature of the process being formed by the system.

3. Outputs are the end produces. The outputs of a total marketing system are the transactions of specified type and quantity, generated by the type of motion. The nature of the outputs and whether they accomplish the goals of the system depend on the manager's skill in arranging the functional parts of the system and in securing needed inputs.

4. Feedback keep the manager informed about the results obtained by the outputs of the system. It helps control the system by monitoring results. If results are not in line with system goals, the manager can alter the inputs, change the goals, or rearrange the functional parts of the system to bring goals and results into harmony.

5. The environment of the system consists of all uncontrollable factors which affect the process. The nature of the environment depends upon the specifications of the particular system being used. As narrower areas of the firm's total activity are viewed as comprising a system the number of uncontrollable variables increases. Cooperate goals may be uncontrollable for a new product development manager and thus, they must be

viewed as a part of the environment. They are external constraints on the activities of the system.

This notion of uncontrollable factors in the environment is the key to understanding the limits of a system model. For example, a firm may be engaged in the marketing process for a particular products which is subject to rigid governmental certification procedures. The firm cannot model would not include it. References would be made, however to such activities as monitor certification process. Thus, the firm would use information about the procedures in its decision-making process.

System Language In this text, system will be represented through the LOGOS languages. In LOGUS, system are represented by rectangles and identified by an action phrase of two to five words. When a system is actually a wholly contained element of a larger system, it is called a subsystem. These five subsystems and their interrelationship constitute a suprasystem. Illustrating the suprasystem with these five subsystems, each of which represents the same of level of activity, is known as defending the system at the first level of detail.

Flows into a system or subsystem are illustrated in LOGUS by a signal path. There is an incoming signal path to "procure inputs" from "Establish criteria". In this particular case the incoming flow is a signal to proceed with the procurement of inputs as well as some parameters for the procurement process. Note that there are no signal paths into "Establish criteria" This does not imply that no signal exist. Rather, there signal have simply remained undefined in this model. A strong case can be made for the universality of all systems, thus requiring the analyst to arbitrarily limits his model at some point. In this case, no signal to or from the larger suprasystem have been defined.

Flows from a system or subsystem are illustrated in LOGOUS by an outgoing signal path. The incoming signal path to "Procure inputs", from "Establish criteria" is an outgoing signal path from "Establish criteria". It is largely through the use of signal paths that the interrelationships of subsystem are illustrated.

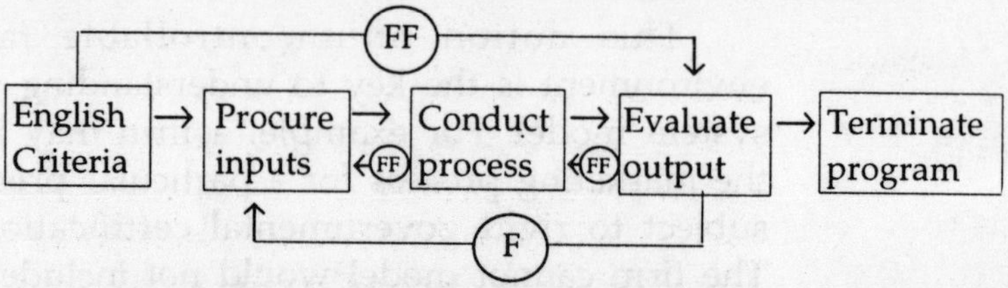

Feedback is illustrated in LOGOS by a signal paths. As mentioned earlier, feedback helps in controlling the subsystem to which it is transmitted. For example, a process is conducted which requires inputs. If the process is initiated, but problems arise, it may be desirable to immediately require a change in the inputs. Thus, the feedback path from "conduct process" will control the inputs procured to improve the implementation of the process. Similarly, the output of the process may be valued in terms of the criteria for successful implementation of the process, It may be determined in "Evaluate out put" that changes are required in the inputs and/ or the process. Thus, feedback from evaluations helps in controlling the inputs and the conducts of the process.

Notices the action verb, "Evaluate." Students of decision making are constantly confronted with the task of evaluation. All too frequently, however, no provision is made for the formal criteria upon which evaluation is based. In the signal path labeled with FF is a feedforward and serves the vital function of providing criteria for evaluation. A feedforward is used when one subsystem produces a vital ingredient for some subsystem positioned further along in the suprasystem. The value of the feedforward will becomes clearer as the decision process is discussed further.

The benefits of the systems approach

What are the major advantage to the systems approach? The systems approach provides a framework for the manager to organize his thoughts relative to the implementation of a given process. It helps him to see the essential elements in a situation and the relationship between these elements. It provides a structure for analyzing, planning, and controlling a given set of activities. In short, he systems approach provides a means for understanding highly complex situations and thereby improving managerial decision making. The systems approach gives organization and structure (a scientific method) to managerial activities and therein lies its major benefit.

THE INFORMATION-DECISION INTERACTION

Making decisions is the basic responsibility of management. The manager must make decisions relative to planning, organizing, and controlling the operation. Where and how are made within the mind of the manager. The individual is required to think and exercise judgment relative to a given situation. The process starts with the recognition of a problem in some specified area. Perhaps new product has been developed, and a base price must be established. This represents a problem which must be solved by deciding on a price. In any decision environment the manager must consider the controllable variables, the uncontrollable variables, and the relationship between them. He or she can manipulate the controllable aspect of the situation within the constraints of the uncontrollable environment in an attempt to solve the problem. With a thorough understanding of the problem and the variables involved, the manager must develop alternative solution and project the outcomes of each possible course of action. Based upon an evaluation of the project outcomes and related goals, the manager must select the best alternative; that is he or she must make the decision.

It is helpful to look at decision making in a systems framework, even though the process is often carried out in the manager's mind. What are the input into the process? The basic input is information two types are needed. First, information about the various aspects of the decision situation is needed. What is the problem? What variables are concerned? What alternatives are available? What is the best alternative given the goals of the manager? Secondly, information is needed relative to the useful frameworks for organizing and understanding the relationship between variables. These frameworks will be referred to as decision models. All of these parameters are formalized as criteria in "Establish criteria". These criteria direct the acquisition of information and provide the basis for evaluating decisions. Decision models are utilized to convert information into decisions. The decision is evaluated using the criteria that have been established.

A noted, information is the basic input for the decision-making system. A decision maker must have some means for obtaining vital decision information. The process of generating such information can be termed the research process. This process includes the activities of collecting data, processing data to transform it into useful information, and transmitting the processing data to transform it in to useful information and transmitting the processed information to the manager. This process can also be viewed in a systems context. In this way, we can see that raw data is the basic input in to the system and information is the output.

Information is the common denominator of both the decision making system and the information management system. The information management system generates an output (information) which is the vital input for decision making. Viewing the information system in isolation can produce a distorted result. The only objective of an information management system is to improve the decisions which are outputs of the decision-making system. The raw data inputs and the structure of the functional parts of the information system must be from the ultimate decision should control the type of information going to the manager, and the information required should dictate the data collection and processing activities.

To summarize the interaction, data is collected for processing by the information management system. Processing transforms the data into useful information which is then transmitted to the manager. The manager use the information to arrive at decisions in his or her area of responsibility. Feedback -from these decisions dictates the modifications needed in either of the joint system.

For example, sales records may be collected and processed to form sales forecasts for future periods. These forecasts are delivered to the sales manager for use in the planning process. A sales manager might use the forecasts to make decisions relative to the allocation of sales people to varies territories and to set sales quotas. The results of this decision in the form of feedback, provide a basis for modifying, if necessary, the information management and/or decision-making systems.

Thus, information and decision making are inseparable if the organization is to be managed effectively, and basic understanding of marketing decision making is a prerequisite for understanding research and information management activities. With this thought in to a review of marketing decision making and decision-making techniques.

The nature of marketing activities and decisions

The successful management of the marketing function is base upon the ability of the firm to match its products and services with existing markets. By developing a frame work for the total marketing process, were can identify the critical decision areas. The reason for developing marketing information within an organization is to improve marketing decisions. Thus, we must clearly define the nature of marketing activities and decisions as a starting point for developing marketing information. Developing information without first knowing for what it is to be used is a futile but all-too-common practice. In most cases knowing exactly what information you need is half the battle. Without a strong orientation toward the need is half the battle. Without a strong orientation toward the needs of the manager, the information system is likely to fail. The decisions which are uniquely marketing related can be conveniently grouped in to two areas: (1) Market analysis and (2) Formulating the marketing mix.

Market analysis is the first important decision area which is uniquely in the realm of the marketing manager. Marketing management is responsible for investigating the nature and structure of the market in order to locate market opportunities for the firm. Relative to this area the marketing manager mist first make decisions involving market segmentation. Market segmentation means breaking the total market in to homogeneous submarkets. Markets can be segmented based on geography, socioeconomic variables, or buyer behavior (shopping patters, usage rates, or buying motives). A basis for segmentation must be established which are internally similar. This allows groups to be appealed to with a single marketing program. After the segmentation is complete, a profile must be developed for each segment. This profile should provide the basic characteristics of the consumers and the major means of competition used by each competitor. The potential for each segment or segments can then be selected based on this evaluation. Many customer and market considerations must be taken in to account in the market analysis process. These include:

1. The nature of the market.

a. Number of potential buyers.

b. Characteristics if buyers-age, income, occupation, education, sex, size, of family, race, life style, psychographics. etc.

c. Characteristics of users if users are different from buyers.

d. Where users and buyers live.

e. Where buyers buy.

f. Size of purchases.

g. When buyers buy.

h. How buyers buy-brand specification or not; impulse or planned; cash or :redit.

i. Why buyers buy-attitude and motivations.

j. Who influences buying decisions

k. Use for product or service.

l. Indications of changes in buying habits.

2. The structure of the market.

a. Number of competitors

b. Market shares of each competitor

c. Characteristics of leading products or service.

d. Differentiation of our product or service from the leaders.

e. Policies an procedures used by the principal competitors.

After the target market has been selected and the nature of the target segments described, programs must be developed to reach the target.

To put the development of a marketing program into perspective it is important to understand the notion of the marketing concept. The marketing concept stress the integration and coordination of many functional decision areas within marketing. In addition, the concept argues that the needs, wants, and values of consumers should be the focal point of marketing. This focal point gives a direction to the formulation of an effective and profitable marketing program. Information from market analysis thus becomes an input in to other marketing decisions.

The information of a marketing program typically involves the integration of four major areas. These includes product, price, distribution, and promotion, jointly they are called the marketing mix. These variables are usually controllable to some degree for marketing management.

Levels of decision making

There is another critical dimension to decision making in addition to the delineation of decision areas. This is a definition of decision levels. All decisions within the advertising area, examples, cannot be viewed in the same way. Deciding to aggressively use advertising as a competitive weapon does not have the same implications or require the same information as deciding on the copy for a given ad. Robert N. Anthony in Planning and Control system presented a very useful hierarchy of decision levels. Anthony noted that it is "apparent that mistakes with serious practical consequences have been made when techniques and generalizations found valid for one class of activities (level of decision) have been applied to the other. "He established three decision levels-Strategic planning, management control, and operational control. The first two of these deal with management decision making and the third with operating procedures. Anthony also breaks Management control in to two divisions; planning and control.

Since this text deals with information for marketing management we will consider only the first two levels of Anthony's hierarchy. For the purpose of description we have labeled the levels of decision making with which we will deal as follows:

1. Strategic planning
2. Management planning
3. Management control.

These correspond approximately to control. Before defining our three levels of decision making, certain terms should be clear; planning, control, strategic, and how to do it. Control means assuring that desired results are obtained. To do this, the manager must set performance necessary. Strategic decisions are those that establish the firm's general position relative to the external environment and the competition. Operational decisions deal with the ongoing administration of the internal organization.

With these concepts in mind, we can define strategic planning as policy formulation with respect to the various decision areas. At this level management is deciding what to do in terms of market analysis and formulating the marketing mix. Policies are strategy-type statement which establish long-term goals or thrusts. For examples, a firm may establish an overall marketing policy of seeking market positions through segmentation. This implies corollary policies in each area of decision making, such as policies of style innovation and price discrimination in the product and prices areas respectively. Note that strategic planning does not lead immediately to implementation, but lays the groundwork for more specific planning.

Management planning involves the process of establishing programs to implement the policies and budgets designed to obtains and use resource in such a way as to accomplish the organization's policies. For example, a firm might set the following specific objective:

> During the next model year, model B will be introduced and attain monthly sales of 1,000 units by the end of third quarter.

Objectives at the management planning level of decision making provides measurable criteria for evaluating short-term performance. These objectives can be attained. For examples, the introductory objectives for model B may call for penetration pricing. Finally, a specific operating plan and budget can be developed. At this point the actual program for model B would be set.

Management control requires decisions to insure that the programs are, in fact, continuing to implement the policies. Thus, the output of management control are corrective actions designed to keep the organization on the desired course. In the case of model B, for example, management control would monitor implementation to ensure that operational plans were being carried out, evaluate the success of management planning, and compare long term performance to policies.

In order to make a clear distinction between the three levels of management decisions it may prove helpful to compare them on a number of dimensions. Presents for each decision level; the level of management typically involved, the nature of the activity, the characteristics of the activity, the tempo, the inputs, the type of information needed, and the output of the given decision level. By breaking each decision area in to these three levels, the manager can more clearly define the nature of the decisions involved and thus the type of information needed.

The marketing decision matrix

Marketing management must deal with many different decision areas on different levels. By looking at these various areas and levels of decisions in conjunction, a marketing decision matrix is formed. This matrix provides the manager with a framework to organize his activities and determine the types of information he needs. In order to effectively manage the form's marketing activities, it is necessary to clearly define the nature of the decisions in each cell of the matrix and to develop useful information for use in each area. This decision matrix is a starting point for developing effective marketing information.

The marketing decision matrix

Level of decision / decision areas	Strategy planning	Management Planning	Management Control
Market analysis			
Product			
Price			
Distribution			
Promotion			

An example of the information/ decision-making interaction

On September 27, 1974, Ford Motor Company introduced two new car lines to the public; Ford Granada and Mercury Monarch, two of the first domestically-produced luxury small cars. At a time when economic conditions were adversely affecting all new car sales. Granada broke Ford Division first-day sales of 1,702 units were the best for a new car introduced by Lincoln Mercury in 14 years."

Ford product planners had earned the right to celebrate these success stories. Granada and Monarch were the result of newly five years of market studies, consumer surveys, design trails, plants made and changed. Their development actually grew out of two separate new car programs launched in 1970. One of these was as examination of the growing luxury, high-priced compact car with 5.254 units sold. Monarch first day sale of 1,702 units were the best for a new car introduced by Lincoln-mercury in 14 years".

Ford product planners had earned the right to celebrate these success stories. Granada and Monarch were the design trials, plans made and changed. Their development actually grew out of two separate new car programs launched in 1970. One of these was an examination of the growing luxury, high-priced compact car market and the possibility of a successful entry in to that market by Ford. Cars in this market include Audi. BMW and Volvo. The other program was a redesign of the Maverick. Ford's economy compact introduced in 1969.

Maverick was produced to compete with the growing number of foreign-built autos sold in the United States. With a long sloping hood and short rear deck, its primary appeals were low initial and operating costs and ease of maintenance-it was a basic machine. While Maverick first-year sales were impressive, the car did not stem the tide of the increasingly popular imports.

In 1970, however, Ford introduced a more suitable competitor for the imports, the subcompact pinto. In addition to its competitive role. The economy Pinto had an immediate effect on Maverick sales. It be came clear that Pinto was actually cutting in to the sales of its "big brother" ion the Ford line-up. Maverick sales also were affected by competition at the upper price range of the compact market. The Valiant, Dart, and Nova-white sharing the compact class with Caught between the two competitive force, Maverick needed a change, and the direction of that change was up-to compete with the heavier, roomier compacts and to move clearly out of Pinto's product range.

With the two new car programs in mind. Ford's design studies began to produce design concepts for the maverick "X" and Comet "X" and the new laxity compact.

Initial research on the luxury model was conducted in Santa Monica, California, in June 1970, with a consumer sample (where consumers were invited to examine and comment on proposed vehicle designs). Ford market researchers wanted to determine the potential of a Ford product in the Mercedes or Audi category, and to get an idea of the features such a car should have. They learned from the sample that consumers would want the car to be small but solidly, with a high level of luxury and substantial interior room. A relatively high price for the car would be acceptable.

In April 1972, another major study was conducted in San Diego, this time to test three actual prototype models, as well as two European Ford cars. The consumers selected for the sample either owned 4-door car or were considered prospective buyers.

The result were decisive, but not promising for Ford's interest in the luxury car market; The consumers did like the cars themselves, but considered the planned price of $6,000 (in 1972 dollars) too high. The response indicated that a Ford entry into the luxury compact marker would not be successful, and company management decided to abandon the program. however, the design features regarded favorably by the consumers were later incorporated in to the development and planning of prototypes being considered as future maverick and comet replacement. The luxury car program, though not followed through to production, made its contribution.

During the first half of 1971, marketing researchers began testing the appeal of new design concepts for maverick and Comet to small car owners and prospective buyers.

Result of this research, too, were not heartening; none of the design concepts developed for the new cars scored as a shown-stopper with the consumers. But some helpful information did come out of the first study. The cars that did receive some favorable attention were the 4-door prototypes. These were considerably more" boxy-looking" than the existing sloping line of Maverick and Comet and carried a more formal image. The 2-door prototypes had styling touches quite similar to the existing compacts and were not perceived as improvements.

In the summer of 1972, consumers in Toledo and Chicago reviewed a new group of 2-door and 4-door designs. The 2-door concepts again were not perceived as improvements over the existing car, but a 4-door styling theme produced by the Lincoln-Mercury Design Studio was received favorable. The consumers considered it a formal style-a family car, but definitely not in the lower price range.

The success of the 4-door Lincoln-Mercury entry directed designers toward adapting the formal appeal to the 2-door car, dropping at that stage nearly all the existing early in 1973 with Maverick, Comet, and Nova owners confirmed that this more formal styling approach was on the right track.

Another significant result of this research was that the participants regarded the new formal approach as substantially different from the traditional compact car with its basic economy and sometimes down right sparse interior-the new models had a definite air of luxury and "foreignness".

After further studies, final design touches were made on the 2-door and in the spring of 1973, company management approved both the 2-door and 4-door designs.

One of the chief characteristics of the cars was "package efficiency"—that is, maximum use of the functional space available with its wheelbase of 109.9 inches. Hip and shoulder room were increased over the standard compact interior dimensions, and entry and exits were improved with the use of titled door hinges, and wider doors. The boxy shape of the tank capacity were enlarged. Ford's interior designers added luxury touches to give the car the traditional big-cat "feel" of comfort and quality.

However, the research indicated that these cars were so different in style and image from the basic, economy maverick and Comet that the existing car names were no longer considered appropriate by the consumers sampled. Just as the product itself had moved away from the original economy compact concept, the name, too, would have to be brought up to date. But, then, what of the Maverick and Comet lines? Did the introduction of this newly developed luxury car signal the end of the economy compact or should both cars be maintained?

In August of 1973, a study was conducted in Atlanta to try to resolve the issue. Prospective buyers of compact, intermediate, and standardizes cars examined the new car along with other Ford and General Motors Corporation cars of all size. The new styling carried a definite appeal across the spectrum of prospective buyers who participated in the research, and was considered to equal intermediate size cars in roominess and to surpass them in luxury. Also, 33 percent of the respondents estimated the sticker for the Granada and Monarch.

More significantly, one third said there was no other car on the road like the new car. It was clearly too distinctive simply to serve as a substitute for the existing Maverick and Comet lines. Also, 1973 marked the beginning of serious fuel shortages and the resulting increase in small car popularity and sales. These considerations all influenced the solution of the issue-the Maverick and comet would be retained as compact economy entire and the new car, in Ford and Lincoln Mercury versions, would be a completely new product offering.

Several possible names for the new cars were researched to find names that consumers considered appropriate for a luxury small car. In the tradition of Mustang and Pinto, Stallion was tested along with Fairmont, Lurene, Eagle and others. However, test participants favored Granada and Monarch as indicating excellence and suitability.

Association with a luxury car, as confirmed by the research, would prove helpful in developing merchandising and positioning strategy, the next step for company management. The functional approach to car design, clearly in demand according to the studies, also became a key part of the advertising for the cars.

Research had shown that the greatest sales potential for the Granada and Monarch was among car buyers looking for functional benefits. These buyers made up 54-percent of the compact marked and 34 percent of the intermediate and standard size car markets, the largest attitudinal segment of buyers. They were interested in value, and the advertising that would get their attention would have to offer that value in straight-forward terms.

In the past, a touch of humor and emphasis on the fun if driving a Ford Motor Company product have been successful advertising approaches, but the practical thinkers that made up the potential Granada and Monarch market would not be so attracted. Three elements were selected as key points of emphasis: the availability of low-priced but well-equipped models, good gas mileage provided by the standard six-cylinder engine, and the value of the cars for their price.

Test print advertisements were prepared an presented to consumer panels. Subheadings broke up the copy and highlighted the practical appeals of the car-The Design. The Economics, The Comforts, The Construction -and photographs and diagrams appeared throughout. Results indicated that this was an effective format. Headlines making big promises, such as "Ford Present the Unexpected", fared poorly; the panelists wanted the facts. Car size comparisons in the copy proved particularly affective when the Mercedes was included.

Consumer samples in Los Angles, reviewing print advertisements that stressed price and fuel economy, described the material as blunt-but that was the kind of frankness they appreciated.

One of the studies included an examination of the car after the advertisement review, to ensure that the actual product would not be a had read the advertisement in the morning newspaper. The reactions were reassuring, as some of the respondent found the car even more impressive than indicated in the advertising.

Plans for the introduction of the new cars were next on the marketing agenda. While the customary aim of new car advertising is to zero-in on the potential Company management wanted to make an impact on all car buyers with the Granada Monarch message. Television commercials announcing the arrival of the new cars were prepared, and during introduction week, these commercials ran in each U.S.T.V household an average of three times.

A newspaper insert was developed to introduced the entire 1975 Ford line, but featured Granada on the cover and prominently inside. Over 70 million copies were distributed during the announcement week in Sunday, daily, and weekly newspapers. Monarch appeared in Sunday supplements such as Parade. Pronouncement advertisement appeared in the major national magazines.

In all, the average American family saw, read, or heard about Granada 16 times during the three weeks before and for weeks after the announcement.

In keeping with the direct, factual advertising approach for the car, the company dropped the customary "tease" aspect of car advertising prior to actual introduction; introduction Granada and Monarch advertisement dealt frankly with the car's features (except for photographs or art), and that included price.

Pricing information caused some headaches since suggested retail prices weren't determined until the last minute before the print advertisements went to press. But early advertising studies had shown that consumers appreciated such information, and making that favorable available.

Merchandising aids for Ford and Lincoln-mercury dealerships were prepared and distributed to the dealers for their introduction day activities. For greater exposure after introduction, Granadas and Monarchs were displayed at major shopping plazas throughout the country and at the major airport terminals. Direct mail advertisement were sent to owners of Ford, Lincoln, and mercury cars as well as owners of competitors' products. Participating Lincoln-Mercury dealers held a "Day of the Cat" sweepstakes, with a 1975 Monarch as grand prize, to promote the Lincoln-Mercury version of the new car with the popular "Sign of the Cat" theme. Ford and Lincoln-Mercury sales districts planned additional programs and displays for the remainder of the model year.

In addition, Granadas and Monarchs were test driven and given highly favorable reviews by the top car-buff-magazine writers. The first domestically produced luxury compacts in the United States were clearly in the public eye. And, as the first day sales results indicate, marketing and advertising efforts for the cars were "on target".

5

SYSTEMS APPROACH TO MARKETING

INTRODUCTION

In the increasingly competitive environment which has developed in recent years there can be little doubt that marketing intelligence has become a vital factor in the organization's ability to succeed. In the past, when change was less rapid then it is today, it was reasonable to assume that the best forecast of the immediate future was a direct extrapolation of past trends. In other words, change was seen largely as inevitable but as a continuous and predictable process. Accelerating technological change and the increase in international competition have resulted in turbulence and discontinuity and demand that we modify this assumption and recognize that to survive under these new conditions we must monitor and analyse our competitive environment continuously. To do so effectively marketing research must be seen as an ongoing process in which the organization's database is constantly reviewed and updated. No longer will is suffice to review sales data (which records what *has happened* rather than what *might happen*) with the occasional dipstick study to confirm out prejudices and expectations. In future the firm's survival will depend fundamentally upon its ability to read and anticipate environmental and competitive change and an essential element of this ability will be the creation and maintenance of an effective marketing information system or MIS.

Of course the existence of an effective MIS cannot guarantee success as this will depend upon the ability of the firm's management to use the available information in developing and implementing an effective marketing strategy. That said, marketing information systems must be seen as a *necessary* albeit not *sufficient* condition for competitive success. In this chapter we will examine the nature of MIS, the needs they serve and the benefits they offer. Next we look at the contribution of market research to the establishment and maintenance of an MIS and conclude with an analysis of the role of MIS in marketing decision making.

In the early 1960s the need for a programmed and systematic approach to marketing research led a number of practitioners and academicians to propose the concept of *marketing intelligence* as an alternative to the traditional view of marketing research. The distinction between research and intelligence was spelled out clearly in and article in *Business Management* which asserted:

> Marketing research usually focuses on a specific problem or project. A marketing research department might seek to discover why the competition has a larger share of the market in certain regions, or it might test consumer reaction to a certain proposed product. Whatever the activity, marketing research projects tend to have a definite beginning, middle and end.
>
> A marketing intelligence system, on the hand does not focus on specific problems. Rather it is a thermostat that monitors the market place continuously so the company can adjust its actions from day to day or month to month. A sound marketing intelligence system should prevent real problems from arising.

According to the *Business Management* article the first marketing intelligence system was established at the Mead Johnson division of Edward Dalton Co, in 1961. Its creator, Dr Robert J. Williams, made the same distinction between the one-off nature of marketing research and the continuous provision of the intelligence system (MIS) in a rather more colourful way when he said.

> The difference between marketing research and marketing intelligence is like the difference between a flash bulb and a candle. Let's say you are dancing in the dark. Every 90 seconds

> you're allowed to set off a flash bulb. You can use those brief intervals of intense light to chart a course, but remember everybody else is moving too. Hopefully, they'll accommodate themselves roughly to your predictions. You may get bumped and you may stumble every so often, but you can dance along.
>
> On the other hand you can light a candle. It doesn't yield as much light, but it's a steady light. You are continually aware of the movements of other bodies. You can adjust your own course to the courses of the others. The intelligence system is a kind of candle. It's no great flash on the immediate state of things, but it provides continuous light as situations shift and change.

The application of the systems approach to marketing management was elaborated on in a seminal article by Lee Adler which first appeared in the Harvard Business Review and has been reprinted many times since 1967.

> There seems to be agreement that the systems approach sprang to life as a semantically identifiable terms sometime during World War II. It was associated with the problem of how to bomb targets deep in Germany more effectively from British bases, with the Manhattan Project, and with studies of optimum search patterns for destroyers to use in locating U-boats during the Battle of the North Atlantic Subsequently, it was utilised in the defeat on the Berlin blockade. It had reached its present culmination in the success of great military systems such as Polaris and Minuteman.
>
> Not surprisingly, the parallels between military and marketing strategies being what they are the definition of the systems approach propounded by The Rand Corporation for the U.S. Air Force is perfectly apt for marketers:

> An inquiry to aid a decision maker choose a course of action by systematically investigating his proper objectives, comparing quantitatively where possible the costs, effectiveness, and risks associated with the alternative policies of strategies for achieving them, and formulating additional alternatives if those examined are found wanting.
>
> The systems approach is thus an orderly. 'Architectural' discipline for dealing with complex problems of choice under uncertainty.

It follows that an MIS is a system for dealing with such problems which occur within the domain of marketing. In promoting the development and adoption of a systems approach Adler perceived it as a substitute for the traditional approach to marketing research which he criticised for leading to:

> dreary chronicles of the past rather than focusing on the present and shedding light on the future. It is particularistic, tending to concentrate on the study of tiny fractions of a marketing problem rather than on the problem as a whole. It lends itself top assuaging the curiosity of the moment, to firefighting, to resolving internecine disputes. It is a slave to technique.

By contrast Adler believes that the systems approach will lead to the development of a system:

> tailored to the needs of each marketer. Such a system would serve as the ever-alert nerve center of the marketing operation. It would have these major characteristics:

Continuous surveillance of the market.

A team of research techniques used in tandem.

A network of data sources.

Integrated analysis of data from the various sources.

Effective utilisation of automatic data processing equipment to distill mountains of raw information speedily.

Strong concentration not just on reporting findings but also on practical, action oriented recommendations.

Alder's analysis and recommendations are as apposite today as they were over two decades ago for, apart from development in the application of computers to marketing, each of the characteristics he specifies is as relevant today as it was in 1967.

Definition The *Macmillan Dictionary of Marketing and Advertising* offers the following definitions.

Marketing Information Systems. The systematic organisation of all marketing data required by a business organisation to provide a reliable, illuminating and timely flow of information to marketing and general management.

Marketing Intelligence Systems. A basic component of the Marketing Information Systems, providing marketing executives with current information about developments and changing conditions in the macro and task environments (competitors, customers, suppliers, etc.). The efficiency of such systems can be augmented by improved training of sales people in their intelligence responsibilities, the development of a marketing intelligence centre, and the purchase of information when appropriate from specialised intelligence services.

Two further definition which have stood the test of time and which were proposed when the idea of the MIS first surfaced as a major topic are:

An interacting structure of people, equipment, methods, and controls which is designed to create an information flow that is capable of providing an acceptable base for management decisions in marketing.

> A set of procedures and methods for the regular planned collection, analysis, and presentation of information for use in marketing decision.

Smith *et al* appear to have combined these two definition when they propose the following in their book of readings on the subject:

> A structured interacting complex of persons, machines and procedures designed to generate an orderly flow of pertinent information, collected from both intra-and extra-firm sources, for use as the bases for decision-making in specified responsibility areas of marketing management.

Several common elements link these definitions. Perhaps the most important is that an MIS is a means to an end and not an end in itself. The marketing information system adds value only if it informs managerial decision making and is used as the basis for future action. Thus one must be careful not to assume that the existence of an MIS will lead to competitive success—only if it is integrated into the management of the organisation will this occur for otherwise, in the terminology of Ames, it is likely that it will remain a trapping' and add little or nothing to the 'substance' of the business. This distinction between trappings and substance is very important as has been shown by numerous investigations of critical success factors both before and since Ames' penetrating diagnosis. Briefly, Ames argues that in their efforts to improve performance managers will examine the activities of other successful firms and conclude that their success is attributable to functions or activities which are present in the other firms but absent from their own. Thus in the 1960s many industrial companies attributed the higher performance of consumer goods firms to the fact that they had a marketing function and so set up one in their own company but with no significant improvement in performance. To refute the latter's claims that 'marketing doesn't work' Ames pointed out that the mere creation of a system or function will have little or no effect unless it is supported by both attitudinal and behavioural change.

Much the same problem attended the establishment of strategic and corporate planning departments in the 1970s. Many managers who survived the recessions and shake outs of the late 1970s and early 1980s diagnosed their problems as arising from the setting up of formal planning departments with the result that they became divorced from the mistaken belief that a service department could discharge this activity for them. It is believed that much the same problem could accompany the setting up of formal marketing information systems in the 1990s as the evidence mounts that sound marketing information is a necessary condition for successful planning.

A second element common to the definition is the emphasis upon the systematic, planned and regular collection and analysis of data involving formal procedures and techniques. The latter procedures and techniques are very much the province of the professional marketing researcher and will be commented on in more detail below.

So much for the definition of the MIS—what needs does it serve? A recent survey by Honours Marketing Students at Strathclyde identified the following problems and pressures which have required the development of much more sophisticated data capture and analysis systems than hitherto.

increased competition, both direct and indirect,

accelerating technological change leading to shorter product life-cycles,

the information explosion and the dangers of information overload,

more regulation and legislation.

Against this background a properly designed MIS offers the opportunity to:

handle effectively the massive amounts of data on products, channels, sales, customers and competition,

integrate the wide variety of data encountered,

co-ordinate the complex relationships between forecasts, plans, schedules and actuals,

collect and deliver information tailored to the precise needs of different users and decision makers,

speed up decision making,

eliminate duplication and reduce confusion, complexity and uncertainty.

Thus the potential benefits to be derived from an effective MIS are considerable. Given access to the system one should be able to obtain timely and appropriate information directly relevant to the particular problem to be solved. Further, if properly designed, the MIS can give advance warning of changes or trends which call for reappraisal of the existing plan and can be used as a control device to compare actual against planned performance.

MARKETING RESEARCH AND THE MIS

The ability of an MIS to serve the needs and deliver the benefits outlined above will depend very much upon its design and the quality of the data captured and stored in it. In turn, this will depend on the principal subsystems and their effective integration. As a minimum one requires a principal subsystem for each element of the marketing mix so that the basic design would comprise the following:

1. Market research information system
2. Product planning information system
3. New product development information system
4. Pricing information system
5. Sales forecasting and planning information system

6. Distribution information system
7. Advertising and promotion information system
8. Service information system
9. Expenditure control information system.

As noted when discussing the differences between longitudinal and cross-sectional research the normative or textbook assumption is that marketing research is undertaken on a regular and continuous basis whereas the reality is that most marketing research is *ad hoc,* intermittent and designed to address a specific problem after it has occurred. In other words, most marketing research is reactive rather than proactive. By contrast the whole idea of an MIS is that it should contain all the data required for informed decision making on marketing issues and that this data should be subject to continuous review and updating. Given the rapidly changing environment referred to earlier it is unlikely that an MIS could accommodate every possible eventuality except at an inordinate and unnecessary expense. It follows that specific, focused *ad hoc* research will always be required to complement the MIS but that the creation and maintenance of the MIS itself must be the primary concern and responsibility of the marketing research function. However, in most organizations sufficiently large and sophisticated to have an MIS of the kind implied above the MIS will only be one element in a much larger and all embracing management information system likely to include corporate planning and research, operations research, financial planning and control, administrative and personnel systems, etc. Integration of the MIS within the larger management information system and the allocation of responsibility for areas of possible overlap are matters for corporate rather than marketing management. In assigning responsibilities the empirical evidence suggests that the marketing research function is likely to cover the following areas:

Determination of market characteristics

Measurement of market potentials

Market-share analysis

Sales analysis

Competitive-product studies

New-product acceptance and potential

Short-range forecasting

Studies of business trends

Audit and panel data

Special projects

Customer demand schedules

Questionnaire replies

Profitability

Life cycle analysis

Inventory analysis

It will be noticed from the above listing that research into advertising is not mentioned, the implication being that such research is undertaken by the advertising agents and media owners rather than by the advertisers themselves.

Organisational structure and the MIS

In order to enable organizations to deal effectively with the challenges of an increasingly dynamic and complex environment there has been substantial shift from the traditional hierarchical structure with a centralization of authority and control towards more flexible, organic and networked structures with considerable delegation of authority and responsibility. Given that in all complex systems, hierarchy, specialisation, and centralization are major sources of distortion and blockage of intelligence one would expect that the new flexible structure would improve greatly information flows within an organisation. Undoubtedly this is so with the possible exception of the complex multidivisional organisation comprising a number of discrete strategic business units.

Examination of such complex organizations (which are becoming increasingly commonplace through merger and acquisition) suggests that the potential synergy which may exist between different SBUs will be lost or dissipated unless there is an effective information system shared by them all. Further, within SBUs a number of studies have indicated that inadequate communication between top and middle management is a major factor leading to poor performance with the implication that an effective information system would help reduce this problem.

Most MIS represent one element within a larger integrated management information system. Without wishing to exaggerate the importance of the MIS over other elements, the increased emphasis upon the marketing orientation does imply that the MIS has a particularly important role to play in enhancing managerial effectiveness. Specifically it is believed that the MIS should be the source of the key data required to inform top management in determining the organizations' overall strategy. To the extent that since the major inputs into the MIS will have originated with line management this should ensure a smooth flow of information upwards through the organisation. Similarly the clear statement of purpose and objectives contained within a formal strategy will inform line management as to what activities are to be pursued, in what manner and to what end and thereby dictate what information is to be added to or deleted from the basic MIS. By the same token marketing research is regarded as a tool essential to the creation and maintenance of the MIS but sill only a part of a much larger and comprehensive intelligence system which derives information from a variety of other sources. This distinction is important for most textbooks and courses present marketing research as a set of techniques and procedures designed to solve specific problems. Such an approach is necessary to communicate the nature of these techniques and procedures but it would be unfortunate if this gave the impression that marketing research is a discrete activity when it should be a continuous and ongoing process as indicated in the above review of the marketing information system.

6

MIS AND MARKETING RESEARCH

A marketing information system is the major tool used by management to aid in problem solving and decision making. And marketing research is a major component in a marketing information system. The use of these tools should permeate every phase of a company's marketing program. For this reason we discuss information management early in this book. We shall be referring to this tool throughout the planning, operation, and evaluation of our organization's marketing program. So let's learn something about a marketing information system and marketing research.

Today many environmental forces, plus changing conditions within companies, make it imperative that every firm manage its marketing information as effectively as possible. Let's consider just a few of these forces-external and internal-and their relationship to information management.

1. There is a shortening of the time span allotted to an executive for decision making. Product life cycles frequently are shorter than they used to be and companies are being forced to shorten the time taken by their entire new-product-development process

2. Marketing activity is becoming more complex and broader in its scope. Companies are expanding their markets, even to the point of engaging in multinational marketing. Our insights into buyer behavior, while limited, are still sufficient to tell us there is a world of behavioral data we need to acquire and understand.

3. Shortages of energy and other raw materials mean that we must make more efficient use of our resources and manpower. A company needs to know which of its products and customers are profitable and which ones should be eliminated.

4. Growing consumer discontent is often intensified because management looks adequate information about some aspect of its marketing program. Maybe the firm does not realize its product is not up to consumer expectations, or its middlemen are not performing adequately.

5. The knowledge explosion (the information explosion) is just fantastic. We have more than an adequate supply of information. We simply need to figure out what to do with it-how to manage it. Fortunately, computers and other data processing equipment continue to improve, thus providing management with fast, inexpensive means of processing masses of marketing information.

At the same time, however, it is unfortunate that a sizable number of companies seem unaware of the importance of managing information in a more sophisticated fashion. Even today a significant number of firms have marketing research department. Another reasonably large segment of firms he only a small (sometimes one person) marketing research department which scope of activity typically is limited to sporadic surveys and other model data-gathering efforts.

In today's business setting, a company needs to add a new dimension to its information management, predicated on the systems approach to marketing. *A marketing information system (MkIS)* is an interacting, continuing, future oriented structure of people, equipment, and procedures designed to generate and process an information flow in order to aid managerial decision making in a company's marketing program.

A marketing information system is

1. The systems concept applied to information handling to

   a Determine what data you need

   b Generate (gather) this information

   c Process the data (with the aid of quantitative analytical techniques)

   d Provide for the storage and future retrieval of the data

2. Future-oriented. It anticipates and prevents problems, as well as solving them. It is preventive as well as curative medicine for marketing.

3. Operated on a continuing basis, not a sporadic, intermittent one.

4. Wasted if the information isn't used.

We are involved in a marketing intelligence operation. To some extent it resembles a military or diplomatic intelligence operation. We are gathering, processing, and storing potentially useful information which currently exists in fragmented, unorganized-but open and available-fashion is several locations both inside and outside the company. In an MkIS, however, we are to suggesting the use of any undercover intelligence methods such as industrial espionage or hiring competitors' personnel to learn their secrets. In most cases a company does not need to rely on such clandestine methods. Frequently they are valueless or even counterproductive. Moreover, the information which a company needs is usually available by socially acceptable means, if the firm will just establish a reasonably simple marketing information system.

A marketing information system is especially characterized by its involvement with the computer and with personnel possessing quantitative analytical capabilities. A modern MkIS would not be possible without a computer because of the masses of data to be handled. Essentially in an MkIS we are using the management scientist and his abilities to apply model building and other operations research techniques to the management of marketing information.

Unless management consciously establishes some communication system to process information gathered from within and outside the company, it is unlikely that the company issuing its marketing information effectively. Unfortunately, experience has shown that information flowing from these primary sources is frequently lost, distorted, or delayed. A marketing information system is of most obvious value in a large, multidivisional company where information is likely to get lost or distorted as it becomes widely dispersed. However, case experiences have shown that use of integrated information systems can also have beneficial effects on management's performance in small and medium-sized firms.

For most small companies, however, a formal, computer-based system probably will not provide sufficient benefits to offset the costs of establishing and operating it. But a small firm can effectively adopt an arrangement which embodies the concept of systematized information handling. Only the small company will probably use less complex techniques in the various stages of its MkIS. The optimal arrangement probably is a noncomputer system which includes (1) coordinated efforts at information gathering and processing by various departments in a firm, (2) the use of data processing equipment other than a computer-mechanized accounting and billing equipment, office copiers, tape recorders, etc., and (3) the periodic, but frequent, use of outside marketing research firms to provide informational aid in problem solving and decision making. In a landmark study, Cox and Good pointed out that an effective MkIS has three operating subsystems related to (1) the control of marketing operations, (2) the planning of marketing activities, and (3) the basic research on particular marketing problem areas. For each of these three subsystems. In sales forecasting, the information system is being used to improve the accuracy of the annual sales forecast. In the sales-force-management project, the goal is to develop better quotas for a new compensation plan for salesmen. We can see that the different projects each may emphasize some parts of the information cycle more than others.

Examples of benefits and uses of a marketing information system

Typical Applications	*Benefits*	*Examples*
Control system		
1. Control of marketing costs	1. More timely computerized reports	1. Undesirable cost trends are more quickly so that corrective action may be taken sooner
2. Diagnosis of poor sales performance	2. Flexible on-line retrieval of data	2. Executives can ask supplementary questions of the computer to help pinpoint reasons for a sales decline and reach an action decision more quickly
3. Management of fashion goods	3. Automatic spotting of problems and opportunities	3. Fast-moving fashion items are reported daily for quick reorder, and slow-moving. Items are also reported for fast price reductions
4. Flexible promotion strategy	4. Cheaper more detailed and more frequent reports	4.On-going evaluation of a promotional campaign permits reallocation of funds to areas behind target.
Planning system		
1. Forecasting	1. Automatic translation of terms and classifications	1. Survey-based forecasts of demand for complex industrial goods can be between departments automatically translated into parts requirements and production schedules
2. Promotional planning and corporate long-range planning	2. Systematic testing of alter native promotional plans and compatibility testing	2. Complex simulation models both developed and operated with the help of data bank information can be used of various divisional plans for promotional planning by product managers and for strategic planning by top management
3. Credit management	3. Programmed executive decision rules can operate on data bank information	3. Credit decisions are automatically made as each order is processed

4. Purchasing	4. Detailed sales reporting permits automation of management decisions	4. Computer automatically repurchases standard items on the basis of correlation of sales data with programmed decision rules
Basic research system		
1. Advertising strategy	1. Additional manipulation of data is possible when stored for computers it an unaggregated file	1. Sales analysis is possible by market segment breakdowns
2. Price strategy information	2. Improved storage and retrieval capability allows new types of data to be collected and used strategies	2. Systematic recording of information about past R&D contract bidding situations allows improved bidding
3. Evaluation of advertising	3. Well-designed data banks permit integration and comparison of different sets of data	3. Advertising expenditures are compared to shipments by country to provide information about advertising effectiveness
4. Continuous experiments	4. Comprehensive monitoring of input and performance variables yields information when changes are made	4. Changes in promotional strategy by type of customer are matched against sales results on a continuous basis

RELATIONSHIP OF MARKETING INFORMATION SYSTEMS AND MARKETING RESEARCH

It may be a bit risky to generalise on this relationship, because it is perceived quite differently by various people. Some folks see a an MkIS as simply a logical computer-based extension of marketing research. The first marketing information systems were developed in the 1960s, while marketing research as separately identified activity predates this by some 50 years. Others see the two as distinctly different activities, related only to the extent that they both deal with the management of information. Firms without an MkIS will perceive broader role for their marketing research group. If a company has a formal MkIS, then the marketing research activity is probably as just one part of the information system.

Contrasting characteristics of marketing research

1 Emphasis is on handling external information

2 Concerned with solving problems

3 Operates in a fragmented, intermittent fashion-on a project-to-project basis

4 Tends to focus on past information

5 Not computer-based

6 One source of information input into a marketing information system

Contrasting characteristics of marketing information system

1 Handles both internal and external data

2 Concerned with preventing as well as solving problems

3 Operates continuously-is a system

4 Tends to be future-oriented

5 A computer-based process

6 Includes other subsystems besides marketing research

The essence of what we mean by "marketing research" is contained in Richard Crisp's definition of the term. Crisp has called marketing research "the systematic, objective, and exhaustive search for and study of the facts relevant to any problem in the field of marketing." This definition suggests a systematic activity, thus sounding like the essence of an MkIS. Yet, as traditionally practiced, marketing research has tended to be unsystematic.

Marketing research tends to be conducted on a project-to-project basis, with each project having a starting point and an end. These projects often seem to deal with unrelated problems on an intermittent, almost "brush-fire" basis, as contrasted to the continuous information flow for decision making in a marketing information system. Marketing research tends to stress the collection of past data to solve problems. Information systems are future-oriented activities designed hopefully to prevent problems from arising. Marketing research is involved primarily with handling external data. Accounting departments and other nonmarketing areas in the firm typically gather and process internal marketing data, as when they analyze sales volume and marketing costs to evaluate performance in various sales territories or product lines.

In firms that have an MkIS, the separate marketing research activity can be extremely valuable. Marketing research projects are a significant source of data entering an MkIS.

Consequently, at this point we shall turn to the subject of marketing research and discuss its scope, the typical procedure in a marketing research investigation, the organizational structures typically used for marketing research, and the current status of the field.

For over 50 years there has been a steady growth in marketing research departments, thus reflecting management's recognition of the importance this activity. In a broad-based study sponsored by the American Marketing Association, about 60 percent of the companies reported having a formal (more than one person) marketing research department. About half of these form departments had been established just during the preceding decade. The most common activities were determination of market characteristics, measurement of market potentials, market-share analysis, and sales analysis. It is interesting to note the sizable number of firm now engaging in research on corporate responsibility.

In marketing research no two tasks are exactly alike, nor is there any single procedure that can be followed in all investigations.

Define the objective and the problem Researchers should have a reasonably clear idea of what they are trying to do in a research job. Usually this means defining a problem. However, the objective of a research job is not always to solve a problem. Often the purpose of a sales analysis is to determine whether the company has a problem and, if so, in what territory, product, or class of customer it lies. To illustrate, a manufacturer of commercial air-conditioning and refrigeration equipment had been enjoying a steady increase in sales volume over a period of years. Management decided to make a sales analysis. This research project of years. Management decided to make a sales analysis. This research project uncovered the fact that although the company's volume had been increasing, its share of the market had declined. In this instance, marketing research uncovered a problem which management did not know existed.

The case history of the Aurora Electronics Company (an actual company, but a fictitious name) may be used to illustrate the first three steps in a marketing research project-namely, problem definition, situation analysis, and informal investigation. The Aurora Company was a small electronics manufacturer, with the engineering department located in Chicago and the production plant and the president's office located in Chicago and the production plant and the president's office located in Phoenix, Arizona. Annual sales volume was $3 million, with 90 percent of this coming from contracts with the federal government. The other 10 percent came almost entirely from sales of the electronic component part used in automatic garage-door openers. This component was sold directly to a large door manufacturer. Joseph Stacy, the president was an engineer, and his company had an excellent reputation. The firm had no marketing department, no sales manager, and no sales force. It had a fine engineering department; the entire company was heavily engineering-oriented. At the time of the case, the firm was interested in diversifying its product line and its market so as to reduce its heavy dependence on government contracts. The engineering department developed an FM auto radio-a tuner and amplifier unit which could be connected to the regular AM auto radio and could use the AM speaker.

Most common activities are determination of market characteristics, measurement of market potentials, market-share analysis, and sales analysis. Note the large number participating in corporate responsibility research.

Research activity	Percentage doing
Advertising research	
Motivation research	33
Copy research	37
Media research	44
Studies of ad effectiveness	49
Business economics and corporate research	
Short-range forecasting (up to 1 year)	63
Long-range forecasting (over 1 year)	61
Studies of business trends	61
Pricing studies	56
Plant- and warehouse-location studies	47
Product-mix studies	51
Acquisition studies	53
Export and international studies	41
Company-employees studies	45
Corporate-responsibility research	
Consumers "Right to Know" studies	18
Ecological-impact studies	27
Studies of legal constraints on advertising and promotion	38
Social values and policies studies	25
Product research	
New-product acceptance and potential	63
Competitive-product studies	64
Testing of existing products	57
Packaging research: design or physical characteristics	44

Sales and market research	
Measurement of market potentials	68
Market-share analysis	67
Determination of market characteristics	68
Sales analysis	65
Establishment of sales quotas, territories	57
Distribution-channels studies	48
Test markets, store audits	38
Consumer panel operations	33
Sales compensation studies	45

The general problem, as presented to an outside marketing research firm, was to determine whether the company should add this product to its line. Breaking the problem down into parts which could be handled by research resulted in the following specific questions.

1 What is the market demand for such a product?

2 What product features are desired, such as push-button turning or signal-seeking turning?

3 What channels of distribution should be used for such a product?

4 What should its price be?

5 What changes or additions in the company's organizational structure would be required if the product were added?

With this tentative restatement of the problem, the researchers were ready for the next procedural step, the situation analysis.

Conduct situation analysis

The situation analysis involves getting acquainted with the company and its business environment by means of library research and extensive interviewing of company officials. The researchers try to get a "feel" for the situation surrounding the problem. They analyze the company, its market, its competition, and the industry in general.

In the situation analysis the researchers also try to define the problem more clearly and develop hypotheses for further testing. In research the establishment of hypotheses is a valuable step in problem solving. A hypothesis is a tentative supposition or a possible solution to a problem. It is something which is assumed or conceded merely for purposes of argument or action.

In the Aurora Company case, the situation analysis suggested the following hypotheses:

1 The company organization is inadequate to take on a consumer product

2 The market for FM radios is limited geographically to a radius of 25 miles from FM stations. (This distance is the approximate sending or receiving limit for FM broadcasting.)

3 Marketing channels should be the same as those used for AM auto radios. Distribution patterns for home radios are substantially different.

Conducting informal investigation

Having gotten a feel for the problem, the researchers are now ready to conduct an informal investigation. To some extent this step overlaps the preceding one, which involves getting background information from within the company or from a library. The informal investigation consists of talking to people outside the company-middlemen, competitors, advertising agencies, and customers.

In the Aurora case, the researchers talked with many people. FM station owners and managers were of considerable help. Wholesalers and retailers of automobile radios were consulted, as were repairmen for auto radios. Long interviews were held with automobile dealers handling German FM auto radios-the Blau Punkt and the Becker. Consumers who had purchased these imports were interviewed. Helpful information was derived from talks with sales representatives of the

Motorola Company. Advertising agencies were consulted regarding their possible future use of FM stations as an advertising medium. The idea was that an increase in the advertisers' use of FM stations would in time increase the quantity of FM programming, and thus make set ownership more attractive.

This important step in a research project will often determine whether further formal study is necessary. Decisions regarding the problem are frequently made after the informal investigation is completed. As a matter of fact at this point Aurora executives decided not to market the FM auto radio.

After the problem is defined and the informal investigation shows that the project is economically feasible, the company determines what facts are needed. The next step for the researcher is to plan how and where to get this desired data.

Select the Sources of Information An investigator may use primary date secondary data, or both (Primary data are original data gathered specifically to the project at hand. Secondary data are those already gathered, having been collected originally for some other purpose.) Thus when researchers stand in supermarket and observe whether people use shopping lists, they are collecting primary data. When they get information from the census of Population or library, they are using secondary sources.

At the same time, secondary sources of information must meet certain standards of accuracy in order to be of optimal usefulness. First, the information must be sufficiently current. If quotas for salesmen in Florida or Arizona in 1980 are set on the basis of data found in the 1972 Census of Business, the quotas with be understated because these are areas of rapid growth in market potential. The information should be classified in a manner useful to the researchers. They may want to make a study of college students, but then find that their desired secondary source classifies the data by age groups of 10-19 and 20-29.

To be useful, the data must be valid (relevant). For instance, sales of aid equipment in Texas is not a valid measure of the size of the Texas ski market, because many Texans who ski in Colorado or New Mexico will buy some equipment at the ski resort. Secondary information also must be reliable. That is, it must be based on a sampling procedure which is statistically sound. Finally, accuracy in the information implies that the original source generated the data in an impartial manner.

Sources of secondary data Several readily available, excellent sources of secondary information are at the disposal of a marketing researcher.

1. *Internal company records*. Companies regularly maintain orderly records of salesmen's daily reports, sales orders, and customers' complaints. Companies also usually keep sales records for each territory, product, and class of customer.

2. *Government*. The federal government furnishes more marketing data than any other single source in the nation. These data are available at very how prices, even though there is a tremendous cost involved in collecting them. Also, the government has access under the law to types of information (company sales and profits, personal income, etc.) which are impossible for a private company to get. The decennial Census of Population, for example, published by the Department of Commerce, contains economic, market, and sociological data in addition to a count of people. The Census of Business, usually taken every five years, provides detailed information about retailing and wholesaling institutions and service trades. The Census of Manufactures, also taken usually every five years, furnishes detailed information for each manufacturing industry.

The Department of Commerce publishes various summaries of statistics. The most inclusive is the annual Statistical Abstract of the United States. The monthly

Survey of Current Business furnishes data on a wide variety of topics. The Minerals Yearbook (Department of the interior) is a comprehensive annual report on mining activities.

The U.S. Department of Agriculture is a fine source of information on agricultural activity. The Department publishes many excellent reports on marketing methods, consumption patterns, prices, packaging, and the like. Agricultural Statistics, published annually, furnishes information on production, consumption, price, and trade of most agricultural products and minerals both in the United States and in many foreign countries.

The Department of Labor particularly its Bureau of Labour Statistics, is another good source. Its Monthly Labor Review carries data on wages, employment, and price indexes. The Monthly Catalog of United States Government Publications lists all federal government publications according to the agency or department which prepared them.

State and local governments provide a wide variety of sources of information. Data stemming from tax records, license applications, and other registration systems furnish much of the state and local information.

3. *Trade, professional, and business associations.*

4. *Private business firms.* Private marketing research firms, advertising agencies, and individual manufacturers or middlemen may be able to pro-information needed by a researcher. Companies such as the A. C. Niels Company (the largest marketing research firm in the world) conduct varies kinds of marketing research. Their findings are published and are available to persons who subscribe to the companies publications. The Niels Company, for example, prepares a food-drug index giving information on client's retail sales and his competitors' sales for particular products.

5. *Advertising media.* Many magazines, newspapers, radio and television stations, and outdoor

advertising companies publish information that marketing researchers may not find available elsewhere. Sales & Marketing Management annually publishes its "Survey of Buying Power." Which cover population, retail sales income, and effective buying power for all state counties metropolitan areas, and cities with populations over 10,000. Many media publish circulation data station coverage maps, and statistics on the trading areas.

6. *University research organizations*. Most large universities operate research bureaus and publish findings which are of value to the business communication.

7. *Foundations*. Nonprofit research foundations and related groups carry of many kinds of research projects. Statistical analyses and reports on special topics are published by such groups as The Conference Board and the American Management Association.

8. *Libraries*. Lest the student forget, a good library is probably the best single all-around source of secondary information. It will contain publications from practically all the sources mentioned here.

Sources of primary data after exhausting all reasonable secondary sources information, researchers may still lack sufficient data. Then they will turn primary sources and gather the facts themselves.

1. *Company sales force*. Frequently marketing analysts will interview sales people in order to get pertinent market information, or they will ask the sale force to interview middlemen, customers, or representatives from competitors. Sales people can often supply quite current and detailed information from their territories and at a low marginal cost. Management should not however, sue expensive sales personnel in research capacities if this divert them from their primary job of selling.

2.. *Middlemen, consumers, and others.* Manufacturers can seek information from their wholesalers and retailers. Wholesalers, in turn, can use their rate customers as primary sources. Middlemen may be asked their opinion of a given product or company program. Sometimes middlemen can give a manufacturer a good indication of the feelings of the ultimate consumer. However, sellers may have to go directly to the consumers to get information about their attitudes, motives, and buying habits.

Determine methods for gathering primary data: There are three widely used methods of generating primary data: survey, observation, and experimentation Normally, to all three are used on one project. The choice of method will be influenced by the availability of time, money, personnel, and facilities.

Survey method A survey consists of gathering data by interviewing a limited number of people (a sample) selected from a larger group. A survey has the advantage of getting to the original source of information. In fact, this may be the only way to find out the opinions or buying intentions of a group.

While the survey is still the most widely used method of collecting primary data, there may be a trend away from it. Not only have methods of observation and experimentation bee improved and their value more fully realized, but the survey method contains certain inherent limitations. There are opportunities for error in the construction of the survey questionnaire and in the interviewing process. Surveys may be very expensive, and they are time-consuming. Another key weakness is that respondents often cannot or will not give correct answers. This is particularly destructive when a marketing analyst is searching for reasons underlying a respondent's behavior. There also are indications that researchers' access to one especially rich data base-business corporations-is declining and will continue to do so unless ways can be found to alleviate growing friction between business people and researchers (particularly academicians). Business respondents object to the sheer number and complexity of questionnaires received, as well as to the misuse of information.

The interviewing or data gathering in a survey may be done by the researcher in person, by telephone, or by mail. These three types of interviews may be evaluated on the following bases: (1) flexibility, (2) amount of information to be obtained, (3) accuracy, and (4) speed, cost, and administration.

Personal interviews are more flexible than the other two types because the interviewers can alter the questions to fit the situation as they see it. They are able to probe more deeply if they are not satisfied with an answer. (Of course, there is a danger that a bias may be introduced into the survey if the original questions are altered.) Ordinarily, it is possible to obtain more information by personal interview than by telephone or mail. Also, the interviewer can be observation obtain data regarding the respondents' socioeconomic status their home, neighborhood, and apparent standard of living. Finally, a statistically sound sample is more easily obtainable with personal interviews.

The major limitations of this method of interviewing are its relatively high cost, the length of time needed to conduct the survey, and the opportunity to introduce errors in the interviewing process. When the personal interview method is used on a broad geographic basis, as in a national survey of magazine readership or shaving habits, the advantage of flexibility pretty much disappears. Interviewers in these situations ordinarily must follow an exactly prescribed procedure.

In a telephone survey the respondent is approached by telephone, and the interview is completed at that time. Telephone surveys can usually be conducted more rapidly and at less cost than either personal or mail surveys. Telephone surveys are less flexible than personal interviews but more flexible than mail surveys. Since a few interviewers can make any number of calls from a few central points, this method is quite easy to administer. Another significant advantage is that a telephone survey may be timely. For instance, people may be asked whether they are watching television at the moment and, if so, the name of the program and the sponsor.

One limitation of the telephone survey is that interviews must be show Lengthy interviews usually cannot be conducted satisfactorily over the phone is virtually impossible to get a complete cross section of the public because some people do not have telephones, others have unlisted numbers, many are not at home when the interviewer calls, and finally some refuse to respond this type of survey.

Interviewing by mail involves mailing a questionnaire to potential respondents and having them return the completed from by mail. Since no interviewer are involved, this type of survey is not hampered by interviewer bias and problems connected with the management of interviewers. Mailed questionnaires are more economical than personal interviews and are particularly useful in broad, national surveys. Also, if the respondents remain anonymous, they are more likely to give true answers because they do not feel the need to impress the interviewer. Finally, it is easier to reach some groups by mail than by either of the other two methods.

A major problem with mail questionnaires is the compilation of a good mailing list, especially in a broad-scale survey. If the sample can be drawn from a limited list, such as property taxpayers in certain counties or subscribers to a certain magazine, the list presents no problem. Another significant limitation concerns the sample reliability of the questionnaire returns, particularly when the returns are anonymous If the respondents have characteristics which differentiate them from the nonrespondents, this factor would negate the validity of the survey results. A mail survey may lack timeliness; respondents are often slow about returning the questionnaire. Furthermore, the questionnaire must bee reasonably short and the questions very simple, there is no way to elaborate or explain a puzzling question. There is also no opportunity to get additional data by observing the respondent. Often the representativeness of the sample is quite doubtful because the rate of returns on mail questionnaires is so low.

Observational method In this research method the data re collected by observing some action of the respondent. No interviews are involved, although an interview may be used as a kind of follow-up to get additional information. For example, customers may be observed buying beer in cans instead of bottles, and then they may be asked whey they preferred one form of packaging to another. This is a valuable research tool, but unfortunately it is often underrated in favor of the interview technique.

Information may be gathered by personal or mechanical observation. In one form of personal observation, the researcher poses as a customer in a store. This technique is useful in getting information about the caliber of the sales people or in determining what brands they push. In another situation, an observer may watch customers at a discreet distance and notice what motivates a purchase. One study was made to determine how people buy beer in a retail store. To some, price was important. ("What do you have on sale this week-end?" "What is a good low-priced beer?") Some had brand preferences. ("Give me six-pack of") Others needed help in selecting a brand. ("What brand do you recommend?") Mechanical observation is illustrated by the use of an electric cord stretched across a highway to count the number of cars that pass during a certain time period.

The observation method has several merits. It can be highly accurate. Often it removes all conjecture about what the consumer does in a given matter. If researchers over a period of several weeks trace the license numbers of cars parked in a suburban shopping center, they have a pretty good idea of the area from which this center is drawing customers. The consumers are unaware that they are being observed, so presumably they act in their usual fashion.

The observation technique reduces interviewer bias, but the possibility of bias is not completely eliminated as long as people are used as observers. However well trained an observer may be, bias may occur and mistakes are possible Another disadvantage is that the technique is limited in its application. Observation tells what happened, but it cannot tell why. It cannot delve into motives, attitudes, or opinions.

Experimental method This method of gathering primary data involves the establishment of a scale model or a controlled experiment which simulates the real market situation as much as possible. The theory is that the small-scale experiment will furnish valuable information in designing a large-scale marketing program.

The experimental method may be used in several different ways. In one instance, a firm may manufacture a few units of a product and give them to employees or consumers to try out. Probably the major application of the experimental method has been in market testing. This technique consists of establishing (1) a control market, in which all factors remain constant, and (2) one or more test markets, in which one factor is varied. A firm may be trying to determine whether to change the color of its package. In city A, the product is marketed in its traditional color. In each of cities B, C, and D, a different color is used. All other factors are presumably kept constant. Thus by measuring the sales in the four markets over a period of time, the manufacturer hopes to tell which color is best.

The outstanding merit of the experimental method is its realism. It is the only one of the three methods of gathering primary data which affords actual market tests and simulates an actual market situation. In testing the relative values of different advertisements. Only the experimental method will tell which advertisement sold the most merchandise. Furthermore, this method holds great promise for the future as marketing research people improve their techniques. For instance, the method lends itself nicely to the use of mathematical models as a device for quantitative measurement.

Two big problems are encountered in market testing: selecting the control and test markets, and controlling the variables. It is difficult-though necessary-to select markets that are identical in all significant socioeconomic factors. Experimental models, which have recently been developed, may be helpful in solving this problem. Some variables are really uncontrollable, and these may upset the comparability of results. Competitors may get wind of the test and try to confuse the picture by suddenly increasing their advertising, for example. Furthermore, the experimental method is expensive; it requires long, careful planning and administration. Tests frequently cover 6 months-2 months during which activity in the test and control centers is measured before anything new is introduced; 2 months during which the variable being tested (new color, new price, new advertising) is placed in the market; and 2 more months to allow for sales which may have been motivated by the test variable but were not made until sometime after it was removed.

Prepare Data-gathering forms Regardless of whether the interviewing observation method is used to gather primary data, the researcher must prep standard forms to record the information. The importance of the questions however, and the difficulty of designing it cannot be over emphasized. In most of the problems in data collection, whether by personal, mail, or telephone survey, center around the preparation of the questionnaire. Marketing research textbooks devote whole chapters to this subject.

Extreme care and skill are needed in designing questionnaires in order minimize bias, misunderstanding, respondent anger, misleading answers, et. Even is a carefully prepared questionnaire, mistakes are bound to occur. This one good reason for pretesting a questionnaire. Some of typical errors occurring in questionnaire design are as follows:

1 *The respondent feels the information is none of your business*: What is you family's income? How old are you? What percentage of your house loan remains to be paid?

2 *Questions lack a standard of reference*: Do you like a large kitchen? (What meant by "large"?) Do you attend church regularly?

3. *The respondent does not know the answer*: What is your spouse's favorite brand of ice cream?

4 *The respondent cannot remember and, therefore guesses*: How many can did you (as a sales rep) make on office supply houses during the past year one for late in the interview. By then some rapport ordinarily has been established with the respondent. A "none-of-your-business" question asked too early may destroy the entire interview.

Pretest the Questionnaire or Other Forms No matter how good a researches thinks the questionnaire is, it still should be pretested. This process is similar to field testing a product. Obviously, engineers think a new model of the automobile is perfect. Otherwise they would not have sent it away from the drawing board. But they know from experience that the only way to test the automobile is to use it. The method used in pretesting the questionnaire is simply to try it out on a small sample of people similar to those who will be interviewed. It is wise to let the research people do some interviewing. By observing the reaction of a few respondents, they may be able to catch number of unforeseen problems.

Plan the Sample Normally it is unnecessary to survey every person who could shed light on the research problem. Before the data can be gathered, therefore the researchers must determine from whom they are going to seek the information. They must plan or establish a sample. As is true of research in general, sampling is no stranger to use because we employ it frequently in our everyday activities. We often base our opinion of people on only one or two conversations with them. We often take a bite of food before ordering a larger quantity.

The fundamental idea of sampling is that "if a small number of items of parts (called a sample) are chosen at random from a larger number of items or a whole (called a universe, or population) the sample will tend to have the same characteristics, and to have them in approximately the same proportion, as the universe." In marketing research, sampling is another procedural step whose importance is difficult to overestimate. Sampling is a source of errors in many survey results. In one study, an opinion on student government was derived from interviewing a sample of fraternity and sorority members. With no dormitory students, off-campus residents, or commuting students included, this was obviously a biased, nonrepresentative sample of student opinion.

To be statistically reliable a sample must also be proportionate. That is, all types of units found in the universe must be represented in the sample. Also, these units must appear in the sample in approximately the same proportion as they are found in the universe. Assume that a manufacturer of power lawn mowers wants to know what percentage of families in a certain metropolitan area own this product. Further assume that in this market one-half of the families live in the central city and the other half in the suburbs. Relatively more families in the suburbs have power mowers than in the city. Now, if 80 percent of the sample is made up of suburban dwellers, the percentage of families owning power mowers will be overstated because the sample lacks proportionality.

Innumerable sampling techniques may be used in marketing research. Many of these are quite similar, and many are used only infrequently. We should be able to get a basic understanding of sampling by considering three types: (1) simple random sample, (2) area samples, and (3) quota sample. The first two are probability samples, and the third is a nonprobability sample. In *simple random sampling*, the sample is selected in such a way that every unit in the predetermined universe has a known and equal chance of being selected. Thus if we wished to use a random sample to determine department store preferences among people in denver. Colorado, we would need an accurate and complete listing of all people within the city limits. If we wanted to use a random sample to determine feed and seed preferences among farmers in the Great Plains states, we would first devise what states to include and then get an up-to-data listing of all farmers in those states.

A variation of a simple random sample which is widely used is an *area sample*. Where it is not economically feasible to obtain a full list of the universe, an area sample may be used. In the above example of a study covering department store preferences among Denver residents, one way to conduct an area sample would be to list all the blocks in the city and then select at random a sample of the blocks. Then every household or every other household in the sample blocks could be interviewed.

A *quota sample* is both a nonprobability sample and a stratified sample. Randomness is lost because proportionality is "forced." Every element in the universe does *not* have a known chance of being selected. To select a quota sample, the researcher must first decide which characteristics will serve as the basis of the quota and then determine in what proportion these characteristics occur in the universe. Thus in selecting a quota sample from among the people who went to Alaska for a vacation, the researcher may decide that the quota will be based upon the state of residence. In one study, it was found that 30 percent of the tourists to Alaska came from California, 10 percent from the state of Washington, and 15 percent from the East North Central census region (Illino, Indiana, Ohio, Michigan, Wisconsin) The sample was forced to the extent that was stratified on a nonprobability basis according to the home state of the tourist. Consequently, of the people included in the final sample, 30 percent were from California, 10 percent were from Washington, and so forth.

Probability sampling has one big advantage: It is the only method the enables the reliability of the results to be measured with mathematical exactness. The mathematical theory of probability may be employed to estimate the size of the sampling error. Furthermore, it does not require a considerable fund of detailed information regarding the universe on the hand, probability sampling can be very expensive and time-consuming, particularly when there wise geographic dispersion of the units in the sample. Adequate listings of units may not be available, and much skill in selecting the sample is required. In simple random sampling these limitations are accentuated.

In quota sampling much reliance is placed on the judgment of those designing and selecting the samples. There is no mathematical way of measuring the accuracy of the results.

Collect the Data The procedural stage during which the primary data are actually collected in the field—by interviewing, observation, or both—normally constitutes the weakest link in the entire research process. Ordinarily, in all other steps reasonably well-qualified people are working carefully to ensure the accuracy of the results. Then the fruits of these labors may be entirely lost if the fieldworkers (data gatherers) are inadequately trained and supervised. The management of fieldworkers is a difficult task because they usually are part-time workers with little job motivation. Also their work is dome where it cannot be observed, often at may widely separated locations.

A myriad of errors may creep into a research project at this point, and poor interviewers only increase this possibility. Bias may be introduced because people in the sample are not at home or refuse to answer. In some instances, fieldworkers are unable to establish rapport with respondents. Or, the interviewers revise the wording of a question and thus elicit untrue or inapplicable responses. Considerable error may be introduced by improper interpretation of answers. Finally, some interviewers just plain cheat in one way or another.

The final in a marketing research project are to analyze the data, interpret the findings, and submit a written report. Today the availability of sophisticated electronic data processing equipment enables a researcher to tabulate and analyze masses of data quickly and relatively inexpensively. The end product of the investigation is the researcher's conclusions and recommendations, supported by any necessary analyses, and submitted in written form.

For their own best interests, researchers should follow up their study to determine whether their recommendations are being followed, and if not, then what are the reasons. Too often the follow-up is omitted. Actually the analysts' future relations with the company can be influenced seriously by this step, whether they are in the firm's own marketing research department or working for an outside agency. Unless there is a follow-up, the company may not pay much real attention to the report. It may be field and forgotten.

ORGANISATIONAL STRUCTURE AND MARKETING RESEARCH

When a firm wishes to carry out a project, there are two ways it can get the job done: by the company's own personnel or by an outside organization.

The American Marketing Association study indicated a strong trend toward companies' having a separate marketing research department, with the manager reporting either to the chief marketing executive or directly to top management. When marketing research is done within the company, the researchers are well versed in company procedures and know what information is available. Also, the firm is more apt to use its research facilities can be expensive, however. Also, unless the company has adequate personnel, needed research projects may be unavoidably delayed.

An interesting mark of maturity in marketing research is the fact that it has already developed many institutions from which a company may seek help in marketing research problems. One group of organizations, which is regularly available for hire in research projects, includes advertising agencies and marketing research or management consulting firms such as the A. C. Nielsen Company of McKinsey and Company. A second group includes, for example, railroads and public utilities which engage in marketing research in order to promote the services they are selling. A third type of outside organization includes trade associations and university bureaus of business research which conduct marketing research on common problems faced by a group of companies.

These outsides employ highly qualified specialists in the marketing research field. Also, they have an objective, impartial approach. Finally, the agencies may bring to a given case the experiences of many other clients who has similar problems.

STATUS OF MARKETING RESEARCH

American business is just beginning to realize the full potential of marketing research. Many firms have long since passed beyond the nose-counting data-gathering stage—the stage where management was hindered by an insufficiency of information. Significant advances have been made in both quantitative and qualitative research methodology, to the point where researchers are making effective use of the behavioral sciences and mathematics. At the same time, however, far too many companies are still spending dollars on manufacturing research for their products, but only pennies, if anything, to determine the market opportunities for these products. In the American Marketing Association study mentioned earlier, about 40 percent of the firms did not have a formal marketing research department, and about one-quarter did not have been even one person formally assigned to the activity."

Several factors account for this less-that-universal acceptance of managing research. Unlike the results of a chemical experiment, the results marketing research cannot always be measured quantitatively. The research director cannot do a given job and then point to x percent increase in sales. Also, because management is not yet convinced of the value of marketing research, it will not always spend the amount of money necessary to do a good job. Good research costs money. Executives may not realize that they cannot always get half as good a job for half the amount of money.

Marketing research is far from perfect. We have noted several limitations marketing research and several areas where major opportunities for error can occur—in sampling, field interviewing, etc. Even when marketing research is accurate, it is not a substitute for judgment. Research gathers, analyzes, and interprets facts, but the executive himself must make the decision.

Marketing research cannot predict future market behavior accurately in many cases, yet often that is what is expected of it. In fact, when dealing with consumer behavior, the researcher is hard pressed to get the truth regarding *present attitudes* or motives much less those of next year.

Even in firms with a sophisticated research capability and a good track record, the predictions of the future can be expensively inaccurate. Witness, for example, the multimillion-dollar market failures of Ford's Edsel. Du Pont's Corfam (man-made substitute for leather), and RCA's venture into computers. In all three of these projects, the estimates of future market behavior proved to be inaccurate by the time the products were marketed.

Possibly a more fundamental reason for the modest status of marketing research has been the failure of researchers to communicated adequately with management. Admittedly, there are poor researchers and poor research. Moreover, sometimes the mentality of the quick-acting, pragmatic, decision making executive may be at odds with the cautious, complex, hedging-all-bets-mentality of a marketing researcher. However, the researchers, like many manufactures, are often product-oriented when they should be market oriented. Thus, they concentrate on research methods and techniques, rather than on showing management how these methods can aid in making better marketing decisions. Executives are willing to invest heavily in technical research because they are convinced there is a "payout" in this activity. Management has not been similarly convinced of a return on its investment in marketing research.

In management's relationship with marketing research today, another basic problem is the apparent reluctance of management (1) to treat marketing research as a continuing process and (2) to relate marketing research and decision making in a more systematic fashion. Too often marketing research seems to be viewed in a fragmented, one-project-at-a-time manner. It is used only when management realizes it has a marketing problem.

One reason why many executives have been unable to relate research and decision making more closely is their unfamiliarity with modern decision-making processes and the informational sources available from related business and nonbusiness fields. Some executives resist the use of research because they fear it is a threat to their personal status. That is, research implies an evaluation of their effectiveness, and it may also invalidate many beliefs fondly held.

7
MIS AND MODELS

We have stressed the nature of the decision-making process, the need for well-defined marketing objectives and strategy, coupled with an appropriate organization for planning and control. Because so much of the marketing executive's success is contingent upon an assessment of market conditions, we have paid special attention to problems of market measurement and the analysis of consumer behaviour. The synthesis of market measurement is expressed in a sales forecast—a central tool in market planning. In the process of emphasizing the importance and vagaries of analyzing conditions in the marketplace, it is possible to understate the need for careful cost analysis. The compilation and analysis of appropriately conceived cost data are also prerequisites to effective marketing management.

All of this has forcefully illustrated the importance management attaches to the collection and analysis of data in making marketing decisions. Our goal will be to suggest how the use of marketing information systems and models and the techniques of marketing research can improve the quality of marketing decisions.

Nature of information systems

Businessmen have always had at their disposal information that they have used more or less systematically in making decisions. In recent years, a more comprehensive and sophisticated approach to data collection and analysis has emerged, exemplified by the use of the word "system". A system implies the interaction and interdependence of elements viewed as a whole. Webster defines system as, "an organized or complex whole; an assemblage or combination of things or parts forming a complex or unitary whole." In our daily conversations, we use the term as we speak of a political system, planetary system, telephone system, missile system, data-processing system, and so on. A system view enables us to conceptualize interrelationships among complex phenomena. We are able, as a consequence, to visualize the whole as larger than its parts. A key to systems analysis is the word "interrelationship."

We can think of systems as made up of subsystems. The business system has a marketing systems component, and the latter has a distribution system subset. It is argued that to understand the function of subsets it is necessary to understand the function of the system as a whole.

When we speak of a marketing information system, we conceive of the selection, analysis, and flow of data compiled from internal and external sources for the purpose of making decisions. We acknowledge that the total system is made up of interrelated bits and pieces of information. To organize, plan, and control a marketing program, executives need a total view of their information requirements. How does one design a marketing information system?

Designing a marketing information system

Because much of the thrust for better management of information has paralleled the use of computers in industry, there has been a tendency to associate the design of information systems with computer expertise. But computer systems specialists have at time placed too much emphasis on the "hardware-software" dimension of information management. Indeed, one should acknowledge that a company can and should design a marketing information system even in the absence of a computer capability. Nevertheless, the emergence of information systems has been precipitated by computer technology. Fredric G. Withington of Arthur D. Little highlighted the relationship as follows:

> The study of information systems—is not the study of computers. It is the study of how the organization communicates and processes

information to maximize the effectiveness of management and further the objectives of the organization. In fact, however, most organizations never devoted great attention to their information systems until they began to consider the use of computers. The flexibility and power of the new tool, as well as its great cost, have caused many managers to think for the first time of formally planning their information flows and processing functions.

Data specification and decision analysis. Information should be compiled for the sole purpose of making decisions. Accordingly, the first step in designing a marketing information system is to examine the kinds of decisions that marketing executives have to make. This exercise should reveal partial answers to questions such as:

Who makes a decision?

How frequently is the decision made?

How serious are the consequences of a bad decision?

How does one decision impinge on other decisions?

What criteria have been used in making a decision?

How accurate and timely must the data be to make this decision?

Answers to these questions should lead to an explicit description of the organization's information needs and decision-making process. It should be self-evident that there is no such thing as a "generalized" marketing information system. Each marketing department will have unique problems, a unique management style, and a unique organization structure. Data for decision making will vary according to company size, centralization, product category, and market coverage. The best the one can do is to acknowledge a number of universal variables that will influence the design of all marketing information systems. How these variables are interpreted and how the information system is ultimately designed is entirely unique to each company.

Significant variables. Some, but not all, of the variables that must be considered in designing a marketing information system are suggested in the following paragraphs.

When and how frequently will particular types of data be required? It costs money to provide information. One has to balance the costs of current and frequently compiled data against the benefits of improved accuracy. And neither costs nor benefits are ever precisely measurable. While the marketing executive may assign costs to the compilation of a quarterly sales forecast, as against a semiannual forecast, he will never know the opportunity cost represented by lost sales effort or poorly planned scheduling that reflects the latter choice.

The timing question is often answered by the firm's unique planning, control, and decision processes. The *annual* sales forecast, the *monthly* sales territory quota, and the *weekly* inventory report are illustrative. Seasonal and cyclical sales patterns, longer planning horizons, or, the opposite, quick response functions may be significant.

How accurate must be information be? As with timing, this variable is influenced by costs. We can almost always increase the accuracy of data if we are willing to spend the money. Be accuracy gas other than information-gathering costs. Data gathering often takes time, and lengthy delays can be the true cost of improved accuracy. In the final analysis, the accuracy question has to be answered in terms of the consequences on inaccuracy. Substantial capital outlays for new plant and equipment and/or advertising campaigns for a consumer packaged good will demand more accurate information. By way of contrast, the fashion-oriented dress manufacturer may add a new style to an established line with little risk. The cost of gathering information necessary to predict the success of a single style is prohibitive, and losses incurred from a single style failure are not that great.

How refined must the data be? Frequency and

accuracy are, of course, measures of data refinement. But most information must be aggregated in some form according to the planning, control, or decision process. Aggregation may be by products, by customer class, by geographical area, or by organizational unit.

Answering the aggregation question calls for an analysis of the disparity of data. For example, does an apparent accurate corporate sales forecast hide significant offsetting forecasting errors within product categories or market areas? Aggregation is also a function of organizational structure and control. The sales force hierarchy is illustrative where data by customer order is the basic unit and becomes aggregated by territory, district, region, and nationally. Again, offsetting sales data may cloud the problem of performance appraisal, as any sales manager will tell you.

Modifying a current information system. Because most companies have on-going information systems, the relevant question of designing a marketing information system is usually, "How do we modify and improve the current system?" The distinction between modification and starting from scratch is important, for it recognizes that innovation will have to be built around information prejudices and tradition. Decision makers are creatures of habit and altering the information form, flow, and source may represent an inconvenience, a threat to status, and a jeopardizing of the executive's decision-making role and skill. This being the case, it is imperative to obtain top management support. Cox and Good in a study of marketing information systems concluded, "One characteristic of the more successful companies is striking. In every case, at least some members of top management have seen the promise of the technique and have viewed its development as a top management responsibility."

Developing a marketing information system thus calls for top management support, which in turn should lead to adequate backing by the various line and staff people who must participate in the design process. As we have implied earlier, this means decision makers at all levels. It also means integrating quite disparate groups within the organization. Designing a marketing information system will require inputs from accounting, finance, production, research and development, personnel, and data processing, as well as from marketing. Not the least of management's problems will be coping with the magnitude of the task. This leads to two important generalizations related to the design problem.

First, it is more than likely that the company will have to work with a "grand plan" but place major emphasis on information subsets. Not only does this approach make the task more manageable, but the benefits from changing information flows, formats, and sources will be more readily apparent. Secondly, new computer-based information systems should be run alongside of older systems for a suitable period of time, often as long as a year. This is necessary to insure debugging of the new system *and* achieving management acceptance.

Basic components of a marketing information system

Although we may not specify the particular characteristics of marketing information system in terms of type of data, accuracy, timing, or data aggregation, we can identify certain basic components of all computer-based systems. They include a data bank, a statistical bank, a model bank, and an input/output capability. Montgomery and Urban have suggested the interrelationship of these components and their function as a link between the manager and his environment. Figure 1 is their conceptualization of the structural design of a marketing information system. We shall use it to illustrate the interrelationship of the data bank, the model bank, the statistical bank, and the input-output components.

Data bank: The data bank is conceived as a storehouse. Prior to the arrival of computer-based data storage on discs, tapes, or cards, the company stored its data in files and reports. Anyone seeking relevant data had to dig out the appropriate memo, survey, customer call report, or what have you. The computer-based data bank assumes this storage function. Data are entered into the bank according to management's conception of the kind of information needed to make decisions.

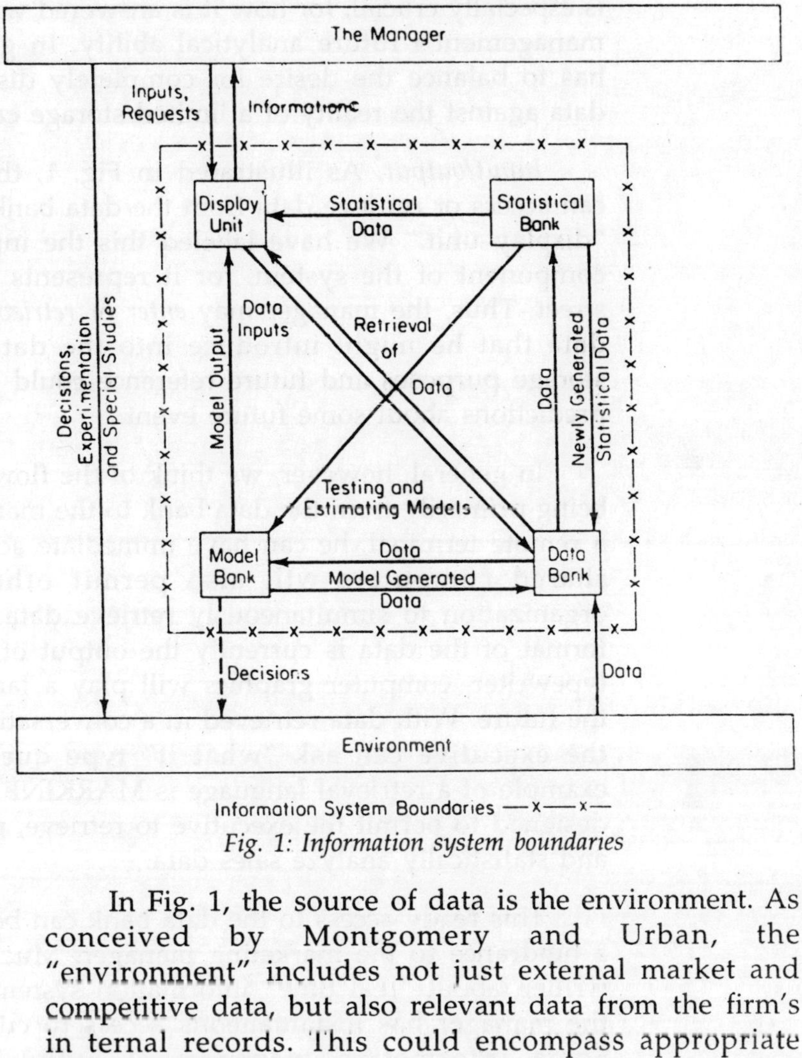

Fig. 1: Information system boundaries

In Fig. 1, the source of data is the environment. As conceived by Montgomery and Urban, the "environment" includes not just external market and competitive data, but also relevant data from the firm's in ternal records. This could encompass appropriate financial and cost data as well as traditional marketing data, such as salesmen's call activity.

Management has to make two decisions, since computers have a limited storage capacity. First, it has to specify the kind of data that will be relevant for future decisions and consequently accessible in the data bank. This exercise should screen out some classes of data and commensurately reduce the storage problem. Second, a decision has to be made on the extent to which data shall be held in aggregated form, which will also have an effect on the storage required. The aggregation question is especially crucial, for how it is answered will influence management's future analytical ability. In general, one has to balance the desire for completely disaggregated data against the reality of a limited storage capacity.

Input/output. As illustrated in Fig. 1, the manager can access or retrieve data from the data bank through a "display unit." We have labeled this the input/output component of the system, for it represents a two-way street. Thus, the manager may *enter* or *retrieve* data. The data that he might introduce into the data bank for storage purposes and future reference could be his own predictions about some future event.

In general, however, we think of the flow of data as being primarily from the data bank to the manager. With a remote terminal, he can have immediate access. Time-shared computers will also permit others in the organization to simultaneously retrieve data. While the format of the data is currently the output of a terminal typewriter, computer graphics will play a larger role in the future. With data retrieved in a conversational mode, the executive can ask "what if" type questions. An example of a retrieval language is MARKINF which was designed to permit the executive to retrieve, manipulate, and statistically analyze sales data.

This ready access to the data bank can be a boon or a hindrance to the marketing manager. Much has been written about "real time" information systems whereby the manager has instantaneous access to current data. Some information management authorities have contended that for most planning and control functions a real-time system is impractical.

A real-time system with a conversational mode would enable a manger to specify only the information he wants, in a format that he designates (i.e. tabular or graphical), aggregated as he would prefer—all instantaneously. Those that argue against such a system feel that this puts an unnecessary burden on the executive to specify his data requirements and that he does not need such current data. It is also reasoned that with top executives having access to performance data at lower levels there will be adverse effects on organizational relationships. Moreover, the high cost of real-time data storage is an important consideration. The merit of real-time information systems cannot be explored further here. Our major emphasis should be on the role of the display unit or input/output component as a critical part of the marketing information structure. We have noted its role as the interface between the manager and the data bank component, but it is equally important in relation to the other two components—the statistical bank and the model bank.

Statistical bank. Using the disaggregated or aggregated data in the data bank, the executive will want to perform a number of statistical routines in the process of data analysis. These routines may be as simple as determining averages or proportions. Standard computer programs would be available in the statistical bank for this purpose. For example, by using sales data by territory from the data bank, he could determine the average order size, call frequency, and the number of accounts opened by territory, by region, and for the company as a whole. The statistical data bank would perform this computational chore for the executive on command and would provide him with appropriate measures of variance. The statistical routine could be one whereby he merely receives data on those units that are, for example, + or -5 per cent of the norm for the period under consideration.

Other statistical routines could permit bivariate cross-classification analyses, goodness of fit measures (chi-square tests), rank ordering, and so on. For sales forecasting purposes, time series analysis and exponential smoothing routines could be accessed.

These examples suggest some of the simple uses of the statistical bank. Other more sophisticated statistical routines would include computer programs for multivariate analysis such as regression analysis, discriminant analysis, factor analysis, such as regression analysis, discriminant analysis, factor analysis, and cluster analysis.

We should note again, by referring to Fig. 1, that data processed through the statistical bank can be directly accessed by the manager via the display unit. At the same time, however, it may be prudent to place some of these newly generated data in the data bank for future reference.

Model bank. The fourth component of the information system is the model bank. In a general sense, a *model* is anything that represents something else. We think of airplane models, fashion models, and model homes. In each instance, we have something other than reality in mind. The typical marketing executive carries around in his head several implicit "models" of his world. He has a model that indicates the response function as he considers a price cut, an advertising budget or a product improvement. He also has a model of what should be the proper allocation of a salesman's day or a media budget. In an organizational sense, he had a model of how the marketing efforts of his firm as a manufacturer should complement those of his marketing channels. At the core of his thinking is a model of consumer behavior.

The basic purpose of a model is to conceptualize relationships. Using a model as an aid to decision making calls for making explicit the variables that are incorporated in that decision. Models force management to focus on assumptions and data. As painful as it may be, a by-product of modeling is the beneficial exercise of moving from some implicit model (assumptions and data) to an explicit model.

As an element of a marketing information system, the model bank permits the executive to examine relationships and response functions in a complex environment. Some of the models developed for company use may be relatively simple and have wide application. An example would be an inventory control model. Other models will be complex, and it may be feasible to utilize only subsets of the total model.

One of the critical problems in developing a model bank is the role that the executive shall play in model design. To the extent feasible, the notion of a user-designed system is highly desirable. By interacting with the model builder in the design of the model, the user will acquire confidence in its capabilities. Marketing executives should not be model builders, but model users. To be intelligent users, they must have a rudimentary knowledge of modeling techniques. Initially, this may call for the development of simple descriptive models whereby the executive can see how his assumptions affect outcomes.

Again, as was true with the statistical bank, data generated from a model bank would be accessed by the executive through the display unit. Some data output from a model, however, could be stored in the data bank for future reference. Because models of the market environment are so central to the analysis of many marketing problems, we shall devote the remainder of this chapter to a review of the major categories of models with special emphasis on selected applications.

Before turning to an examination of marketing models, we should emphasize that the preceding comments on marketing information systems represent a broad review. The design, control, and evaluation of such systems is one of marketing management's biggest challenges. And at times, this truism is ignored as management becomes engulfed in day-to-day operating problems. A better information system could have either eliminated those problems or expedited their solution.

Major categories of model

Management scientists have had a semantic field day as they have sought to classify models. Without too much difficulty, one can find models categorized as implicit, explicit, descriptive, normative, stochastic, deterministic, heuristic logical flow verbal, mathematical, static, dynamic, and predictive. We shall try to clarify this nomenclature without contributing to it. *Explicit models* as distinct from *implicit models*, are those that have been represented in some communicable form. We can communicate an explicit model through *verbal, logical flow*, or *mathematical* means. Montgomery and Urban have suggested this distinction as illustrated in Fig. 2. The verbal model indicates the behavioral patterns assumed in a pricing decision, i.e., "If I change may price my competitor will match my price unless it would cause him to lose money." Another verbal model might have assumed that the competitor would not change his price. The logical flow model seeks to diagram the verbal model. It makes explicit a sequential relationship between the model's components. The next step is to quantify the model's components and their relationship. This mathematical model indicates not only sequential relationships, but the magnitude of interrelationships.

Mathematical models can be described in terms of time and risk *Static* models do not consider time effects, in contrast to

dynamic models. Models that consider risk, and are stated in probabilistic terms, are *stochastic*. *Deterministic* models assume certainty of events and outcomes. Mathematical models have the virtue of making assumptions and relationships more open to debate, testing, and revision. And it is largely through quantification that we can make progress in the measurement of market phenomena.

A further distinction among models is based on their function. Here we have *descriptive*, *predictive*, and *normative* models.

In a *descriptive* model, we seek to provide a detailed and accurate representation of a system. A system here could be consumer or competitive behavior. Models of consumer behaviour, for example, seek to show purchase rates, brand loyalty, and brand-switching patterns by significant demographic characteristics. They provide the analyst a framework that is useful in specifying the variables to be measured when gathering new data and testing hypotheses.

Predictive models are useful in that they not only describe, but forecast the system's future behavior. Predictive models can be used to test the sensitivity of output to varying inputs and model parameters. Thus, predictive models can be used to answer "what if" type questions. These conditional predictions are useful in exploring the consequences of alternative combinations of the marketing mix or the impact of alternative forms of competitive retaliation.

LOGICAL FLOW MODEL:

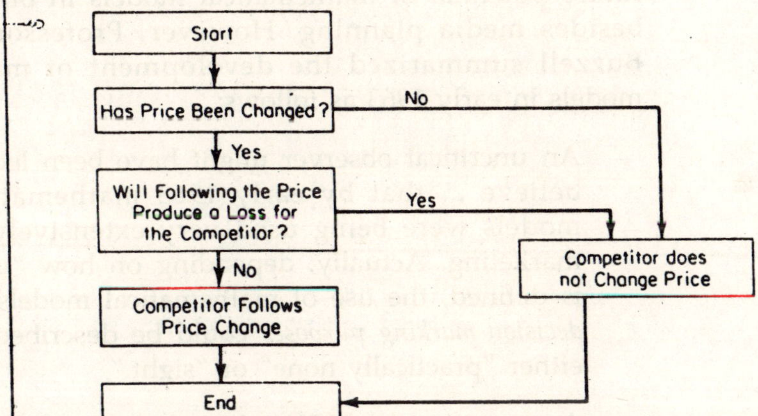

MATHEMATICAL MODEL:

$$\bar{P}_c = (1 - I)P_c + IP_m$$

$$I = \begin{cases} 0, \text{ if } P_mQ_c - C_c < 0 \\ 1, \text{ if } P_mQ_c - C_c \geq 0 \end{cases}$$

$\bar{P}_c$ = competitor's new price
P_c = competitor's old price
P_m = price of firm ("my" firm)
Q_c = quantity of sales competitor could sell at P_m
C_c = competitor's total cost of producing and selling Q_c

Fig. 2: Logical flow and mathematical model

A *normative* model attempts to specify how the system will operate to achieve a given objective. Here the model is designed to select the best alternative course of action based on some previously determined criteria that are also included in the model.

Applications of models in marketing

In the early 1960's, there was considerable publicity given to the potential merit of marketing models. In 1961, the advertising agency Batten, Barton, Durstine, and Osborne, Inc., announced the development of a model for determining the "optimal media schedule." There followed a great debate in the trade press over the merit of media models. Other advertising agencies and a number of management consulting firms proclaimed the future potential of mathematical models in other areas besides media planning. However, Professor Robert Buzzell summarized the development of marketing models in early 1963 as follows:

> An uncritical observer might have been led to believe ... that by early 1963 mathematical models were being used very extensively in marketing. Actually, depending on how "use" is defined, the use of mathematical models *for decision-marking purposes* could be described as either "practically none" or "sight."

As we enter the 1970's, there is not much evidence that mathematical models have gained wide acceptance in industry. Direct access to computer facilities through remote terminals rather than batch processing, simplified computer languages, and the development of time sharing have all contributed to the adoption of modeling and other management science techniques. Certainly, the efforts of educational institutions in the 1960's, and especially the graduate business schools, have been directed toward the preparation of future executives for jobs where an integral part of the decision environment is mathematical models and computer facilities. But the adoption process is often a slow one, and this is especially true where one is seeking to change long-standing decision making processes. Martin Ernst of Arthur D. Little at a conference at Dartmouth College in 1963 described the evolution of mathematical techniques for decision making in marketing as going through three stages: a "shouting" stage, in which many claims are made but little acceptance is achieved; a period of growth, during which claims are moderated and some solid contributions are made; and a final stage of assimilation where the techniques are no longer new but are routine parts of the executive's decision-making process. He suggested that it would take a generation before the latter stage arrived. This would be the late 1980's, depending on how you define "generation." The basis of this forecast was the assumption that the business school graduates of the early 1960's would by then be in responsible executive positions, and management would be conditioned to think in terms of mathematical models. As we noted in Chapter 6, all forecasts are subject to some degree of error, and perhaps Martin Ernst's forecast did not take into account the development and adoption of time-sharing and remote access teletypes. Nevertheless, the adoption of marketing models in the early 1970's, is still very much in the early stages of "growth". Only the largest of corporations have personnel on their staffs that are qualified to design and implement the use of these techniques. Top management is still being "sold" in their utility. But progress is being made as William Clark and Donald Sexton have noted:

> Although the marketer may be unwilling to go on record as giving the computer credit for being of help, he has now been getting such help for a long enough time to know he wants more. He has begun to trust the output from some models the way he trusts *some* accounting information. He also knows that if the computer has done nothing else for him, it has given him generous helpings of time for the crucial part of his work. By sparing him tedium and by doing some of the interpretation of his data, it has let him consider more alternatives and still make decisions promptly. With each small success has come an increment of courage to try something a little more advanced.

This review of the evolution of marketing models and the current state of the art has been included in this section on applications to provide perspective. We can now turn to a brief summary of specific marketing model applications. More detailed treatment will be presented in subsequent chapters where models will be illustrated in the context of specific marketing policies and decisions, e.g., product policy, advertising policy, and so on.

To review the extent to which specific marketing models have been used as parts of a marketing executive's decision-making process requires some assumptions about what is a "model" and what is "use." Much of the contribution of computers has been to expedite data processing. Thus, sales forecasting and the processing of marketing research data have been made easier. But this activity will not fall under the umbrella of "modeling" unless the data are being used to test hypotheses about the merit of alternative solutions. By the same token, computer programs are being widely used to prepare income statement, but unless the analyst uses these programs to test alternative marketing strategies, sales, and profit forecasts, it is debatable whether this can be called modeling.

Another area that is more data processing than modeling is the handling of manufacturing schedules, inventory levels, and transportation systems. Again, computer programs have been widely used for this set of data-processing activities. The opportunity to use optimization techniques, such as mathematical programming, has been recognized in this class of problems, and to this extent models have had widespread application among larger firms.

When we move to problem areas that are more behaviorally based, we find that the application of marketing models is less widespread. And it is in this area that the marketing executive would most appreciate help. Here we have models designed to aid in making advertising, product mix, and marketing mix decisions. Although the detailed application of the models used fro these types of problems must be left to later chapters, we can usefully review their general characteristics.

Advertising models designed to cope with budget size and media allocation problems have commanded much attention. For many firms in the consumer packaged goods field, the sums involved in these decisions are substantial, and there has been a justification for the costly development of models. Solution of the media mix problem has been especially tantalizing, for there is presumably a wealth of data on circulation, readership, audience size, and audience composition. Unfortunately, early applications of linear programming (as in the case of the BBD & O model cited earlier) were disappointing. This form of mathematical programming seeks to maximize some "objective function," e.g., the reach or total audience size. It permits setting certain "constraints" (inclusion of a particular magazine, size of ad budget, minimum exposure rates to different groups of buyers) and assumes that these constraints and the objective function are straight-line relationships. The input data for linear programming media models could be a combination of objective and subjective values. Page rates in print media would be objective inputs (if discount structures could be ignored), while the relative value of a page in *Life* magazine versus a thirty-second TV commercial could be a subjective value based on executive judgment. The assumption of linearity, lack of good objective audience size data, and reliance on subjective judgments for many constraints caused this technique to fall from favor in media modeling.

As a substitute for an optimal solution, analysts turned to simulation where the model permits non-linearities and changes over time. For example potential customers may be viewed as reacting differently to second and third exposures to an ad, and their receptivity may be changed after purchase of the product. In general, simulation techniques have shown some promise in media analysis problems.

Advertising budget models have had a more checkered record even than advertising media models. To simplify the analysis, most of these models have assumed that advertising is the sole independent variable and have measured responses to varying levels of effort in terms of consumer predisposition to buy, sales, or profits. Often, they have depicted static rather than dynamic situations and have ignored competitive responses. Some attempts have bee made to use regression analysis. Thus, Palda analyzed the effects of advertising on Lydia Pinkham drugs sales over a fifty-three-year period incorporating in his independent variables a measure for advertising copy and personal income as well as advertising expenditures. This analysis of advertising effects using historical sales/advertising patterns may not have resolved the eternal question: Were sales a result of advertising or was advertising a result of sales? In attacking the advertising budget problem, experiments have been used where advertising expenditures were varied over time. In addition, analyses have been made using different geographical areas that have been exposed to varying advertising expenditures. Each of these techniques chips away at the problem, but as yet there is no simple solution to the determination of the advertising budget question. The great virtue of models will be to force more explicit and rigorous descriptions of the behavioral process in response to advertising expenditures.

New-product models have commanded much attention because of the substantial risks associated with new-product introductions. These models have also used subjective and objective input data. They have often been applied in the consumer packaged goods field where the input would be early results from test markets. When simulation has been used with new-product models, the executive has had the opportunity to incorporate judgmental information on how the market will react to various factors such as promotion or price. One example is the risk analysis model. New-product introductions usually call for some financial criterion such as expected return on investment or profit over some pay-back period. If the criterion is return on investment, the risk analysis model may incorporate forecasts of a number of variables as follows:

$$\text{ROI} = \frac{(D \cdot S)p - (C + X_1 + X_2 + \ldots X_5)}{F + W}$$

where D = Total market demand for the product

S = Market share for the firm

P = Selling price

C = Cost of goods sold

X_1 = Advertising expense

X_2 = Sales promotional expense

X_3 = Other marketing expense

X_4 = R and D expense

X_5 = Administrative expense

F = Fixed investment

W = Working capital

This model does not take into account the time value of money, an additional factor that could be included. Obviously, each of the elements in this model is subject to some forecasting error. Forecasts of market share are not likely to be as accurate as forecasts of advertising expense. To cope with this, the analyst can combine these forecasts, not as precise numbers, but as frequency distributions. The end product will then be a frequency distribution that suggests the likelihood that the return on investment will be above X per cent, between X-Y per cent, or below Y per cent. These models are helpful in sensitivity analysis, i.e., finding which subsidiary forecasts have to be improved in order to increase the return on investment. The model permits the analyst to look at the effects of price increases on market share or the substitution of advertising expenditures for sales promotion expenditures.

Marketing-mix models follow the same general pattern of new-product models. The goals of the marketing process are the same, but the inputs are likely to differ. For the on-going product or company, the input data may be more reliably estimated. By way of contrast, if the new product is one that is very responsive to marketing stimuli, the use of modeling may be easier.

Only the largest of firms have ventured into the costly development of comprehensive marketing-mix models. Obviously, as the number of variables to be considered is increased, the task becomes more complicated. Often, data are not readily available, for the firm's records may not break out cost, revenue, and profit information in appropriate product subsets. Joint costs and delayed effects of marketing efforts present especially knotty problems.

Simulation and marketing models

We noted that simulation had often been turned to as a technique in the process of modeling marketing problems. Because of its potential promise, we shall develop the concept of simulation and illustrate its application in greater detail.

When the analyst turns to solving a problem using simulation, he explores the implications of alternatives, but he does not find a best alternative, as he would in an algorithmic procedure. Thus, mathematical programming provides an optimal solution. The analyst would prefer, of course, to find *the* solution through formal mathematical analysis.

Unfortunately, most marketing problems present such complexities that they remain intractable to ordinary mathematical solution. Under these circumstances, the use of simulation presents an attractive alternative.

A great benefit of simulation is the opportunity to ask "what if" type questions. For example, management might turn to simulation prior to an actual market test for a new product. Through simulation, the assumptions that have been made in designing a marketing program could be tested and modified. Not only is simulation less expensive and risky than real world experimentation, but it also permits testing many more alternatives than would be the case in an actual market test. It also yields answers in a relatively short period of time, and given the short operating time horizon for many marketing decisions, this is a significant plus factor. Under time pressures, the alternative to simulation may be a "gut feel" of the situation, not an experiment. Simulating a market environment and the marketing mix also avoids the problem of revealing to competitors the strategy that is being considered, as must be done in a market test.

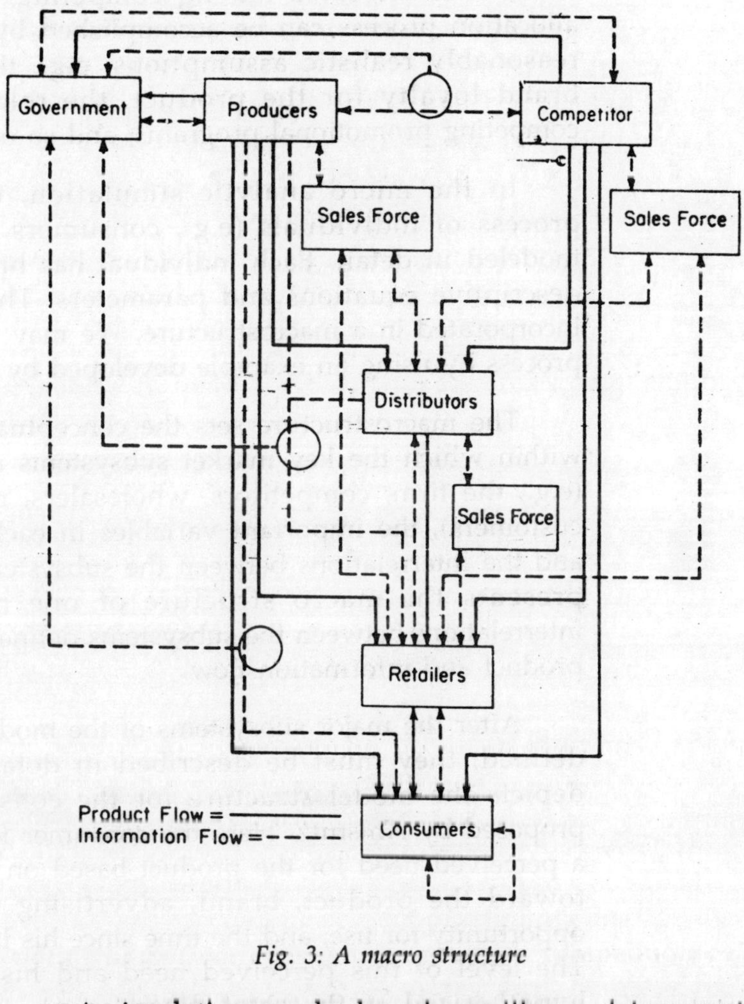

Fig. 3: A macro structure

A simulation can be based on either a deterministic or a probabilistic (stochastic) model. Probabilistic simulations have used Monte-Carlo procedures as a tool for analysis. This technique involves specifying as probability distribution over the set of possible alternatives and then sampling from this distribution.

In the use of models and simulation techniques, two different approaches have been used. They are macro and micro analytic stimulations. In the macro approach, the behavior of individual consumers is not explicitly modeled. For example, a total market demand for a time period may be assumed. Once this is done, the total demand is allocated among competing brands. This allocation process can be accomplished by using some reasonably realistic assumptions, e.g., the degree of brand loyalty for the product, the relative size of competing promotional programs, and so on.

In the micro analytic simulation, the decision process of individuals (e.g., consumers, retailers) is modeled in detail. Each individual has his own set of descriptive equations and parameters. These are then incorporated in a macrostructure. We may illustrate this process by using an example developed by Amstutz.

The macrostructure sets the conceptual framework within which the key market subsystems are specified, (e.g., the firm, competitors, wholesalers, retailers, and customers), the important variables in each subsystem, and the interrelations between the subsystems. Figure. 3 presents the macro structure of one model, with interrelations between the subsystems defined in terms of product and information flow.

After the major subsystems of the model have been defined, they must be described in detail. Figure. 4 depicts the model structure for the consumer sector proposed by Amstutz. Here the consumer first develops a perceived need for the product based on his attitudes toward the product, brand, advertising appeals, his opportunity for use, and the time since his last purchase. The level of this perceived need and his income are hypothesized as the chief determinants to shop. The selection of a particular retailer will reflect the consumer's attitudes toward alternative retail outlets. The decision to purchase will depend upon the availability of the product in the retail outlet, the price of the product, the sales push at retail, and the consumer's attitude toward the brands available. If the purchase takes place, the model allows the generation of word of mouth communication to other consumers.

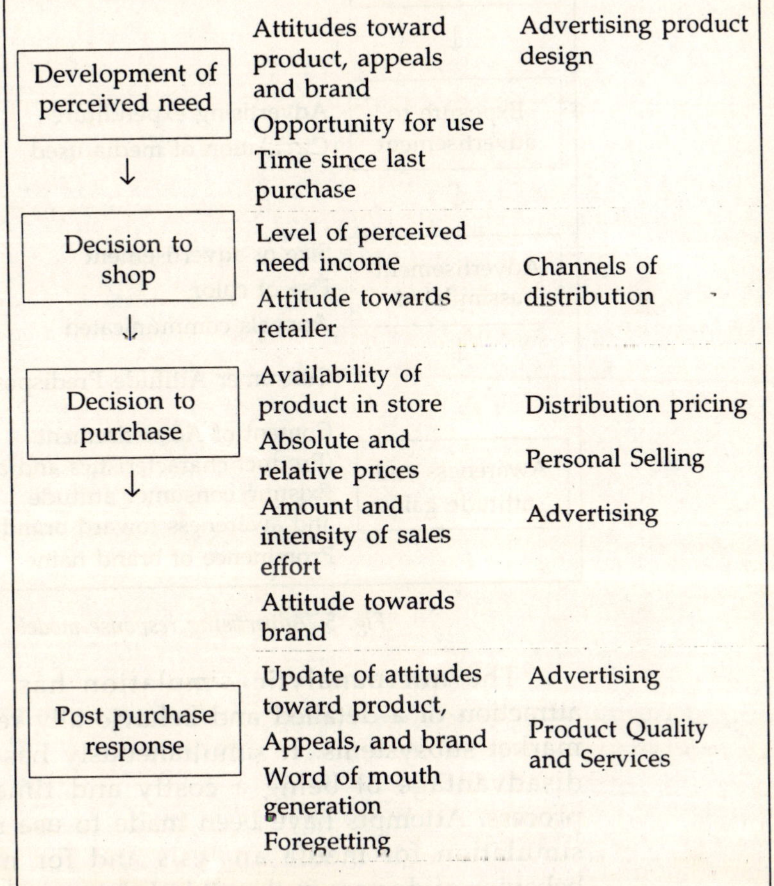

Fig. 4: Structure of microunit consumer response

In the development of the microunit model, each of the actions must be modeled in detail. For example, Amstutz's description of the effects of advertising on the consumer is presented in Fig. 5. All aspects of the consumer's decision process must be described in a similar fashion and expressed in mathematical equations. Similar structures and subrelationships have to be developed for the retailer, wholesaler, manufacturer, and other systems in the macrostructure.

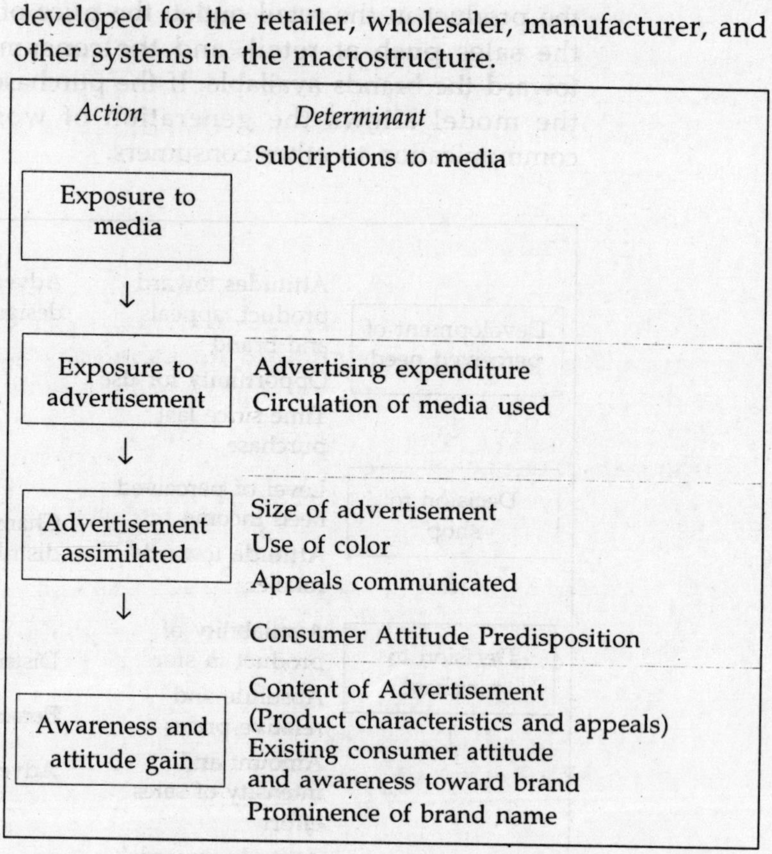

Fig. 5: Advertising response model

The microanalytic simulation has the obvious attraction of a detailed and behaviorally realistic of the market subsystems. It simultaneously has the obvious disadvantage of being a costly and time-consuming process. Attempts have been made to use microanalytic simulation for media analysis and for modeling the behavior of doctors in the ethical drug market. The latter model used a simulated population of a thousand doctors in which the doctor's professional life, prescription history, and his exposure to information through professional journals, direct mail, detail men, and professional interaction with other doctors were all incorporated. The output of the model for each doctor was an estimate of how he would prescribe drugs in a simulated period and an estimate of his attitude toward various drug brands. These outputs permitted aggregate conditional sales forecasts based upon the marketing actions of a firm and its competitors.

As one can imagine from this example, the use of microanalytic simulation techniques has had limited application for a total marketing system. However, there have been significant contributions to subsets that have been analyzed in this manner.

8
INFORMATION TECHNOLOGY AND MARKETING RESEARCH

The paradox of information technology is that whilst the phrase is upon everyone's lips there is surprisingly little of it to be found in practice save in a relatively uncomplicated and unsophisticated form. Thus whilst there are frequent references to the concept of the paperless office 'one per desk' (a reference to the fact that every manager and office worker would have a personal computer or terminal on their desk) electronic mail and the like all the evidence points to an explosion in the volume of paper-based information in circulation.

APPLICATIONS OF INFORMATION TECHNOLOGY

Consideration of these trends would seem to suggest that information technology will have a very similar impact but as an innovation it is still at a very early stage in its life cycle. In the great majority of instances the application of computing to business decision making has been confined to an extension of earlier data processing applications. Lucey suggests that:

> computers can be used to best advantage for processing information which has the following characteristics: a) a number of interacting variables b) speed is an important factor, c) there are reasonably accurate values, d) accuracy of output is important, e) operations are repetitive, f) large amounts of data exists.

These conditions or characteristics describe well the accounting and other records kept by commercial organizations. It is to these applications which the power of the computer has been harnessed, a development which is unsurprising on the grounds that 'innovations pursue the line of least resistance'. In other words innovations will be adopted most quickly where they can be substituted most effectively for an existing method or solution to a consumption need. It seems likely, therefore, that having established the benefits which computing can bring to business management the extension of computing and telecommunications from basic database and data handling applications into decision support systems (DSS) will soon follow.

Lucey states that:

> there is abundant evidence from numerous surveys both in the UK and USA that existing MIS, often used in advanced computer equipment, have had relatively little success in providing management with the information it needs. The typical reasons discovered for this include the following:
>
> — lack of management involvement with design of the MIS.
>
> — narrow and/or inappropriate emphasis of the computer system.
>
> — undue concentration on low level data processing applications particularly in the accounting area.
>
> — lack of management knowledge of computers.
>
> — poor appreciation by information specialists of management's true information requirements and of organisational problems.
>
> — lack of top management support.

Support for these findings is to be found in a recent case study describing the development of home office banking systems (HOBS) by the Bank of Scotland. Writing in the Summer 1989 edition of the *Journal of Marketing Management*, Lannon and Scarborough discovered that the application of IT in the bank was being impeded for most of the reasons cited by Lucey.

Perhaps the major problem of all was that management was seeking to use IT in a tactical way and was ignoring its strategic potential. Given that the Bank of Scotland has very few outlets in England and Wales and its wish to move into this market required either that it replicated the branch network of the other major competitors or that it provided an alternative means of access to the banking services which it had to offer. HOBS offered this potential. It is interesting that Lannon and Scarborough report senior management in the Bank of Scotland as stating that this was an area where no marketing research could provide any sensible input to the strategic decision. But, once top management had perceived the opportunity IT offered it adopted it as a main plank in its competitive strategy.

Indeed it is probably true to say that the organizations with the greatest experience of the application and management of information technology are the world's major financial institutions. Consideration of their experience underlines that while return on their investment has been disappointing there is equally wide agreement that *not* to have investment would have resulted in a loss of competitive edge and a decline in market position. Much the same is likely to be true of the adoption of IT in marketing and market research—while such investment may lead to only a transient comparative advantage failure to invest could lead to a permanent loss of market share.

While banks may have come late to marketing they have responded with enthusiasm. Further, because of their experience with large scale data processing with account management they are familiar with the potential of information technology and have the resources to extend it to the marketing realm—particularly in the growing battle for 'retail' financial services. In doing so they face two major problems. The first has already been referred to in out comment on Lannon and Scarborough's case study, namely, the organisational and attitudinal barriers to extending IT from a control function to an input to decision making. The second is that early entrants to the field of information technology often face significant problems and expense in updating their software. As Alan Kane observed in a *Financial Times* survey.

> the banks, trusts and building societies have a common software problem. They have an abundance of elderly software, most of it creaking at the joints and out of tune with today's competitive requirements.
>
> Their files, for example, are mainly arranged by account rather than customer. Such an arrangement makes it extremely difficult to readily extract information about customers for the purposes, for example, of special product initiatives or cross selling.

As with other realms of marketing the main challenge is the development of an integrated database. In 1987, for example, Lloyds Band announced an initial commitment to invest £570 million to upgrade all the bank's branch technology and build a new integrated voice and data network. Among the main benefits expected from the project are speedy and integrated access to any customer file, improved marketing information, sales prompts, assistance with lending control and the ability to provide self service banking and interfaces with Lloyd's other systems. According to the *Financial Times*:

> Using a computer to assemble and analyse information such as customer age groups, income levels, occupations, savings, home ownership and so on, provides a valuable marketing tool. Successful targeting of different age and income groups for such services as pension schemes, mortgages, life assurance policies and sayings plans depends on first identifying the relevant groups and having on file sufficient information to target accurately.

Clearly the same is true of marketing any other good or service and emphasises the importance of creating or gaining access to suitable databases.

From the above discussion it is clear that information technology is an enabling innovation in that it allows some tasks to be done more easily, more quickly, more efficiently and, possibly, more effectively. In his contribution to *The Marketing Handbook* Alan Melkman proposes four broad areas of IT application as shown in Table.1. These may be described as follows:

Table 1: An IT applications framework

		Marketing activities	
		Existing	new
Focus of activity	Internal	1 Enhancing	2 Changed methods
	External	3 Enhancing customer	4 Market
innovation			

service

1. *Enhancing operating efficiency* '...those marketing activities which are already carried out in one form or another within the company. Typically, these include maintenance of customer records, budgeting, preparing and making presentations and analysing sales statistics, scheduling meetings and so on'.

2. *Changed methods* '...enabling the Marketing Department to carry out internal functions which were not possible before'. This will usually start with an extension of applications in the first quadrant such as using databases for segmentation and positioning studies, more sophisticated forecasting and modelling, better and faster communication with a field sales force, etc.

3. *Enhancing customer service*. This will be made possible by better and faster communication with customers the application of CATI to obtain timely and relevant data on changing market needs, etc.

4. *Marketing innovation*. The use of video cassettes to make sales presentations and demonstrate product use, access to and use of large on-line databases

such as DataScan, Information Line and Dialog, direct mail services, market identification studies such as Pinpoint, Acorn and Market Location. EPOS (Electronic Point of Sale) has already had a significant impact on retail store management and is likely to develop into EFTPOS (Electronic funds Transfer at Point of Sale).

Melkman's four areas of IT application illustrate the likely sequence which organisations will follow in exploiting the potential benefits of information technology. A constant and recurring them of this book is that increased competition has resulted in much greater awareness of the value of timely and relevant data. In parallel with other changes these have helped to accelerate the take up of IT. Amongst these changes may be numbered:

(a) The availability of much less expensive hardware.

(b) The availability of much more sophisticated software.

(c) Greater user friendliness in both.

(d) Growing familiarity with visible applications and all the output of IT based systems, e.g. detailed retail receipts generated by EPOS systems, access to and use of automatic telling machines (ATM), extensive use of word processing, etc.

(e) The availability of more skilled and trained manpower.

(f) The establishment of specialist service and software houses.

A description of the services offered by one of the leading companies in the field—Pulse Train Marketing Systems Ltd—will help illustrate the scope and contribution which IT can make to the marketing function.

The research machine

Pulse Train Technology Ltd (PTT) is an international company specialising in services and software for survey research and telephonic business applications. It is a leading supplier of data collection and tabulation systems to specialist computer bureaux and survey research organizations in 14 countries and is the creator of a new generation of integrated hardware and software which they have designated the research machine.

The thinking behind The Research Machine is that early applications of IT tended to remove control from the decision maker with the result that research tended to become a stereotyped activity with canned solutions looking for the appropriate problem to solve. With The Research Machine the user has instant and personal control over all aspects of the research process. Using the system it is possible to undertake research from the users own desk. The software allows the user to design their own research instrument—the questionnaire—check out with the user or client via electronic mail or on-line access to high quality printer, select a sample and commence interviewing for a pilot study within minutes of getting the approval of the questionnaire.

While The Research Machine is itself an integrated entity it is also capable of further integration to standard packages such as the SAS and SPSS statistical and graphics packages and can also provide largely automatic interfaces with the user's own software. The system also has the major benefit that while it is compatible with industry standard modern conventions it is also compatible with older standards as well. Further, if the user is currently using multipunch card formats and data in their existing installation they can still use The Research Machine software immediately and convert the more convenient character reference formats at their leisure.

The designers claim that the real corner stone of the system is a new special computer language which they have developed called the Questionnaire Specification Language or QSL. QSL is a language which was designed from the ground up to be used for research applications. Its objective is to enable the user to write and design research questions and is designed to be easy to learn and use. It is a simple free format language and does not need special control forms. You can write out the QSL notation on any convenient piece of paper or type it directly into the computer via a VDU. The questions generated may be used for both printed questionnaires or for presentation on computer assisted telephone interviewing VDU screens.

- Using The Research Machine it is claimed that once you have written your QSL specification then you can do all of the following things:

- Start conducting a CATI survey. You can send the completed specification from your own terminal to the interviewing room and then watch selected interviews taking place from your own terminal!

- Produce a publication quality printed questionnaire, with multicolumn formats, grids, of any description whatsoever, attitude scales, etc. You can forget about boring details like question numbers, column and code assignments, pagination and layout, etc. The Research Machine will do all of these things for you, automatically.

- Produce a file of interviewer's lists and prompting materials, which are cross referenced to the printed questionnaire and lettered or numbered automatically.

- Book in your returned questionnaires as they come in from the field (or post), carrying out QSL specified quota controls automatically.

- Start key-entry and coding. No key entry specifications have to be written by a supervisor. You do not need to specify a list of edit checks. They are all built into the QSL specification, and control the entry and coding processes automatically.

- Produce (when the data are collected) an elegant top-line report. This is the printed questionnaire with the columns and codes removed, and counts and percentages in their place.

- Produce a questionnaire database, which is added to a permanent data base of all surveys you have ever carried out. The Research Machine has a special high-speed searching-module that enables you to see and review any or all questions on any topic that you have ever researched. You do not have to prepare an index. It is all automatic.

- Make additions to the question library (which you may have used in the first place), allowing your QSL specifications to be used again in future without any retyping.

- Go straight into tabulations (when the data are available) using the on-line menu driven system. You do not need to learn another language for this. Just call up the system, and select what you want from the menu. You do not have to enter labels and text as they are taken from your QSL specification. The menus themselves are tailored to your personal requirements for analysis, and can be changed or added to at any time by your own data-processing staff.

- Use packages such as SAS or SPSS if you have them installed, and produce factor analyses, regression analyses, cluster analyses, or many other kinds of statistical analyses. Your data file will automatically be compatible with those industry standard packages and the Research Machine will have written the major part of your SAS or SPSS set up specification for you!

- Carry out simple analyses of your major research findings and use the extensive on-line graphics facilities in SAS and/or SPSS to produce presentation quality professional graphics. You can preview the results on your own VT240 or VT241 colour graphics terminal, and if you are happy with the results, produce hard copy on a plotter, or go directly to 35 mm slides and overhead projector films.

- Produce special analyses, written for you by your own data-processing department, in the widely used COBOL language. All that you have to do to use such a facility on a repeated basis is adopt conventions for naming your key questions. You can change your questionnaire as much as your want, but the COBOL program should not have to be changed. The Research Machine actually writes out the data-division COBOL source code, which is merely tacked on the procedure division (the report part). The two parts are recompiled, linked and run to give you your own special reports on the new data.

QSL was designed after careful analyses of the known and likely future requirements of users. This research indicated that it would not be possible to design a menu driven system for questionnaire design that had sufficient flexibility. Research questionnaires are simply too diverse and it was also apparent, that the single language offered major benefits in accuracy and efficiency throughout the entire research process from conception, design and execution through to analysis and interpretation. The designers also started from the premise that the researcher was not a computer expert but that they were likely, to be brighter than average and motivated to do their job as well as they could. Thus, to accommodate all the technical problems involved in question construction and questionnaire design discussed. QSL provides access to an on-line library of previously written QSL constructions access to which ensures that the questionnaire conforms with the technical requirements.

It is claimed that the basic QSL language can be learned in one day and this clearly creates enormous opportunities for the organisation to undertake its own in-house research. This facility is greatly enhanced by other modules in the software package. Of particular significance is the database and search them at very high speed. A further facility is that upon payment of a modest fee to the Market Research Society the user can have access to a magnetic tape of the market research abstracts compiled by the MRS which go back to 1965 and are the only series of abstracts published anywhere in the world which cover all fields of marketing and advertising research as well as relevant papers in statistics, psychology and sociology. Nearly 400 papers and articles are abstracted each year from some 40 different English language journals. The abstracts include as regular section headings: survey techniques; statistics models and forecasting; attitude and behavior research; personality and social psychology; communications; advertising and media research; specific applications of research; industrial market research; market research and general applications; and new product development.

A third major module of The Research Machine is concerned with data entry and coding. As a technical aspect of marketing research this has not been discussed in any detail in this text which is intended largely for the user. However, the beauty of The Research Machine module is that it gives the ordinary user access to all of the essential expertise which is so important in ensuring that all data is coded and entered correctly into the database for subsequent analysis.

The Research Machine in designed for use on the VAX family of computers. These are available at quite a modest cost. As a major computer manufacturer DEC provides extensive support and maintenance systems as well as providing access to the networking facility called Decnet which provides a worldwide information technology capability.

9

DECISIONS, SYSTEMS AND INFORMATION

Marketing activities account for an immense of expenditure in the economy. According to the United States Department of Agriculture, for example, the total farm value of food products produced in the Untied States in 1971 was estimated at $36 billion. Marketing added $75 billion to this amount-thus the consumer spent $111 billion. The value added (Calculated from the cost) of marketing was three times the farm cost of he food. In 1972, one consumer spent about $728 million in marketing activities out of total expenditures of about $2.7 billion.

It is evident that extremely large amounts of money depend on marketing manager's making correct decisions. These decisions in turn depend on the decision makers being able to make intelligent appraisals of their alternatives and the consequences of their information about customers, competitors, and one's own activities. Obtaining this information and aiding decision makes in forming intelligent appraisals is the role of marketing research.

A typical case in point is the brewing industry in the United States. A number of examples of the need for good information are provided by this industry. In 1935 there were about 750 breweries most of which were small. Brew brands met only limited success in other than local markets-and success appeared to be more due to luck and intuition complemented by haphazard trail and error, than to knowledge. In the local markets, the beer drinkers had grown accustomed to "their" brewmaster's brew and he to their beer preferences.

However, this marketing pattern proceeded to changes as several breweries grew more sensitive to the market and particularly to outlying market opportunities. These breweries pushed into more distant markets with different brews and marketing programs. They used more market information to plan their products and their marketing efforts. And they increasingly used information to gain more control over their operations. These firms began tracing sales (and even some distribution costs) by types and size of container and by market (for competitors activities as well as for their own) they began testing advertising campaigns and other promotional activities through evaluations of costs and benefits and in general they relied more on marketing information.

During this time, many of the breweries that were oriented around brew masters sold out and closed as more informed firms won away their markets. In fact, by 1963 there were fewer than 225 breweries left and by 1973 the number had dwindled to less than 0 with the largest four companies getting 51% of the output and the largest 10 accounting for 73%. And this activity has all occurred since repeal of the Eighteenth Amendment to the constitution in 1933.

The Hamm experience

This marketing shakedown is still in process. The intelligent use of marketing information alone, obviously will not guarantee success. However, it is one of the prime requisites that frequently has been neglected and has consequently led to marketing failures. For example, the Theo B. Hamms Brewing Company, formerly an independent, Minnesota-headquartered brewer successfully penetrated large sections of the Pacific Coast market in the 1950's with a nostalgic reminder to transplanted Midwesterners of the "beer from the land of sky blue water". In the 1960's this "tested and proven" campaign and market-penetration program was moved almost in total into New England, It was a colossal failure. The people, accustomed to Cape Cod Bay and Nantucket Sound, formed the Minnesota appeal meaningless, if not insulting to their preferences.

The Hamms successor, huge Huiblein, who has successfully marketed distilled liquors, wines, and fried chicken, lost countless dollars and sold out. Success and failure are not merely a function of size.

There are numerous other specific cases in point. However, only two more will be offered.

Carling Brewing Company purchased one of the Criesedieck Breweries of St. Louis and apparently tried to eliminate the very popular (in the Midwest) Stag brand beer and put in its place the favorite carling brand, Black Label. Untold dollars apparently were lost before key managers gathered and used marketing information. After consumer attitude information was obtained and used, the stag brand was successfully reintroduced. The same mistake by the same company was apparently Tacoma in the Pacific Northwest. Carling bought Heidelberg brand with Black Label. The marketplace was ignored until the profit and loss statements demanded greater market sensitivity. Heidelberg beer was reintroduced into the product line and soon outdistanced the Black Label brand. A new chapter of this small Carling episode was Company in Phoenix, Arizona, and immediately expanded the marketing program for the existing brand, A-1. However, by 1972, Carling had slipped to ninth position in the United States and was one of only two of the 10 top breweries to lose sales in 1972.

One of the clearer testimonies to the importance of marketing information is provided by the sales battle between Anheuser-Bush and the Joseph Schlitz Brewing Company. Since the late 1940's the two giants have both continued to expand their market shares and to battle for first place. Anheuser-year and then Schlitz took the lead until a devastating strike in 1953 caused them to lose the lead to Anheuser-Busch had developed a strong marketing team founded on a superb research and marketing information program (for that day and age)

In the meantime, as stated by one writer:

The old Schlitz was an efficient beermaker but a

> *backward beermarketer.....virtually no use was made of marketing research.*

This picture started to change in the early 1960's when a new president was credited with building a "new scientific, capable management was on marketing founded on relevant marketing information. Their Vice-President of Marketing said:

> *We research and, out of research, develop specific things, develop the best programs we can, carry them, out and then do an evaluation. Our objective is to find out what makes the beer drinker tick and how to get to him—on his terms, rather than the brewer's.*

Objectives of the Schiltz research group according to its manager.

> *......are mainly to supply information to management to enable them to make better decisions. The computer is our number 1 tool.....because the mass of data which we have accumulated...is almost impossible to use unless you can reduce it to some from that management can look at and base decisions on.*

Schlitz apparently has developed a marketing information program equal to that of anheuser-Busch. Achlitz sales and profits have increased considerably. In 1972 Schlitz increased its dollar sales 16% to almost 19 million barrels (32 gallons/barrel) and lifted its market share by 1.2% to 14.3% as it improved earnings by 30%. Anheuser-Busch appears assured of more years of sales and profit leadership however, as it increased dollar sales by 8.6% market share from 19.1 to 20% and earning increased by almost 7%.

DECISION MAKING

In the past 20 years there has been massive progress in the development and application of computers and information systems. The new technology and concepts permit operating systems that in years past were not feasible. But before looking at marketing information systems, marketing research and computers it is important to realize that they exit to provide the information is used to recognize problems to evaluate alternatives and to execute the results of decisions. Therefore, the first look is a at the decision making process.

The process The various phases of the decision making process have been explained by many authors with Simon providing some of the explicit descriptions. The first phase of stage *intelligence,* is concerned with gathering information and perceptions about the current status (problems and opportunities) of the decision environment. The second stage is completed and the probable payoffs and consequences of the various alternatives have been examined the best alternative must be chosen. Hence, the third stage is *choice.* A fourth stage, that has been added onto Simon's three stages is *plementation.* This involves the development of a program to carry out the chosen alternatives.

Major decisions involve a great deal of effort. Initially, most problem-opportunity situations appear quite unstructured and require large amounts of time and effort to establish the goals and objectives of the decision. Even more demanding is the task of setting out alternatives and evaluating them. In this phase it is common to forecast the likely results of each alternative. Each of the decision stages is full of smaller decisions. In each stage the decision maker must make a series of decisions to be able to continue to the next stage. For example, as a firm attempts to prepare a marketing plan for a newly acquired product line, decision makers must decide whether the first year objective will be maximization of their profits return on investment, sales market share, or some combination of these. Then they must consider virtually hundreds of alternatives and work these down to a manageable set that allows some in depth consideration of each of them. Typically while many of the alternatives can be discarded there is no one best, clear-cut alternative based on the available information. Instead, the decision maker must finally agonize through to a choice.

The purpose of a marketing information is to provide data and transform it into usable forms to aid in the decision making process. During the intelligence stage, for example a decision maker needs enough information on the environment of the specific situation to be able to structure a view. The design stage calls for information both to enumerate and evaluate alternatives. Finally, there must be information feedback from the implementation so that the actual results can be compared to the described results.

Types of decisions

Although there are many different types of decisions made in organizations, it is helpful to divide them into three distinct types, because each one has different information requirements. The most common terminology refers to the decisions that are either (1) operational activity (2) managerial control, or (3) strategic planning.

Operational activity decisions

These are the decisions that are apart of the day-to-day operations of the organization. For example, a wholesaler may notice he needs to recorder several beverage lines, prepare the order, follow up to see that they are received and properly placed in his inventory. A salesman may look over his customer and prospect lists to decide which ones he should call on and the order and length of each call. He must also make the myriad of minor decisions involved in calling on them. Finally, he needs to analyze the accomplishment of the calling activities.

Operational decisions in general require highly detailed and accurate information that is regularly and very frequently available. Much of this information comes from sources internal to the organization.

Managerial control decisions

These decisions are largely concerned with the monitoring of alternative uses of resources within organization. They are not day-to-day decisions instead there is a greater interval of time between them. Examples of these decisions would be to allocate more or fewer salesmen to a set of customers to change the duties of some of the personal to change the advertising allocation among various markets or media and so forth.

Managerial control decisions allow data to be collected over longer time periods. The decision maker wants to see what has been happening over time and is not as concerned with what has just accurate as for the action-oriented operational decision. Finally, the originally collected data is substantially transformed into information for use by the decision maker. The decision maker wants to see more trends, relationships, and forecasts. Consequently much more analysis and synthesis is involved.

Strategic planning decisions

These decisions are principally concerned with developing goals and objectives and allocating resources to obtain them. These decision processes normally take a relatively long time, considerable resources, and have quite serious consequences. Some examples would be decisions about adding or deleting products lines; the amount of dollars to be allocated to marketing efforts for the year; allocations of funds among personal selling and advertising centering or withdrawing from markets; and so forth.

Strategic planning decisions normally involve a great deal of information in summarized forms that has been collected and analyzed over relatively long spans of time. The recency and the detailed accuracy of the information are not nearly as crucial as with the other types of decisions. Finally more of the information inputs are secured from the organization's external environment because of its influence on the outcomes.

The location of the decision maker in the organization is related to the type of the decision. In general the strategic planning decisions are made by a few people in the top managerial level of organizations. They may be assisted by Managerial control decisions are normally located with middle managers while most operational control decisions are made by lower-level managers. For example decisions to enter new markets, add new products or double marketing expenditures are the realm of the chairman of the broad, the president and perhaps the executive vice president and the marketing vice-president. Involved in the decision regarding the allocation of marketing efforts among alternative uses is the marketing vice-president along with the sales manager and the advertising director. The salesman as, we noted earlier, frequently makes most of the day-to-day operating decisions.

THE ROLE OF THE COMPUTER

The computer has provided the mechanism by which vast quantities of data can be stored and analyzed in a small amount of time. The importance of the computer to the modern economy is highlighted by the fact that the International Business Machines Corporation, a medium sized producer of accounting machines before World War II, in 1973 ranked sixth in size (by sales) in Fortune magazine's list of the 500 largest United States corporations and third in net income. Control Data Corporation another manufacturer of computer equipment did not even exist in 1956, but was 208 on the *fortune* list in 1973.

At first, application of computers was confined to activities that had preciously been performed in some other manner, such as keeping payroll records. Soon, however, the computer came to be widely employed is such diverse uses as controlling the operation of an oil refinery planning the routing of salesmen, and determining the configuration of aircraft.

The computer in marketing

Proper, arrangement of marketing as already suggested, requires the gathering analysis storage, and dissemination of an immense amount of information. Decision makers need frequent, if not continuous, measures of potential sales and costs by products (often by package size and type) and by markets. Often on a less frequent reporting basis this information must be available by customer order size channel of distribution, or other breakdowns.

The sources of data, the reporting parties and the types of information numerous-far more numerous than in the production cost accounting system, which focuses on the major analysis by type of product. Furthermore, these sales and cost data must be taken apart and put together in numerous different shapes and forms for analysis and use by planning and operating managers at different levels and locations. Before widespread computer and transmitting facilities became available, the routinized task of sales and cost analysis, for example for even a limited product line company was overwhelming because of immense processing, analyzing and feedback time requirements. Data were out of date before they could be used.

A large national brewery (which sells almost exclusively through independent wholesale distributors) requires that weekly distributor sales reports (itemized by product, by type and size of container and by type of account) be in the headquarters office by each Saturday night. By Monday morning the information has been combined, synthesized partially analyzed and made available to marketing throughout the organization.

One of the largest department store chains requires each of its retail units to report daily activities by products to its information center. These daily reports, analyzed and compared with both past performances and planned performance, aid both top management and individual store managers to perceive the company's response to the market.

A large manufacturer, which markets a line of women's clothes nationally keeps track of both its marketing costs and its sales on a weekly basis. Such close contact with the market permits the company to make timely response to market demands and to check production and distribution on slow-moving offerings.

These information programs certainly are not unique. In all programs these sales and distribution cost analysis programs account for only a part of larger, more complete marketing information programs.

The systems approach to management

A recent development in management thinking and one that probably would not have taken place without the informational storage, analysis and retrieval capacity of the computer, has been the emergence of the concept of the firm as a system. Instead of treating the company as a conglomerate of activities that can be handled more or less independently; the systems approach is to treat the firm as a network of activities that are related.

Groups of activities which for some decisions can be considered to be relatively independent of other activities may be regarded as subsystems. Marketing activities can be considered as one such subsystem of the firm as a whole. Although it is obvious that marketing decisions will affect other activities in the firm the relative homogeneity of the types of decisions to be made, the common data base required for many marketing decisions and the specialization of personal involved in making marketing decisions and carrying them into effect make it convenient to regard the marketing system as a subentity. Of course, the marketing system must at some stage be considered in its relation to other subsystems within the firm, particularly when fundamental decisions regarding goals, policies and overall budgets are formulated.

The marketing information system

The information function plays a role in the marketing system that in many ways is analogous to the role played by radar in artillery or by a temperature sensing device in a heating system. Since the automatic heating system for a home is easily understood this analogy shall be employed to give some perspective to the marketing system and the part played by marketing information.

Installation of a system

Suppose that one were building a home and had reached the stage where a heating system must be designed. The first would be to establish the decisions that are to be made within the system. If the answer were "decisions about heating the home," the set of choices would be confined to various furnace capacities and heating systems, such as forced air or water.

As frequently occurs in marketing situations, however, it may well be that the set of decisions has been stated too narrowly. In this case, it would be more appropriate to define the decision as follows:

1. Decisions about increasing the temperature.
2. Decisions about decreasing the temperature.

3. Decisions about increasing the humidity.
4. Decisions about decreasing the humidity.

Once the decisions have been defined, information must be obtained for each decision about the relevant environment the objectives to be met, and the possible alternative courses of action. All of these steps together are often referred to as "formulating the problem" and are a part of the intelligence stage and the early phase of the design stage.

The objectives may be defined in terms of ranges of humidity and temperature that are regarded as comfortable. For humidity decisions the alternative courses of action are the devices that increase of decrease humidity. For temperature decisions the alternative courses of action are the device that increase or decrease temperature. It should be noted that *these two decisions should not be regarded as independent*, since some devices (such as air conditioners) affect both humidity and temperature. This lack of independence is also true of many marketing decisions (A such as promotion and price), and in such cases decisions should not be made separately.

A decision is now required on the devices to be employed: an air-conditioner-furnace combination versus a heat pump; oil versus electricity or natural gas as the energy source; forced air versus water systems; and the associated requirements in humidifying and dehumidifying equipment. An information search of suppliers should now be undertaken to establish costs, dependability and performance. Other informational sources, such as consumer reports, may be consulted for independent expert appraisals of the various alternatives. This is a part of the design stage of the decision making process.

The ongoing system Once a "comfort" system has been installed, the problem is removed from that of the "special problem" category to that of making routine, current or, in other words operational activity decisions. For simplicity only the heating aspects of the problem will be considered.

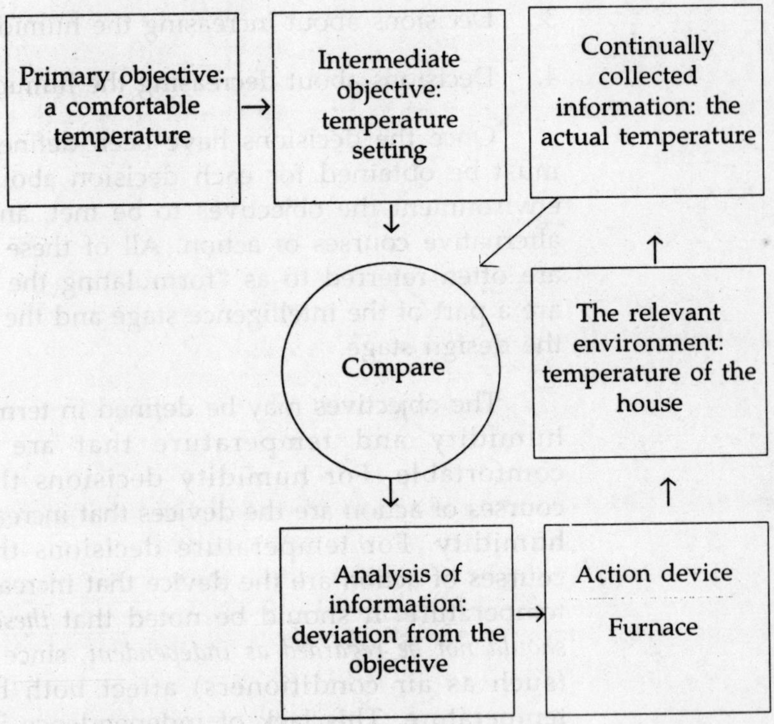

The above figure illustrates the system by which an ongoing heating system works in a house. The first necessary step here is to set the intermediate objective (temperature). (The fundamental objective comfortable temperature, is not operational-i.e., one cannot make decisions to affect comfort without first defining comfort in terms of something controllable). This objective depends primary on the temperature that the members of the household find comfortable but when set, it is not static but is subject to environmental changes. For example a temperature of 72° Fahrenheit feels cooler in the winter than in the summer because of body radiation. The walls of he house, being colder in the winter than in summer, absorb more radiated heat.

The firm sets many intermediate objectives (i.e., objectives that are met in order to attain some more fundamental objectives), such as market share promotional budgets and sales. It is obvious that a great deal of information in necessary in the establishment of these objectives. In particular, management is interested in the relationship between the attainment of intermediate objectives and the primary objectives such as profits and growth.

It is evident that the intermediate objectives of the firm are analogous to the temperature setting on the thermostat and that each is a strategic planning decision in that the setting of objectives is not a regularly recurring problem.

Once an objective is set, it is necessary to sample the pertinent environment to see if this objective is being attained. This is accomplished in a heating system by measuring the temperature of the air in the region of some sensing device. The answer obtained, are used to make operational activity decisions for the heating system. Such information is regularly or continuously gathered.

Once obtained about actual temperature is acquired, it is compared with the information about actual temperature is acquired, it is compared with the goal and decisions made based on the results of the comparison. If all is well, the decision is to do nothing. If the temperature is below some preset figure, the decisions will be turn on the furnace and leave it on until the temperature reaches some other present figure. For example, the furnace may be turned on at 71° and turned off at 73°. In the marketing system, one of the objectives of concern may be market share. If so, the informational system must yield information on the market share being attained, most likely for each market segment. Based on this information it may be necessary to take action in terms of product price promotion or channels of distribution if we see that the objective is not being attained. A similar analysis is pertinent for each objective.

The decision in terms of information, strategies and models

The purpose of information is to reduce uncertainty with respect to the consequence of a decision. Clearly, if for every decision we knew in advance the resultant outcome of each alternative course of action and if each outcome could be ranked in terms of its contribution to meeting the established objectives, we would always make a correct choice from the available course of action. Unfortunately, in the real world we are seldom sure of the outcomes of an action. A decision to market a product may result in a profit or less, or a promotional campaign may be successful or unsuccessful.

The elements determination information value

Three elements determine the value of information to business decision:

1. The degree of uncertainty regarding the outcome of the various possible courses of action.
2. The economic consequences of making an incorrect decision (i.e., not choosing that course of action which unknown to the decision maker at the time of the decision, would lead to the "best" outcome).
3. The amount by which the information is expected to reduce the initial uncertainty; if obtained.

The greater the degree of uncertainty; the economic consequences of making an incorrect decision and/or the greater the amount by which the information is expected to reduce uncertainty, the more valuable the information becomes.

This implies, of course, that when the cost of information is greater than the value of that information, obtaining information is not worthwhile. It also suggests a scheme for choosing between various "packages" of information. For example, a firm may be considering obtaining information from a consumer panel, maintained by some research firm or maintaining its own consumer panel. Or a firm may be considering various different sample sizes in a survey. That particular information package which yields the greatest excess of value of information over the cost of the information should be selected. Choosing between various information packages is part of the decision of selecting a strategy.

In the heating described earlier, the thermostat may be "programmed" to do the following:

> Measure air temperature. If the temperature is less than to equal to 70° Fahrenheit and the furnace is off, turn it on. If the temperature is greater than 70° but less than 72°, leave the furnace in its current state (either on or off). If the temperature is greater than or equal to 72° and the furnace is on, turn it off.

Such a completely specified plan of action may be termed a strategy. The task of the decision maker is to select one strategy from the collection of strategies available to him. The strategy selected completely specifies both the information that is to be obtained, and a decision rule that dictates the action to be taken for each possible information return.

Consider the following example from marketing research. A soft-drink firm, having developed a new flavor has to make a decision whether or not to market the new-flavored drink. Such a decision may involve a very large investment, particularly in promotional expenditures, hence the company would undoubtedly seek information before making a decision.

The firm might begin with a consumer taste test. If acceptance were above some previously specified level, the firm might test-market the product. If results of the test-marketing were satisfactory, the firm might market the product.

The whole sequence is a particular. If any part of the sequence was altered in some manner (perhaps by raising the level of sales for satisfactory results in the test market or by using some other test market, this would constitute a new strategy. As will be shown in chapter 12, the strategy that yields the greatest "expected value" is selected.

If testing new flavors is not a regular activity of the firm, the situation is likely to constitute a strategic planning decision. The necessary research might even be designed and performed by a consulting marketing research firm. It should be evident that the firm that regularly tests new flavors and has perfected a routinized decision process is likely to obtain better information with a lesser allocation of management resources. In general, it is to the advantage of a company to move from the category of strategic planning to managerial or operational control when it is feasible to do so. Such feasibility depends on the frequency with which the problem recurs, but the reader will appreciate the fact that managerial decision-making talent is most efficiently employed in the solution of new and unusual problems not in the solution of recurring problems where clear decision rules may be formulated.

We have so far assumed that the decision maker has a clear picture in mind of the problem or opportunity he faces. That is he, knows his alternative courses of action, all the possible outcomes of his actions the relationship between these outcomes and his objectives, the sources and kinds of information he may wish to obtain, and which outcomes are likely to result from which actions. In fact, the decision maker may possess only a vague idea of any of these elements basic to the decisions he must make.

At this point we may loosely define what has been termed a "picture of the problem" as a *model*. Good models are basic to good decisions. They enter in at each stage of the decision process. No information system can be well designed without adequate models of the problems to be solved, since without an adequate model it is impossible even to specify the information that should be collected.

10

DETERMINING INFORMATION NEEDS

The purpose of the marketing research process is to generate information which will help management answer questions related to decision areas of current interest. The informational activities inside the marketing division of an organization play a major support role for marketing management. Information is needed to improve marketing decisions. If informational activities within the marketing system lose their managerial orientation, they become pointless and without direction. Planning for research to generate either a continual flow of information or one specific set of information should start with an evaluation of the decision-making system.

The first step in the process of providing information must involve an assessment of the decision areas, problems, and decision makers within the organization. The activities involved in such an assessment can be called a marketing information audit.

THE MARKETING INFORMATION AUDIT

A marketing information audit is a comprehensive review and evaluation of the complete decision making and information producing activities within the organization. It should include all basic decision areas and levels. The objectives of the audit are:

1. To determine the exact nature of the marketing decisions considered within the organization.

2. To determine who in the decision-making, system is responsible for each of the required decisions.

3. To define the exact information needs of each decision maker.

4. To locate the sources of the data required to develop the needed information.

5. To determine the type of processing (analysis) needed to transform the data into usable information.

6. To locate inefficiencies within the existing system.

The marketing information audit can be divided into three major phases: (1) demand audit, (2) supply audit, and (3) information management audit. The demand audit looks at the decision making side of the organization. This effort should be directed at isolating the marketing decisions, decision makers, and information needs. The information needs should be specified in terms of type, form, and amounts of information for each decision maker. The supply audit deals with locating the sources of data from which the needed information can be generated. The information planner needs to be familiar with the organizational units and their ability to supply data internally. If the data is not available internally, then it must be developed from external is not available internally, then it must be developed from external sources. This may involve either tapping secondary sources or designing procedures to collect primary data. Finally, the management audit investigates the efficiency of operation within the information management system. Do the components of the system adequately carry out the functions of-data collection, data processing, and information transmission? This is the equivalent of asking can the system efficiently carry out the research process?

The focus of this chapter is the *demand audit* portion of the total marketing information audit. Elements of the *supply* and *information management* audits are discussed in later chapters. One of the vital outputs of the demand audit is a comprehensive statement of information needs within the organization. After the demand audit, the researcher should be able to fill-in each cell of the matrix with the information needed to make the decisions in that decision area and on that decision level. Data requirements can then be derived from the information needs.

In order to understand the information demand audit, two facets must be explored. First, the conceptual nature of the decision-making process must be understood along with the modifications necessitated by the organizational structure. Secondly, operationalizing the audit through situational analysis must be considered. These areas will be discussed in turn, followed by a discussion of when information needs do and do not call for marketing research.

THE IMPACT OF ORGANISATIONAL STRUCTURE ON INFORMTION NEEDS

The decision-making process occurs in the context of a decision making or organizational structure. According to one source, "An organizational structure may be defined as a vertical pattern of work, people, and physical resources that contributes to the attainment of the enterprise missions. It is not enough to know what decisions are to be made or how to make a decision. An analysis of information requirements is incomplete without a knowledge of where (by whom) decisions are made. Regardless of its size, virtually every organization has a structure which determines which members make specific decisions. In this section, some basic considerations in organizational structure and their impact on decision making and information needs are examined.

Regardless of the size or complexity of an organization someone is ultimately responsible for making each specific decision. Along with this responsibility, the individual assumes a position of authority which enables him or her to perform in the organization. The organization exists because one person is not able to make all the decisions required in a particular enterprise. While retaining primary responsibility, the top manager must delegate many decisions to others. This delegation process generates many basic requirements for information in terms of both decision making and reporting. The persons responsible for each decision must have information on which to base their judgments and their superiors must also have information to evaluate their performance. Thus, delegation causes a decentralization of information needs throughout the organization.

Although the terms centralization and decentralization are used in varying contexts, most writers concur that the terms refer to "the degree of delegation of duties, power, and authority to lower levels of an organization." Since the degree of centralization and decentralization is a function of delegation, it is not necessarily reflected in the organization chart. Furthermore, the degree of delegation in different departments and functions of an organization may vary. For example, if a large consumer goods company is organized by product lines, the marketing staff functions may also be decentralized. On the other hand, the marketing staff functions could be centralized.

There is nothing intrinsically good or bad about decentralization. On the positive side one may argue that decentralization allows participation by lower levels of management in decision making. On the other hand, however, centralization allows top management to exercise more direct control over the organization and also provides uniformity and integration of inputs for planning purposes. No organization would be meaningful if centralization were carried to the extreme. Similarly, a completely decentralized organization would have no central leadership and poor coordination of efforts. Although most authorities agree that every firm operates at some point along a continuum between extreme centralization and extreme decentralization, there is considerably less agreement as to which direction is more popular.

Although a positive correlation between information technology and centralization is an intriguing possibility, it is only fair to point out arguments to the contrary. It can be argued, for example, that delegation is more a function of the need for specialized decision-making talent than for information. That is, getting better information to the decision maker is of no use if the decision maker is not capable of utilizing it.

Luthans points out:

> ...organizational centralization-decentralization is much broader than mere information flows. Growth, homogeneity of personnel, and the—environment may all play a role in the eventual organization structure. Whether the computer is of such significance that it can override these other variables is yet to be seen. But one conclusion seems certain. The computer *will* have an impact on structure as on all other areas in organization and management. The only question is *when* and *how much*.

Regardless of the influence of information technology and the computer on organization structure, the degree of centralization does affect the information requirements of an organisation. For example, the span of control in highly centralized organization is narrower than that of a highly centralized organization is narrower than that of a highly decentralized organization. In the decentralized organization management control decisions are made at lower levels in the organization structure. Therefore, information related to these decisions flows upward through relatively few levels of management. On the other hand, in a highly centralized organization this information is frequently transmitted to the highest levels of management. Since it is often difficult to determine the degree of centralization by examining an organization chart, one must be aware of the informal organization structure. That is, the formal structure is revealed through the organization chart, but the informal structure reveals the manner in which decision making actually takes place. The information planner must take both into account.

In addition to delegation, the type of organizational structure adopted by the firm will have a significant impact on the structure of information needs. There are two widely used organization structures the line and staff structure, and the matrix structure of information needs. There are two widely used organization structures the line and staff structure, and the matrix structure.

The line and staff structure was developed to accommodate the need for specialized support services within organization. Basically, the distinction between line and staff is that of decision making versus support. Marketing research, for example, is usually a staff activity, while sales management is a line activity.

The matrix organization structure includes both functional departments (vertical lines) and a project orientation (horizontal lines). Obviously, this structure violates the unity-of-command principle. Assigning specialists to projects, while retaining their places in functional departments, creates and environment in which confusion easily arises. The difficulties involved in coordinating personnel and resolving problems are the primary disadvantages of the matrix structure. On the other hand, the concentration of specialized talent in project ventures constitutes the primary advantage. According to Luthans, "Many modern organizations which are facing tremendous structural and technical complexity have no choice but to move to such an arrangement."

Information needs in a matrix organization are complicated by the lack of unitary upward accountability. That is, a member of a project group is accountable to both the project manager and the manager of the department from which he is assigned. The assignment of specialists to the project, however, provides a more direct link for the interaction between research and decision making. Assume for example that a researcher is accountable to both the project manager and his immediate superior in the marketing department. If this relationship problem is handled well, the commitment of research staff to the project insures the availability of information as it is needed for decision making.

Discussion in the preceding section was devoted to fundamental considerations in organization structure as they relate to information needs. These fundamentals must also be considered in the light of specific structures which are common in marketing organizations. The most typical marketing organizational structure are: (1) functional, (2) territorial, (3) product-based, and (4) customer-based. Each of these forms will be discussed briefly in terms of its informational implication.

Marketing organization based on functions. In the functional organization, decision making is departmentalized along activity lines such as promotion, distribution, new product development, and so forth. Functional organization is most appropriate when a firm's activities are highly centralized (geographically), the product line is relatively narrow, and the target market is not segmented. When these conditions exist, each functional department is able to service the entire marketing operation with its respective contribution.

Functionalized departments suffer from one primary disadvantage. That is, they tend to be myopic in their view of the company. Specialists in promotion tend to concern themselves primarily with the problems of their own department or, at best, their own contribution to narrow measures of corporate performance. This problem is particularly difficult to overcome since the chief marketing administrator is the only executive with a multifunctional perspective. A considerable amount of horizontal information flow, both formal and informal, is required to attain effectiveness from this type of organizational structure.

Marketing organization based on geographic area. Firms with widespread geographic markets are frequently faced with the necessity of organizing along territorial lines. Generally, this orientation is the result of building the organization up from the lowest field unit—the salespeople. In some cases, however, even those firms without extensive personal sales efforts find it desirable to organize along geographic lines if there are noticeable differences in their buyers among two or more geographic regions.

In the geographically-based organization, information tends to be gathered in its most disaggregate form at the sales level. As the information proceeds up through district and region management, it is aggregated and changed to meet the needs of decision makers at teach level. In terms of the levels of decision making discussed, sales people, and possibly district managers, are concerned primarily with management control decision making. District managers and/or regional managers tend to be concerned with management planning. The region manager and/or marketing administrator tend to be primarily concerned with strategic planning. Information at the sales level needs to be current and extensive in terms of individual customers within each territory. The district manager, however, requires a more aggregate report in order to anticipate any needed changes in operating strategy. The marketing administrator requires summary information about the entire marketing operation, usually broken down by provided to other top level administrators to evaluate and revise corporate policy.

Marketing organization based on products. In discussing both functional and territorial organizations, key assumptions were made concerning the nature of the firm's products. In each case the firm was assumed to have a single product line or, at least, relative homogeneity among products. In many firms, however, product offerings are sufficiently diverse to require specialized treatment. An organization which proves to be effective for one product line might prove ineffective for a different product line. When this situation arises, the marketing organization is usually built around products.

In a relatively decentralized line and staff organization based on products-advertising, distribution, product development, and cost and price analysis are all line-oriented functions which produce decisions relative to the implementation of marketing strategy for the product. Although information does flow between departments at the product level and the corporate level, the information needs are very specific to individual departments. Thus product-based organization structures usually generate highly segmented information requirements.

Marketing organizations based on customers. A number of situations exist which cause many firms to organize their marketing decision making based on customers. For example, a firm may sell its product lines to different customer types. The marketing manager assigned to a consumer-oriented market would probably not do a good job of simultaneously managing marketing strategy in an industrial market. Thus a separate organization is created for each type of buyer.

The information requirements of organization based on customers are often quite unique. They may require a high degree of cooperation between customers and sellers in order to maintain a meaningful flow of information. The manufacturer must be aware of the needs of the customer in order to provide the highly technical and/or specialized products which lead to the seller-client relationship. Similarly, the customer must be provided with a sufficient amount of information about the manufacturer's goods or services in order to asses their inadequacies. This situation may lead to a cooperative relationship in which information is exchanged on a frequent basis. It is not uncommon under these conditions for manufacturers to develop entirely new products, or make substantial alterations in existing products, in order to meet the specifications of a single customer.

OPERATIONALISING THE INFORMATION DEMAND AUDIT

Now that we have discussed some of the conceptual and organizational considerations which influence the information demand audit, let us turn to basics of actually conducting such an investigation.

The most critical aspect of a demand audit lies in the interface between a manager's problem and the development of a clear and relevant statement of information needs. This interface provides the source of direction for research. From the manager's perspective a need for solutions is the most important view of the situation. The researcher's view, however, is different but related. The researcher must translate the manager's problem situation into a specific set of information needs. At the point where the researcher attempts to aid in the delineation of the managerial problem and information needs, he or she is involved in *situational analysis*.

Situational analysis deals with the definition and structuring of problems which require a decision by management. The key term is "problem". What is a problem, and particularly, what is a marketing problem? The lack of emphasis in business studies on problem definition may lead one to believe that real management problems are usually obvious and that solving all of these problems would result in business success. To the contrary, problems only become real when they are defined, and the difficulties of problem definition are among the most serious faced by managers and researchers.

For the purpose of this discussion we will use the following definition:

> A management problem is any business or administrative situation in which the difference between the desired state of affairs and the actual state of affairs is of sufficient magnitude to warrant action.

Upon closer examination this definition can be used to cover every area of marketing decision making. Thus, while the definition may fall short of the desired level of scientific rigor, it does reflect the state of the art in marketing today. Notice that the key to problem identification is a difference between the actual and the desired states of affairs.

A state of affairs, such as a market share level, exists in reality. In and of itself, this state of affairs has no particular meaning. Only when compared to some desired state of affairs, such as market share objective, can a problem come into existence. Furthermore, it is only when this difference is "of sufficient magnitude to warrant action" that we technically recognize a problem. For effective problem definition, management must specify both the desired state of affairs and the amount of difference which would warrant action.

It is important to note that our ability to determine a difference between actual and desired states of affairs is usually limited to the measurement of symptoms. When a problem is recognized, however, the action which results must relate to the underlying causes rather than those symptoms. Thus, we can view a management problem in terms of two major components: (1) the symptoms through which the existence of a problem is recognized, and (2) the true cause of the problem, or that area of activity in which a decision must be made to arrive at a solution.

Symptoms and the symptoms syndrome. Symptoms are further described by two characteristics: (1) they must be expressed in terms of management needs, goals, or objectives; and (2) they must be observable, preferably empirically measurable. Therefore, the need for a product development plan qualifies as a symptom. The underlying problem is the absence of a vehicle through which management can attain meaningful product development. Thus, a need exists. Furthermore, the plan itself is observable, and management can determine when the need has been satisfied. The quality or success of the plan is another matter. Similarly, a sales chart which illustrates actual performance and an established objective could produce a symptom of a problem. The chart indicates the current sales levels as well as a sales target; in reviewing the chart, management may see the symptom of a problem. Notice that in both of these cases the symptom itself does not lead directly to problem definition.

One of the most common difficulties faced by both the manager and the researcher is the "symptom syndrome." That is, managers and analysts all too easily fall into the trap of approaching a problem in terms of its symptoms, rather than its underlying causes. The single symptom which is most frequently cited is some measure of sales. Sales may be decreasing unchanged, increasing at too slow a rate, or otherwise failing to meet some criteria for success. In every case, however, the mere knowledge that sales performance is off the mark does not constitute the definition of a problem. Rather, sales performance is an indicator through which management can become aware of problems. Obviously, there are as many indicators as there are performance criteria. Other common indicators include various measures of profit and market share.

When any performance measure deviates from the desired pattern the result is a symptom of a potential problem. As a personal analogy, assume that you are not feeling well and discover that you have fever. Normal body temperature for most people is 98.6 degrees Fahrenheit. Thus, a reading of 98.6 degrees on a thermometer becomes a performance criterion. When a reading above or below the criterion is registered, we are alerted to the presence of a potential problem. Just as a physician considers high body temperature as a symptom of a potential health problem, the manager should consider poor sales performance as a symptoms are not always cast in a negative context. We are also interested in symptoms of unexpectedly good performance; e.g., the medical profession's interest in unusually healthy, elderly individuals, or a marketing manager's interest in sales or profit performance which significantly exceed the criteria for success.

If the physician is able to diagnose symptoms of an illness correctly, and at an early onset, the probability of a serious health problem is reduced. The same principle holds for the marketing analyst. If an information system is well conceived and implemented, symptoms of potential problems are discovered and diagnosed before a crisis develops. Management's ability to incorporate such safeguards into its information system is an indication of good problem definition techniques and system design.

Problem causes and decision areas. The second major component of a problem, the underlying causes, is much less familiar territory. A potential problem exists for every marketing related variable. Problems can be caused by changes in consumer perceptions or attitudes, a change in the legal environment, the action of a competitor, an numerous other external factors as well as the internal decision making of management. There is no simple procedure for defining a problem. Marketing management includes components of both science and art. Thus the marketing practitioners must strive for an effective blend of creativity along with the scientific method.

The "scientific method" is the distinguishing feature of science as we know it today. While science itself refers to a body of knowledge, the scientific method refers to the manner in which that body of knowledge is changed. Carlos Lastrucci has defined science in terms of scientific method as follows:

> An objective, logical, and systematic method of analysis of phenomena, devised to permit the accumulation of reliable knowledge."

Notice that the first part of this definition is concerned with the manner in which the accumulation of reliable knowledge will occur. Thus, if our work is objective, logical, systematic, and replicable, it is scientific. Obviously, the business person is frequently forced to make decisions under conditions which do not meet these criteria.

Scientific methods are more readily used in later stages of the marketing research process. We are concerned here, however, with the delineation of a marketing decision area for which a problem is deemed to exist. We could be relatively scientific at this point only if an extensive body of knowledge were available from which to draw solutions to recurring problems. This is generally not the case. In fact, attempts to emulate science at this stage can often be undesirable.

The scientific method by its very nature has distinct advantages and disadvantages. On the plus side it provides the framework for the orderly accumulation and analysis of data to produce information. On the other hand, it is all too easy for the scientific method to lead to rigidity in the way various situations are viewed. This phenomenon is described by Kuhn in his paradigm theory of the evolution of science. Scientists in the days of Copernicus, for example, maintained a paradigm which was currently accepted than it would have been to universe. It was easier for an astronomer of that day to expand upon the paradigm which was currently accepted than it would have been to break away from the trend of thought. Therefore, if a problem arose which related to the earth's position relative to the planets and stars, the existing theory would be the basis for problem definition. Copernicus questioned that paradigm at great personal and professional risk.

As an analogy in marketing, assume that retailer is interested in relocating his store. If marketing were a fundamental discipline, a body of knowledge supported by research findings would exist. From these findings the retailer could draw a decision as to the best location. Since this is not the case, the retailer can at best hope to gain some insight from the body of knowledge that exists and to explore his problem with an open mind. In order to be meaningful, problem definition frequently requires imagination and creativity which break away from commonly accepted thinking. "Pat" definitions and stereotype solutions based on particular symptoms should be avoided. Creativity is the watchword for effective problem definition.

After the problem has been creatively defined, the information needed to make a decision can be determined. To illustrate the specification of information needs, let us examine an airline case. The airline is not in trouble, but recent shifts in economic conditions have resulted in a reassessment of policies and strategies for the next two to five years. One of the decision areas facing top level executives of the airline concerns the allocation of resources and effort between business and pleasure travel market segments. Management is well aware from experience of the distinct differences in operating characteristics and profitability of service for these two segments. They discovered, however, that a study of these two segments in the airline's system of routes has not been conducted for several years. For example, management will need to know the difference in profitability between business and pleasure travel, expressed in revenue-passenger-miles (RPMs). They will also need to know the projected level of RPMs in the business and pleasure segments of the market. Furthermore, management will need a summary of operating statistics, such as load factors and share of RPMs for both business and pleasure segments throughout the airline's system. This type of information would ultimately lead to strategic planning decisions related to the market. Management might then adopt a policy of seeking market share penetration in business travel segments. Similarly, this part of the analysis may result in a policy of maintaining a systemwide return on investment of 5 percent.

In the context of the overall decision problem, further information needs for market analysis at management planning and management control levels of decision making are illustrated. For example, district managers would need summaries of activity. This might be required on a monthly basis to detect seasonal or cyclical trends. In addition to the summaries, the district manager would probably request projections of business travel within the district. Anticipating the types of decisions to be made, both district managers and station managers would request information concerning penetration goals by segment for their corresponding responsibilities, as well as reports of penetration performance, probably on a quarterly basis.

Notice that the nature of information needs at each of the three levels of decision making is different. For example, information needs at the management control level of decision making are ongoing as opposed to one-time at the strategic planning level. Also, keep in mind that these are not intended to be exhaustive lists of information needs for this type of decision-making problem. You will recall that the levels of decision making, while associated in general with levels of management, may be carried on at all levels of management. That is, management control information needs may exist at the corporate level, the district level, as well as the field level. The information needs discussed thus far all pertain to market analysis. Decisions resulting from type of information might narrow the scope of alternatives available in remaining decisions. For example, the policy stated earlier concerning market share penetration in business segments might require a high priority for allocations of product and distribution to those segments. At the management planning level, decisions might be made classifying specific route segments as "business" or "pleasure." This would result in a different treatment for each of those routes in an allocation of the marketing mix at the district level. Finally, at the management control level, the task may become one of refining penetration policy based on market performance over time.

A clear statement of information needs is the starting place for effective marketing research. Providing information which can improve the decisions made by marketing managers is how research gains value. Even when information is thought to be needed, however, research may still not be justified.

Before proceeding with research, the marketing manager and researcher should be confident that certain basic conditions are present. Perhaps the best way to approach the question—to research or not to research?—is by considering situations where research should *not* be conducted. Lee Adler provides an excellent list of such situations in A *"Dissident"* View on *Marketing Research.*

When the cost of research would exceed its value

Each proposed research effort, whether it is designed as a one time project or for ongoing implementation, should be subjected to a cost/benefit analysis. Only if the benefit (value) of the information exceeds the cost should research proceed. For example, the research department of a large chemical firm developed a new coating for aluminum window the door frames which could prevent stains from concrete during construction. It was estimated that a study of market potential using depth interviews with a sample of 100 firms would cost approximately $12,000. The production cost of the product was very low, however, and would require no extra equipment. Management estimated that going into limited production for one year and including the product in the existing line would cost only $15,000. Since the market potential study was intended only for use in deciding whether to enter limited production or not, it was dropped as too expensive relative to its potential value.

When there is an insufficient budget to do a technically adequate job

Technical problems may arise with research relating to inadequate sample size, lack of pretesting, lack of trained interviewers, and so forth. When budget limitations prevent a reasonable level of accuracy in a research project, it is better to avoid research and the false impressions that can be created. A common problem arises in the case of industrial marketing research where personal interviews are often required to get the technical data and careful diagnosis needed. Personal interviews can be very expensive per interview, thus the size of the sample may be restricted. This is acceptable if there is no need for conclusive results. Some very useful hypotheses may be developed, but the need is often to project to the total market. This may not be possible when the sample is too small due to budgetary constraints.

When time is an enemy

Information, however accurate, has no value if it is not timely. If the decision must be made before the research can be completed, then no research should be undertaken. Time is a particularly serious enemy in highly competitive fashion markets. The decision to introduce a new product may be urgent if the product life cycle is known to be short and a competitor is on the brink of introducing a similar product.

When conducting research would lip hand to a competitor

This problem is most often encountered in relation to new product testing. Open-field testing in test markets may give important product information to competitors before the actual product introduction. This would allow them to formulate a competitive response more quickly than would otherwise be the case. Such a possibility should not be allowed to prevent necessary data collection, but it presents a very real risk. One way to avoid the problem is to conduct tests in controlled distribution systems or in computer simulated markets. Testing products with friendly customers should also be considered, particularly in industrial markets where trial use under normal working conditions is often required for effective evaluation.

When research findings would not be actionable

If for any reason the information produced through research could not be acted upon, it would have no value. Information gains value as an input to managerial decision making, thus, if the decision cannot be affected by specific information, research should not be undertaken to produce the information. Many factors, physical and mental, can lock management into a specific course of action. Where this occurs, research is useless. For example, the advertising group for pool chemicals with a rather large company did an extensive study of customer attitudes toward one of the company's products. The intent was to provide a basis for deciding on the copy appeals for proposed advertising. After the study had already been completed, it was discovered that the new product development department was almost finished with the design of a new product which had a totally different dispensing system and chemical base. The consumer attitude survey was thus wasted, since advertising of the old product was dropped. The key to overcoming this general problem is to get agreement from the decision makers, before doing research, as to the courses of action to follow, assuming various research results. If such an understanding is not possible prior to the design and implementation of research, both the researcher and the manager should exercise caution.

When research is politically motivated

Marketing management is a competitive game. Different managers are trying to advance tneir careers, to win others to their way of thinking, and in some cases, to boost their egos. In this environment it is quite possible that pseudoresearch will be proposed for political rather than decision-making purposes. The manager of a sporting goods store in a downtown urban area wanted to relocate in a newer building in the same area. His company had several other stores located in the suburbs. In order to support his position, he commissioned a study of the "higher" sales potential at the new site. His mind was made up, and he had to convince top management. If the study had not supported his position, he would have discredited the results by finding fault with the sample, questionnaire, or analysis. The research was clearly not intended to improve objective decision making.

When the problem is not clear and the objectives not well defined

Both managers and researchers often contribute to this situation. Managers tend to emphasize symptoms rather than problems, a most common statement as mentioned earlier being that "sales are down". This is only a visible symptom of some deeper problem. The researcher must probe the situation and the decision maker to uncover the real issues and problems. This requires that the manager and researchers work closely; particularly in the early stages of the research process. Many researchers seem to be tempted to substitute their own judgments for those of the decision maker or to cast the problem in a mold that fits their particular methodological expertise. The specialist trained in experimental design may want to conduct an experiment, whatever the problem. This can lead to waste, inefficiency, and information which is not relevant to the decision maker. No research should proceed without a clearly stated managerial decision as its point of departure. This managerial decision must be defined with ample and meaningful management input.

When a test does not represent later reality

This can be a very serious problem in experimental research. Favorable experimental results in product or advertising copy testing may not project to the marketplace. Advertising research often shows copy, graphics, and so forth, doing well in isolated tests, but doing poorly when combined into a total ad. The parts do not harmonize when used together. In such cases, researching isolated parts does not get the desired results.

When findings are intended for use in legal proceedings

Attempting to use marketing research as legal evidence has many potential pitfalls. For example, what constitutes good research from a technical or management point of view may not be acceptable from a legal standpoint. Also, research results may be subpoenaed for use by the adversary.

In a recent survey by an advertising agency, 90 percent of the sample correctly understood an ad. The FTC argued that this was proof that some portion of the audience was deceived and that ads with the "capacity to deceive" are unlawful. In this case, the research proved very damaging.

When what is to be measured changes slowly

Some variables change very slowly over time. For example, corporate image studies on an annual basis for large companies are generally not necessary because their images are very resistant to change. An appropriate time span between such studies is usually five years or so, unless some major event has occurred which may cause the image to change.

Many facets of consumer behavior are also reasonably stable. The average percentage of the family food dollar spent on various categories of food for home consumption has changed very little over the last ten years, for example. When behavior patterns are this stable, there is little need to research then on a regular basis.

When the information already exists

Reinventing the wheel may be great fun at times, but it has very little value. When data already exist in the corporate data bank or in external secondary sources, there is no need for primary research. Searching secondary data can be extremely tedious work, but is an essential element of an effective information program.

Proposals to conduct research should be carefully evaluated before serious design efforts are undertaken. This can avoid considerable waste and enhance the potential for research to have significant benefits when it is undertaken. Research should not be designed or implemented when any of the conditions described above exist.

11

ANALYSING MARKET OPPORTUNITIES

In this chapter we will focus on research for market analysis, particularly in terms of identification of market opportunities. The basic decision in market analysis is selection of the target market or market opportunity, but a considerable amount of information is typically needed to do this effectively. This information is not only useful in the target market decision: it also becomes a vital input into decisions related to the marketing mix.

Since it is not possible to cover every aspect of market analysis, this chapter concentrates primarily on information for market segmentation and target market selection. The target market is the group of customers or potential customers that the firm has selected to attempt to do business with. The marketing mix will be designed to meet the needs of this target market. Thus, the nature of the target market holds implications for all marketing decisions. Information produced through research must identify and describe the target market in a manner which allows management to formulate a competitive marketing mix and successfully implement its marketing strategy. The identification and selection of target markets is a complex task. In this chapter we use a two-step procedure involving: (1) the identification of alternative market segments and (2) the screening of those alternatives to select the most desirable target.

The thrust of the discussions which follow is the information needed for effective market analysis. These information needs are the link between decision making and research. In order to provide a clearer picture of these information needs, the basic concepts of market analysis will be explored. Illustrations of research designed to produce various types of information for market analysis will also be presented. This union of research methods and decision making through defined information needs is essential if research to be discussed relies on secondary and survey data. This is due to the nature of the market analysis task. Qualitative research also has important applications in this area in discovering directions for quantitative work.

THE STRATEGY OF MARKET SEGMENTATION

Implicit in the concept of market segmentation are the assumptions that (1) the customers in any given market are different and (2) that this heterogeneous segments. We must also assume that some of the ways in which the customers differ are related to purchase behaviuor. It is obvious, for example, that the total group of people who buy hamburgers from fast food franchises contains a wide range of ages, incomes, physical sizes, and political beliefs. Furthermore, subgroups could be formed based on similar ages, incomes physical sizes and political beliefs. If one of these characteristics is related to the purchase of hamburgers, however, little is gained by the exercise.

In the process of selecting target markets through market segmentation, the first step involves identifying the bases for segmentation. The bases for segmenting markets must be selected for their relevance to purchase behavior. These approaches are basically one of two types analysis of consumer characteristics and analysis of consumer response. A meaningful profile of segments usually requires a combination of these approaches.

It would be reasonable to assume for example, that virtually all of the serviceable market for facial cosmetics (e.g., lipstick eye liner, powder etc.). Falls within the 'female' segment of the population. On the other hand, a particular cosmetic manufacturer might need to identify segments in terms of income occupation age brand image product usage, and price sensitivity in order to select the best target market for a specific product or produce line.

The purpose of identifying segments is to provide

better information for planning (and implementing) the marketing mix. The segment is unique and wants shared by members of a segment can be satisfied by a marketing mix which is unique from those used for other segments. Second each segment will usually exhibit characteristics behaviors which prescribe an appropriate marketing mix. The problem facing management however, is often complicated by the existence of multiple segments all of which cannot be serviced within the limits of the firm's resources. Strategic planning therefore requires goals and objectives. Therefore mush of the success of a firm's marketing strategy depends on the care with which targets are identified and selected.

RESEARCH FOR IDENTIFYING MARKET SEGMENTS

In measuring market segments it is important to keep three information needs in mind. As mentioned earlier each segments must be unique in terms of its specific needs or buyer behavior. Second, segments must respond differentially to specific marketing mix. Finally, segments which meet the first two criteria must also be readily identified. The first need is usually met by segmenting the total population into various categories of buyers or nonbuyers; regardless of the segmentation classification used, the primary basis for segmentation is actual or potential product usage. The second criterion, differential response to specific marketing strategies may be met by a number of measures particularly in the area of consumer response or behavioral differences. Finally, the third criterion is most easily most if segments are identifiable in terms of socioeconomic or demographic measures. Thus, we seldom find meaningful segment identification based on only one type of segmentation classification. When a particular classification is illustrated in the following discussion, it may be in terms of any one or more of the three criteria. Several will be illustrated with emphasis on some of the more important categories.

Segmentation based on consumer characteristics

The two earliest bases used for segmenting markets were demographic and geographic. Demography is the study of population and demographic variables; it includes such measures of a population as the distribution of age, sex religion family size and life cycle categories. These variables are relatively easy to measure particularly since the advent of the decennial census.

In the past, demographic and geographic variables have been particularly useful in monitoring the changes in population characteristics for large market areas. For example, if a product is known to sell particular well in urban markets. It is useful to know where new high density population centres are emerging. In recent years markets of baby food products have been concerned with the declining birth rate in this country. Demographic research provided these manufacturers with new potential market segments in the growing elderly groups with new special dietary requirements. Demographic and geographic research may also be combined to point out regional variations in ethnic subcultures. For example kosher food products have a limited market, primarily among Jews. The density of Jewish population which makes the distribution of kosher products feasible exists only in certain large urban areas. Similarly, the demand for hot, spicy. Mexican/Indian dishes is concentrated in southwestern United States.

Socioeconomic data refer to characteristics of a population which have not traditionally been included in demographic studies. The inclusion of socioeconomic variables such as social class, and more of normally defined as a composite of income, education and occupation. Much has been written about social class structure in the United States. It is beyond the scope of this test. However, to provide detailed insight into this subject. The socioeconomic dimension of this first set of segmentation variables is important however, for two reasons. First, socioeconomic variable imply smaller group structure and thus, a more finely turned basis for identifying market segments.

Some studies have shown that the members of the various social class strata in this country have differing media habits and purchasing behaviours. Although it is difficult to generalize that social class strata themselves are large market segments this information can prove useful in relating other factors to market segmentation. If for example the users of a particular producers are found to exhibit the socioeconomic and demographic characteristics of a lower class stratum and are restricted to a particular geographic area, this useful information can be brought to bear in devising marketing mixes for the segment. Obviously, a furniture retailer located in the inner city in Cincinnati would be faced with a different problem in terms of product line strategy and communications strategy than a similar type of retailer located in a newer suburb. The former faces a broader geographic market area (29 versus 19 tracts) and a better educated younger clientele with significantly higher incomes. Residents of the newer suburbs also occupy more white collor jobs and live in homes which are better maintained than inner city residents.

The data for the Cincinnati study researchers were not concerned from secondary sources, e.g., U.S. Census. The researchers were not concerned with identifying segments which are "better" or "worse" than others, but segment may be more or less appropriate for a particular firm depending on the nature of the products and brands involved.

The discussion of demographic socioeconomic and geographic segmentation has thus far centered on the use of these measures as primary segmentation variables. Their value in this regard has decreased in recent years. There is a mounting body of evidence pointing to the need fro a more direct analysis of the perceptions and behaviour of buyers in segmenting markets. As a result, the role of demographic socioeconomic and geographic variables has become one of description. That is these variables are still the most desirable means for describing segments which have already been identified using some other basis.

An excellent example of the use of demographic in segmentation is provided in a study reported by Garfinkle. The purpose of this study was to assist the manufacturer of a brand of toothpaste in devising better media strategy. A national sample of female heads of house holds was asked to indicate which brand they buy most often, which brand is their second choice and then to specify their attitudes toward other major brands of the product category. The respondents were asked to provide information concerning media use and certain socioeconomic and demographic characteristics. Analysis of the findings yielded the following information:

> The largest group of new customers came from those who previously considered the brand their second choice. The conversion rate from second choice to regular use was closer to 20 percent as compared to less than 5 percent for people who rated the brand their third choice. Equally significant, the conversion rate from second choice to regular use varied from as low as 10 percent fro some brands to as high as 80 percent for other brands in the same product category.
>
> These findings permitted the advertiser to identify his prime targets: Current customers, to maintain their loyalty and to keep the switch away rate to a minimum and customers who considered the brand their second choice, to maximize the conversion rate thereby gain the largest possible group of customers.

This finding satisfies the first criteria for segmentation. That is the segments were identified in terms of their purchase behavior and brand preference. This insures that segmentation is based on a factor which might ultimately relate to purchase.

Each of these segments was then analyzed in terms of their state of preference for 44 television programs and 15 magazines. There was a considerable amount of difference in the preferences for media associated with each of the segments. This finding meets the second criterion for segmentation, the ability to determine varying responses to specific marketing variable. In this case the marketing variable of interest is media.

The prime importance in this section however, is the

application of socioeconomic demographic and geographic variables. The same segments were finally analyzed in terms of these variables. One segment was clearly a higher income, higher class and more urban market than that associated with the other brands. Another segment appeared to occupy the other end of the spectrum. By identifying the location and type of market in the demographic and socioeconomic data, the marketer can create the right appeals and select appropriate media for reaching the target segment.

Psychological bases Psychological bases for segmentation tend to be related to either personality or motivation. Although an extensive amount of research has been conducted on the basic behavior of buyers, the useful application of psychological studies in segmentation are somewhat limited. These variable tend to be used to satisfy the second criterion for identifying segments. That is they provide the basic for developing strategies to which a particular segments response will differs from the study of motivation these bases for segmentation will be discussed separately.

Personality and psychographics. Some of the earliest attempts to segment market in terms of behavioral characteristics involved personality research. Typically researchers attempted to utilize established personality inventories, such as the Edwards Personal Preference Schedule, the Thurstone Temperament Schedule, and the Gordon Personal Profit to identify characteristics of market segments. The difficulties encountered in these studies were discussed by Evans in a classic article which pointed out the frustrations involved in personality research. Although researchers found personality to be a difficult basis for segmentation analysis, work in this area has continued. The two basic problems which have conformed researchers in the past involved meeting the first criterion for segmentation and defining personality measurement.

Based on this data, the housewives were divided into six segments labeled: homemakers, materials, variety girls, cinderellas, glamour girls, and media conscious glamour girls. The researchers then determined which personality scores were statistically different between segments. For example, the difference in mean scores for ascendancy and sociability between "homemakers" and materials" is statistically significant. In terms of using personality traits for gaining insight into segment behavior, this finding suggested that matriarchs perceive themselves as on the way up and tend to socialize to a greater extent than homemakers. Combining this information with the product related information in the study, we might conclude that matriarches are interested in expressing their rising place in the world through the acquisition of a variety of material objects. Similarly, promoting these various products to this segment should utilize social themes when possible.

On the other hand, homemakers tend to express themselves through products related to food and food preparation. This is consistent with their view of stable social status and limited social activity. In meeting the third criterion for identifying segments, the researchers provided information on several demographic and socioeconomic variables. Using the same two segments as examples, we note that slightly more homemakers are white than black, of more moderate means, and married to husbands whose occupations are considerably down scale relative to that of materials. Furthermore, homemakers tend to be slightly closer in ago to the age of their husbands and overall, slightly older than materials. Thus, a manufacture of say refrigerators or stoves could use the socioeconomic and demographic information to targets his efforts toward the different segments and utilize the personality trait information to vary the theme and approach in marketing to each group.

Although Greno, Sommers, and Kernan were able to satisfy the three requirements for identifying segments there are still problems in utilizing personality traits distinguish segment behaviors. A concept which has been developed over the last ten years represents efforts to circumvent some of the problems associated with personality research. The concept is known as psychographics or life-style analysis. It should be noted that life-style analysis is not wholly derived from the area of personality research. The two are closely related, however, and a detailed examination of their differences is beyond the scope of this discussion. The reader should consult the list of suggested readings at the end of the chapter for additional sources. Although the terms are sometimes used interchangeably psychographics is more closely related to the concept of personality and life-style analysis is more closely related to measures of activities, interests, and opinions.

It is the multifaceted aspect of life-style research that makes it so useful in segmentation. A prominent life-style researcher, Joseph T. Plummer, summarizes the concepts as follows:

> The new construct life-style patterns combines the virtues of demographics with the richness and dimensionality of psychological characteristics and depth research.
>
> Life style is used to segment the marketplace because it provides the broad, everyday view of consumers.....life style segmentation can generate identifiable whole persons rather than isolated fragments."

A good illustration of life -style segmentation research is provided by work toward the development of a national advertising campaign for Schlitz beer. "With Schlitz as one of its major accounts the Leo Burnett Agency was concerned by the late 1960s that its existing campaign needed revitalizing. At the at time the campaign was built around the concept line of "When you are out of Schlitz, you're out of beer." The creative director assigned to the account conducted some informal life style research by leaving his corporate office and touring taverns on the street to at a feel for the life style of the heavy beer drinker.

> ...As the creative man saw him, the heavy beer drinker was "the man who belongs to that 20% of the population that drinks 80% of the beer. A

man who drinks a case a week or even a case a day... he is a guy who is not making it and probably never will. He is a dreamer, a wisher, a limited edition of Walter Mitty. He is a sports nut because he is a hero worshiper... he goes to the tavern and has 6 or 7 beers with the boys... if we are to talk to this man where he lives, in terms he respects and can identify with, we must find for him a believable kind of hero he inwardly admires."

A word which Schlitz has used earlier and felt that it "owned" seemed to represent the life style of the heavy beer drinker. The word was "gusto." After conducting a literature search of previous research on the word, it was concluded that "Gusto has been a powerful, hardworking word and had conveyed many relevant meanings to consumers about beer, about taste, and about life." The idea for a new campaign which resulted from the initial research was the "Gusto man, and gusto life" approach.

By the time the campaign idea has been formulated, the results of the Leo Burnett 1968 Life-Style Study was available for male respondents. The agency would feel confident in entering the new campaign if life-style segmentation confirmed the gusto man/gusto life approach. In meeting the first criterion for identifying a segment, the initial segmentation basis was to identify the heavy beer drinker, or heavy user. Notice that respondents were segmented as nonusers, light users, and heavy users, as a primary segmentation basis. Life-style data was then used to provide a picture of the heavy beer drinker. The following summary statement confirmed the image of the heavy beer drinker:

...The major life style patterns that emerged indicated that the heavy beer drinker was probably more hedonistic and pleasure-seeking toward life than the nondrinker. He seemed to have less regard toward responsibilities of family and job. More than the nondrinker he tended to have a preference for a physical/male-oriented existence and an inclination to fantasize. Finally we found, not surprisingly, a great enjoyment of beer drinking, especially beer which he saw as a real man's drink.

Meeting the third criterion for segmentation, the research also provided demographic data on the heavy beer drinker. The significant demographic features indicated, "that the heavy user is middle class economically, but derives his income from primarily blue-collar occupations. He is young and has at least a high school education." Armed with this rich picture of a target market, the agency produced and successfully implemented the "gusto man" campaign.

Motivation as a basis. Motivation is a concept which is difficult to define. In fact, the difficulty of defining motives and dealing with motivation in consumer research accounts for the limited application of this basis for segmentation. For the most part, the applicable work in motivation research involves "patronage motives." Patronage motives typically concern the consumer's reasons for shopping at a particular retail outlet. Consumers are classified, for example, as price conscious, convenience oriented, service oriented, or in terms of some other motivating feature.

A study of bank selection criteria for residents of Austin, Texas revealed different motivations for each of two segments. One group appeared to be convenience oriented, and the other group appeared to be service oriented. The segments were further defined in terms of socioeconomic, demographic and other variables. The most significant finding in this particular study was that the convenience oriented group perceived all banks to be essentially the same. This segment is therefore, relatively immune to patronage appeals. The service oriented segment, however, does see meaningful differences between banks and their service offerings. Further analysis of this group indicated that it included fewer single persons and more families with young children slightly higher 'annual family incomes a higher percentage of both heads of the household employed full time, and greater reliance on word-of-month promotion in banks election. Although considerable additional information is required for strategy formulation banks in Austin and similar communities could benefit from his segmentation research.

Another study of patronage motives in bank selection involved a larger, and perhaps more representative sample, than the Austin study. Again, however, a word of caution is required in interpreting the results of segmentation based on motivation. Motives are such broad and pervasive aspects of behaviour that it is difficult to formulate specific strategies without a considerable amount of additional information. Therefore motivation research may uncover useful information for formulating the major theme of a marketing strategy but a considerable amount of additional information is usually required to respond to a target segment.

Segmentation based on consumer response

Referring to our earlier discussion, recall that the bases for segmentation are divided into two major groups, consumer characteristics and consumer response The former is most useful in describing general behavior differences between groups of people or listing their attributes. The latter, however, is more directly concerned with the behavior of consumers in direct response as a primary segmentation basis, for segmentation. Several of the research examples cited in the previous section included consumer attributes for completing the segmentation identification process. It would be difficult within the constants of this section to illustrate all of the consumer-response research categories. A few have been selected however, to illustrate the concept.

In the complex world within which contemporary marketing decisions are made the customer's perception of products and marketing strategy is more important than management's perceptions of these variables. A product is defined purpose by a manufacturer. Similarly, the success of a brand name is often dependent upon the meaning of the brand perceived by customers. Assume, for example, that a firm markets a consumer convenience product which competes with a number of brands. The firm is concerned with its general lack of ability to increase and maintain market share. A question arises as to the possibilities of identifying market segments for the various brands and then utilizing that information to solidify strategies specifically for a target market segment.

Haley introduced a concept known as benefit segmentation which may be used as a primary basis for identifying market segments in terms of the benefit which they perceive in products. If in the above example the product happened to be toothpaste, Haley's benefit segmentation approach would have provided some meaningful information at the time of introduction. Notice that "principal benefits sought" heads the list. One group of respondents to the survey indicated that they seek brightness of teeth as a principal benefit of toothpaste. To complete the other criteria for segment identification we find that this group is highly sociable and active, and tend to smoke cigarettes. The predominant demographic characteristics of the groups that they are teenagers and young adults whose profit suggests the segment name, "The sociables." Furthermore, we find that this group disproportionately favour Macleans, Plus White and Ultrabright.

It is important to note that the same segments may not have been identified on the basis of usage of toothpaste per se, or specific brands purchased. Rather, the groups were primarily formed on the basis of the benefit they seek in the various toothpaste products. With this information management can formulate more accurate promotional strategies which are aimed specifically at a particular target market.

The preceding examples have focused on the segmentation problems of product manufacturer. In a series of interesting studies, Martineau introduced the concepts of retail store image as a factor in marketing strategy. As the postwar populations shifted from urban to suburban living the downtown department store was faced with the problem of retaining and if possible, increasing sales. For the retail store executive the possibility of store image segments presents opportunities for marketing strategy formulation. Rich and Portis identified three segments for nine major department stores in the New York City area and in Cleveland. Based on the responses from 4,5000 randomly selected female shoppers the researchers identified three types of stores, high fashion price appeal and broad appeal..behavioral differences between the store image segments and descriptive characteristics indicated that members of the high-fashion segment have a relatively high interest in fashion, are less likely to look for bargains, and stop less at discount stores. Furthermore, the high fashion segment tended to have a relatively high income, have no children at home, and live in the suburbs. Although this research did not provide extensive detailed information, the three criteria for segment identification are met. The information can be used to assist retail store managers in designing marketing strategies for their respective target segments.

RESEARCH FOR ESTIMATING MARKET POTENTIAL AND SELECTING TARGET MARKET SEGMENTS

The process of identifying opportunity involves more than the identification of market segments. Serving a segment is only an opportunity if it enables the firm to meet its goals and objectives. The opportunity, therefore is usually measured in terms of the profitability associated with a particular segment. Furthermore, a firm may be faced with resource constants which force it to select a target market from two or more alternative segments. The basis for selection is usually a financial criterion such as profit.

In order to assist the attractiveness of a segment as a target market, management must have a projection of the criteria (profit, sales, market share, and so forth) and related information upon which it will make a decision. This need usually requires forecasts of sales and costs associated with serving the segment. The remaining discussion in this chapter will thus be divided into two parts. First, a brief discussion of forecasting will illustrates the techniques and problems associated with this type of research. Second, the use of grids to analyze the profitability of segments will be discussed.

In this analysis of marketing opportunities the problem of forecasting focuses on the methods to be employed. That is, management should have knowledge of the objectives and criteria upon which decisions will be made. These factors determine the areas of information need. Furthermore, the process of identifying segments provides the researcher with the significant variables or factors which may be forecasting is to determine the appropriate method given the set of known constraints.

Forecasting methods have been classified in a number of ways by various authorities. One, for example, explains that "Three are two main approaches in forecasting :.... (1) noncausal methods; and (2) causal analysis. The former involves analyzing historical data in order to project its pattern of movement through time. The latter involves an analysis of the factor to be forecasted as well as factors which are causally related in an attempt to define that relationship. Using the defined relationship the factor is forecasted for future time periods.

While it is useful to consider the causal and noncausal nature of certain methods, another important classification distinguishes between "objective" and "subjective" forecasting methods. According to Bolt, "Objective forecasts tend to be of a statistical/ mathematical nature and subjective forecasts tend to be intuitive based on the application of experience, intelligence, and judgement. Since the two classifications just discussed are not mutually exclusive, a third one is particularly useful for our limited discussion. In this approach:

> ...We have grouped the techniques into three basic categories (1) judgement technique) time-series analysis and projection, and (3) causal models. The first category uses qualitative data (e.g., expert opinions) and information about special events, and may or may not take the past into consideration. The second focuses entirely on patterns and pattern changes and thus relies entirely on historical data. The third uses highly refined

and specific information about relationships between system elements. It is powerful to take special events formally into account and it also uses the past as an important input.

Judgemental technique

Jury of executive opinion. The most common judgmental or subjective technique used in forecasting: Jury of Executive Opinion. As the name implies this technique involves gathering a panel of experienced executives who together to develop a forecast or the basis for forecasting. The disadvantages of this technique are obvious. It is not specific and relies solely on individual opinion. Less obvious but perhaps more important are the advantages of the jury or panel approach.

If properly conducted the jury of executive opinion can take advantage of the observation and experience of talented executives. It is not correct to assume that this method is devoid of historical trends or anticipations of the future. The executive's ability to assimilate past experience and a knowledge of a dynamic environment in which the market operates are vital assets in this process.

Forecasts derived the executive panel tend to decrease in quality with the passage of time. That, is they are most accurate for the short term and least accurate for the long term. Finally, the Jury approach offers the advantage of a forecast which can be developed in a relatively short period of time.

Delphi Technique. A more structural method for utilizing executive opinion the Delphi Technique. As in the case of the jury of executive opinion, a panel of experts is used, but their opinions are collected through a structural questionnaire. Each set of responses is processed and a new questionnaire developed which is returned to each of the executives. With each new questionnaire the objective is improved closure of opinions by the executives.

In practice the Delphi Technique applied to the panel of executives suffers the same basic disadvantages as the jury of executive opinion. That is executive opinions as opposed to direct market factors, are the basis for the forecasts. The Delphi Technique offers an additional advantage, however, in that it is more systematic or scientific. The executives do not communicate with each other, and their response are systematically processed to develop a consensus.

The primary disadvantage of the Delphi Technique is the length of time required to develop a forecast. Whereas a jury of executive opinion can be developed within a matter of days, the Delphi Technique can easily take several months. Although forecasts developed in this manner are still not particularly useful for the long term, the overall quality is usually improved.

Time-series analysis

Regardless of the statistical methods employed time-series analysis involves attempts to project historical patterns into the future. Time-series generally contain one or more of four types of movements:

1. *Secular trend*-Multi-year general upward or downward movements in a time series.
2. *Periodic movements*-Movements in a time series which recur within a given period of time, such a year and generally referred to as seasonal movements.
3. *Cyclical movements*-Movements which are similar to periodic movements but are of longer duration than a year and often irregular in the period of repetition.
4. *Irregular variations*-Movements in a time series which are the result of either a one-time specific event or minor causes which, although they may be repetitions, are of no particular significance.

The most common technique for time-series analysis is the moving average. The purpose of the moving average is to remove cyclical movements seasonal variations or irregular movements. This is accomplished by calculating average points from the time-series data.

The average point will tend to provide a smoother time-series plot reflecting the nature of the series without undesired variations. The length of the moving average is arbitrary. Forecasts based on moving average for future periods. Moving averages are actually more useful as warning indicators for short-term movements in a time-series.

Although time-series analysis has evolved into a fairly sophisticated area of investigation, such forecasts are based on historical data only. This leaves them vulnerable to changes in the underlying conditions of the marketplace. The months of October, November, and December are not plotted because the following January, February, and March are not available for calculating through the December point. Since the quality of the forecast will deteriorate rapidly over time, the value of moving average for developing actual forecast figures is questionable. Finally, some of the more recent sophisticated time-series analysis techniques are relatively expensive and highly complicated. Given the inherent problems of using moving averages it is questionable whether the benefit exceeds the cost in many decision making situations.

Causal methods of forecasting

Both the judgmental and time-series analysis methods dealt directly with the factor to be forecasted. That is, executive opinion or a sales trend were directly examined in order to forecast sales. When using causal methods, the researcher is seeking a better understanding of the relationship between the factor to be forecasted and other factors which cause that behaviour. If a tire manufacturer wishes to forecast sales, the question might arise as to the relationship between new car sales and the demand for tires. If the sale of automobiles leads to the demand for tires in later period, tire sales forecasts might be developed based on automobile sales as a causal factor. Although there are a number of causal methods, we will only examine three in this section. These include correlation regression models intention-to-buy and anticipation techniques surveys and leading indicators.

Since the research techniques discussed in this

group of forecasting models were all covered in earlier chapters, they will not be redefined at this point. Rather each, will be illustrated to review briefly earlier discussions which relate to these methods.

Correlation/Regression methods. Most commonly used of the causal methods are the various least squares associative analyses known as correlation and regression techniques. Regression analysis in particular offers many advantages for forecasting. It estimates an equation which can be used to determine the value of a dependent variable (the forecasted factor) given known quantities for the independent variables (the causal factors).

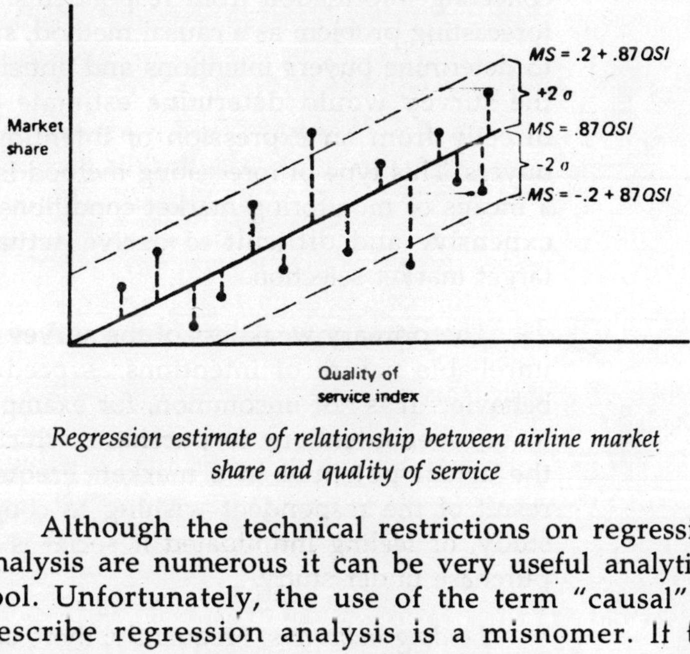

Regression estimate of relationship between airline market share and quality of service

Although the technical restrictions on regression analysis are numerous it can be very useful analytical tool. Unfortunately, the use of the term "causal" to describe regression analysis is a misnomer. If the regression results do in fact describes a causal relationship it is only because the researcher detected the relationship when defining the original model. Thus the regression line is nothing more than a statistical phenomena. Nevertheless, a well-conceived and carried out regression analysis can provide useful forecasts for analyzing market opportunities.

Using the equation for the regression line, we can develop a confidence interval for the value of market share in a future period. Since the coefficients in the regression equation are estimates, each of which has a probability distribution, we are able to forecast a range of possible values. It remains to be seen whether the forecast is useful given the which of the confidence interval. Since the researcher relies on systematic and logical thought in order to determine likely causal relationship regression analysis may at times be little more than an extension of the jury of executive opinion. At least it is always an extension of someone's opinion.

Intention-to-buy and anticipation surveys. Surveys were described in general in terms of quantitative methods for collecting information from respondents. Applied to the forecasting problem as a causal method, surveys are used to determine buyers intentions and anticipations. That is the survey would determine estimate of future sales directly from an expression of intentions by potential buyers. This type of forecasting method is most useful as a means of monitoring market conditions. It is relatively expensive and difficult to derive actual forecasts for target market selection.

The primary weakness of the survey approach is the unreliable nature of intentions as predictors of actual behavior. It is not uncommon, for example, for a survey to uncover intentions to purchase, which vastly exceed the actual potential in a market. Frequently, this is a result of the respondent wishing to cooperate with the study, or feeling intimidated if social is attached to the purchase under study.

Leading indicators. Frequently; there are factors which relate to the sales or costs associated with a product but their impact occurs after some period of time. There appears to be such a relationship, for example, between the rate of change in Gross National Product and the demand for air travel. When the domestic economy began to show signs of instability in the late, 1960s, it was only a matter of months before the impact was felt in the application as opposed to a technique. That is, the techniques included in regression analysis and surveying are frequently used to develop leading indicates.

One of the problems associated with the use of leading indicators is complex. Single indicates seldom prove to be of much value. A forecast of the demand for steel must take into account not only general economic conditions but specific trends in a number of industries. Some composite leading indicator indices are published by the Census Bureau and other government and nonprofit agencies. They tend to be of greatest use to primary goods manufacturers and of value as products approach the consumer stage.

Obviously, the type of forecasting problem, the amount of time available for forecasting the nature of available data, and the amount of resources all affect the selection of a·forecasting method. The brief discussion in this section covers only a few of the many forecasting methods which have been developed. Nevertheless they will illustrate a variety of techniques and the types of trade -offs which the researcher faces in selecting a research approach.

Analysing segment profitability

The identification of segments and the problem of forecasting have already been discussed. What remains are the other steps in the decision process which ultimately result in the selection of a specific target market. This section deals with the information needs of managers who are faced with this selection decision. The discussion will emphasize the financial analysis of segment profitability. We will assume for the purpose of this discussion that forecasts have been provided for not only market potential but also competitive positions and market share. Furthermore, analysis of profitability requires assumptions as to the marketing mix strategy and tactics adopted to serve each segment.

The problem of selection is thus reduced to one of estimating the profitability of each alternative segment. This subject is treated in two steps. First, the general subject of assessing segment profitability provides a background for discussing this type of information need. Second, the application of segment profitability analysis to potential markets constitutes the basis for decision making.

The major problem in assessing the profitability of individual market segments is the availability of meaningful revenue and cost information. Usually, cost information is developed for the accounting information system and must be converted at length.

The first step is to devise a matrix breakdown of the company's market segments. Assume that we are concerned with a manufacturer of computers, calculators and adding machines. Notice that the matrices imply that marketing manager are responsible first for profitability by product line, and second by geographic region. This requires the identification of segments which are geographically based and then expressed in terms of customer types by product line. Information for profitability analysis would originate at the region level with details provided for customer type and product type within the product line. This information would then be aggregated to provide company totals.

Recall from the discussion that costs are not necessarily assigned in direct proportion to sales revenues. That is the assignment of salesmen's salaries and other assignable costs to say the full-keyboard models, is not in proportion to the sales generated by that models. For example, the full-keyboard model generates half of the adding machine sales, but based on salesmen's effort per unit sold, this model is assigned 48 percent of salesmen's salaries on the other hand the full keyboard model is assigned 67 percent of the product advertising expense based on the actual proportion of advertising devoted to this model.

We are ready to examine the contribution to profit derived from each customer segment. A particular primary customer-oriented segment has been identified for each model of adding machine. That is most full keyboard machines are targeted to banks, deluxe ten-key machined to manufacturing firms and basic ten-key machines to small retailers.

We can see sales to the manufacturing and retailers segments account for virtually all of the profits for the deluxe ten-key and basic ten-key models respectively. In the case of the full keyboard model, however, over half of the profits are generated from sales outside the bank segment. Although the high profitability of no-segment sales for full-keyboard can be attributed in part to low salary allocations and the lack of advertising expenditures, the fact that these sales are occurring suggests that additional segments for the model exists. Since the analysis described thus far concerns an existing product line and its historical market segments, we are not necessarily concerned with eliminating existing target markets. This would be the case if we discovered that the profitability of an existing segment falls significantly below corporate objectives. If further research failed to provide information upon which profit performance should be improved the manufacturer might seek other markets for this products.

In the actual case of the adding machine line, further research should be conducted to determine the nature of nonsegment sales for the full-keyboard models. This could well reveal that those sales are concentrated in another identifiable segment. The new segment would thus constitute an opportunity for expanded sales and profit.

Although the above example concerns a firm and the segments which it already serves the same from of analysis would be conducted to screen new prospective target market. If resource models this analysis would enable the firm to determine that segment which best meets its criteria for success. Although the full-keyboard model might have the largest sales projection an analysis of the marketing strategy for serving those segments might indicate a high cost of entry. On the other hand, the deluxe ten-key model might provide an easier segment entry and still meet the profit objectives of the firm.

The process of identifying market opportunities generates numerous information needs. The discussion in this chapter has emphasized the market segmentation approach to target market selection. In general, this approach involves three major components related to information needs. First, market segments must be identified second relevant information about market segment potential and marketing costs must be forecasted; and third each segment must be analyzed to determine which best meet the goals of the firm.

Basically the concept of market segmentation assumes that any relatively, heterogeneous group can be divided into two or more relatively homogeneous groups. Furthermore, segments must respond differentially to varying mix strategies and be identifiable in a manner which allows marketing managers to develop effective strategies. If information identifying market segments is to be used for screening target markets three criteria must be met. First, it must identify the manner in which a segment is unique in terms of the specific needs of buyer behaviour. Second it should provide insight into the manner in which different segments respond to specific marketing mix strategies. Third, it must provide identification information through which strategies can be devised to reach the members of the segment.

Numerous bases exist for meeting the criteria set forth for segment identification. Socioeconomic demographic and geographic measures are traditional approaches to segment identification which most commonly meet the third criterion. That is these variables are most commonly used today to provide a picture of segment members through which marketing communication can be addressed to the potential customer. Psychological bases, such as personality type and buyer motives are most useful in meeting the second criterion for segment identification. Measurement of this type helps provide understanding of the manner in which the members of a segment respond differentially to the same marketing mix strategies. Finally, measures of consumer responses, perceptual factors and usage factors are most useful in meeting the first criterion for segment identification. These bases relate moat directly to actual purchase behavior and typically provide the most meaningful distinction between segments.

Once market segments have been identified it is necessary to project the market potential available within each segment. Marketing strategies and the costs associated with those strategies can be forecasted along with sales to provide the basis for an analysis of segment profitability. In this chapter three types of forecasting techniques were discussed. Judgmental techniques such as Delphi method and jury of executive opinion rely on the experience and wisdom of executive is or experts as the basis for forecasting. Obviously these methods tend to be less scientific than quantitative analysis.. Nevertheless, they enable the researcher to incorporate a wide range of information into the environment. Time-series analysis such as moving averages use historical records to forecast the future. The primary weakness of these approaches is their total reliance on the statistical analysis of past history. Their usefulness for short-term forecasting low costs and the availability of data make these techniques useful in many forecasting situations. Finally, causal techniques (regression analysis leading indictors, and intention-to-buy surveys) help the researcher better understand the factors which cause changes in the forecasted item. These techniques vary greatly in their accuracy, costs and data requirements. They are particularly useful, however, in identifying turning points in tends and in helping the researcher to better understand the environment in which forecasts are made.

Given identifiable market segments and forecasts of sales and costs associated with strategies for reaching those segments target markets can be selected. Screening criteria usually relate to profitability although other company goals may be involved. Analysis of segment profitability provides better insight into the nature of existing segments as well as the selection of target markets from potential segments. The major problem facing the researcher in this screening process involves the reclassification of accounts to provide useful financial information for marketing decision making.

